AF184256

Waves in Contract and Liability Law in Three Decades of Ius Commune

Editors:
Anne Keirse
Marco Loos

Waves in Contract and Liability Law in Three Decades of Ius Commune

intersentia

METRO

Intersentia Ltd
Sheraton House | Castle Park
Cambridge | CB3 0AX | United Kingdom
Tel.: +44 1223 370 170 | Fax: +44 1223 370 169
Email: mail@intersentia.co.uk
www.intersentia.com | www.intersentia.co.uk

Distribution for the UK and Ireland:
NBN International
Airport Business Centre, 10 Thornbury Road
Plymouth, PL6 7 PP
United Kingdom
Tel.: +44 1752 202 301 | Fax: +44 1752 202 331
Email: orders@nbninternational.com

Distribution for Europe and all other countries:
Intersentia Publishing nv
Groenstraat 31
2640 Mortsel
Belgium
Tel.: +32 3 680 15 50 | Fax: +32 3 658 71 21
Email: mail@intersentia.be

Distribution for the USA and Canada:
International Specialized Book Services
920 NE 58th Ave. Suite 300
Portland, OR 97213
USA
Tel.: +1 800 944 6190 (toll free) | Fax: +1 503 280 8832
Email: info@isbs.com

Waves in Contract and Liability Law in Three Decades of Ius Commune
© The editors and contributors severally 2017

The author has asserted the right under the Copyright, Designs and Patents Act 1988, to be identified as author of this work.

No part of this book may be reproduced, stored in a retrieval system, or transmitted, in any form, or by any means, without prior written permission from Intersentia, or as expressly permitted by law or under the terms agreed with the appropriate reprographic rights organisation. Enquiries concerning reproduction which may not be covered by the above should be addressed to Intersentia at the address above.

Cover image: Artistdesign29 – Shutterstock

ISBN 978-1-78068-602-8
D/2017/7849/127
NUR 822

British Library Cataloguing in Publication Data. A catalogue record for this book is available from the British Library.

CONTENTS

Anne L.M. Keirse*
Rudolf M. Renting
Marco B.M. Loos

INTRODUCTION: THE WAVES OF CONTRACTUAL AND TORTUOUS LIABILITY

1. 35 years of European private law in Europe

As the 21st *Ius Commune* conference on European private law coincided with the 35th anniversary of the Maastricht law school, it was deemed a good occasion to look back at the evolutions that have taken place in the European law of obligations since 1981. More particularly, this book is the result from a discussion about how particular changes or developments have impacted both fields of contract law and tort law, either in the same or in diverging or even opposite ways.

Think, first of all, of the evolvement of different perceptions, for example in terms of (the need for) protection of the weaker party (*e.g.* consumer protection, and more recently small and medium-sized enterprises (SME) protection) and in respect of 'freedom' (*e.g.* the freedom to contract, the fault principle, *etcetera*). Secondly, in both fields of contract law and tort law it seems that there is an increased level of Europeanisation and constitutionalisation (with the 1991 Maastricht Treaty – celebrating its 25th birthday in the week after the Ius commune conference that took place in the city from where it takes its name – as one of the starting points). Hardly existing in the 1980s but currently at the core of scholarly attention in private law is the need to adjust the law to the growing impact of digitalisation. More and more, the law of obligations emerges from different (growing/evolving) sources of law. It emerges from all directions: top down, bottom up, but also crossing-over and diagonal. The law of obligations is not only the product of national lawmakers but also of supranational lawmakers and it concerns different types of actors. Norms of the law of obligations are not only being made by national legislators and courts, but also by European institutionalised lawmakers and (increasingly important) by private actors, organisations and networks. So too, in both areas of the law the focus seems to have shifted away from mere comparisons of national contract or tort law systems respectively to a growing call for European (or perhaps world-wide) harmonisation. Thirdly, in both fields of law there seems to be an emergence of new forms of regulation and of new kinds of remedies.

* Prof. dr. Anne L.M. Keirse is professor of Private Law at Utrecht University, director of the Utrecht Centre for Accountability and Liability Law and a part-time judge at the Court of Appeal in Amsterdam. Rudolf M. Renting is a (Legal Research Master) student at Utrecht University. Prof. dr. Marco B.M. Loos is professor of Private Law at the University of Amsterdam.

The contributions in this book all revolve around the question of whether there are parallels between or opposite changes of contract and tort law in respect of the particular developments that can be found in the last 35 years. More specifically, an important theme concerns the differences between both fields of law with regard to the integration of knowledge regarding the development and/or prevention of new (technological, environmental or financial) risks. *Hage's* contribution on autonomous systems takes up this issue by questioning the very foundations of our private-law systems. The impact of (behavioural) economic analysis on both fields of the law and the development of new forms of dispute resolution form another theme. *Voet's* contribution on the emergence of a European form of collective redress should be mentioned here. The continuing process of Europeanisation, internationalisation and transnationalisation is further taken up by *Jansen and Somers*, whose contribution addresses the influence of the principle of equality on the Belgian law of obligations, and *Lazić*, who discusses the position of 'weak' parties in the Brussels Ibis Regulation. While these contributions show how the international legal order has influenced the development of domestic private law, one must bear in mind that this influential relationship also works in the opposite direction. Reminding us of the latter, *Okany* deals with international state responsibility for acts of non-governmental entities that carry out decentralised governmental functions – a field of law that apparently draws heavily upon analogies with domestic tort law. On the whole, the focus lies on the changing interrelationship between contract and tort law. *Królikowska's* contribution clearly addresses this topic by focusing on the European influence on the doctrine of concurrence of claims under both fields of law.

2. Development through waves

2.1. Legal development (not) as a linear progress

Although some changes – *e.g.* the growing importance of autonomous agents – mark the end of an era and put a stop to a certain rule or approach, this book is based on the idea that private law does not evolve in a linear progress. Rather, in contradistinction to popular belief, the evolution of private law must be perceived as a continuing process of waves. It often looks back at the past, returning to old solutions in order to solve new problems. Four recurring issues in the development of legal systems should be mentioned to illustrate what is meant here.[1]

First, legislation is drafted seldom only with a view on the (linear) progress of the law. Often, extra-legal considerations play a role as well. Think of the reasons that led governments to the decision of making national codifications of private law: political objectives arguably played a larger role than the aim of substantively better rules. Research has revealed how the great codifications of the late eighteenth and nineteenth

1 A.L.M. Keirse, 'Golfbewegingen in het verbintenissenrecht', J.H.A. Lokin, J.M. Milo, C.H. van Rhee, *Tweehonderd jaren codificatie van het privaatrecht in Nederland. Opstellen over (de geschiedenis van) het privaatrecht naar aanleiding van het tweede eeuwfeest van het Wetboek Napoleon Ingerigt voor het Koningrijk Holland*, Groningen: Chimaira 2010, pp. 121–123.

centuries were primarily aimed at reaching politically more unified nation states.[2] Qua substance, however, the codified law can be seen as more or less a continuation of the law that had been developed in the preceding ages.[3] The latter can also be observed in the more recent codifications, such as the New Dutch Civil Code of 1992 – which celebrates its 25th anniversary in the year when this book is published. As these codifications pin down the doctrines that have been achieved by legal scholarship, they tend to have a conservative effect on the law, whose natural development through case law and legal scholarship is obstructed. This also holds true for contemporary EU legislation. Directives are rarely changed, and if they are, their implementation into national law takes a lot of time. For this reason the Product Liability Directive,[4] which is based on insights of the 1970s, is criticised for slowing down the development of the law.[5] In future, the academic sets of principles of European private law[6] could, if given an official status by the EU, result in another stagnation in private law development. And currently progressive and forward-looking legislative initiatives, such as the proposal for a Digital Content Directive,[7] may over time evolve into backward legal instruments regulating the problems of the past instead of offering solutions to then contemporary matters.

Secondly, it happens more than once that judges are reticent in adopting innovative interpretations of the law. This happens especially when the case at hand concerns a politically sensitive issue. Rather than forwarding the law by itself, the judiciary then tends to await the solutions reached in politics. Controversial new laws can be interpreted somewhat conservatively for the same reason, as a consequence of which they do not always have the desired effect on society. The law then needs an external stimulant – social acceptance of the new solution – to achieve the right effect.

Thirdly, legislators often draft changes of the law under the silent presumption of unchanged circumstances. As the real world does not constitute a *ceteris paribus* situation – many legal and non-legal factors influence the way a rule works in practice –, new laws often do not reach the desired effects. Even large-scale empirical research

2 See P.A.J. van den Berg, *Codificatie en staatsvorming. De politieke en politiek-theoretische achtergronden van de codificatie van het privaatrecht in Pruisen, de Donaumonarchie, Frankrijk en Nederland, 1450–1811*, Groningen: Noordhoff Uitgevers 1996; P.A.J. van den Berg, 'De paradox van codificatie: over de gevolgen van codificatie in Europa voor de rechtsvinding', *Rechtsgeleerd Magazijn Themis* 163 (2002) 4, pp. 195–203.

3 Think, for instance, of the writings of Pothier that greatly influenced the French *Code Civil*.

4 Council Directive 85/374/EEC of 25 July 1985 on the approximation of the laws, regulations and administrative provisions of the Member States concerning liability for defective products.

5 P. Machnikowski (ed.), *European product liability. An analysis of the state of the art in the era of new technologies*, Cambridge: Intersentia 2016, p. 687.

6 Think, in particular, of the Draft Common Frame of Reference (DCFR). Cf. Chr. von Bar & E. Clive (eds.), *Principles, definitions and model rules of European private law. Draft Common Frame of Reference (DCFR). Full edition*, Munich: Sellier 2009. On the development of the DCFR, see M.B.M. Loos & A.L.M. Keirse, 'The Optional Instrument and the Consumer Rights Directive: alternative ways to a new ius commune in contract law – Introduction', in: A.L.M. Keirse & M.B.M. Loos (eds.), *Alternative Ways to Ius Commune. The Europeanisation of private law*, Cambridge/Antwerp/Portland: Intersentia 2012, pp. 1–20.

7 Proposal for a Directive of the European Parliament and of the Council on certain aspects concerning contracts for the supply of digital content, COM(2015) 634 final.

into the effectiveness of a law cannot rule out the existence of unforeseen factors that can influence the workings of a law.

Fourthly and lastly, change often meets resistance. Think of the body of consumer law that emerged under EU legislation: whereas consumer protection once was a main goal of the EU, recent legislation shows the opposite development in favour of freedom of contract and the demands of the free market. So much so, even, that voices are heard again in favour of the original goal of consumer protection.[8] This kind of development via actions and reactions is characteristic for legal development in general.

2.2. *Waves in contract law*

The claims made above can be illustrated by looking at the development of Dutch contract law over the last two centuries. In short, this development can be characterised as starting from egoism (first three quarters of the nineteenth century) through paternalism (last quarter of the nineteenth and first half of the twentieth century) to fraternalism (second half of the twentieth century).[9] Originally, in the nineteenth century, the focus very much lay on the principle of party autonomy and freedom of contract. The assumption was that contracting parties were equal to each other in their negotiations and could act free from external factors influencing their will.[10] During the nineteenth century, with the rise of mass production in factories, however, this view slowly changed under the influence of sociological insights in the differences between social classes in society.[11] As the substance of a contract can be heavily coloured by the difference in economic, social or cultural status of the contracting parties, lawyers became aware of the fact that the principle of party autonomy does not necessarily lead to just contracts. This awareness gradually led to a socialisation of contract law, as a consequence of which contracting parties now had the obligation to take into account the interests of society in general, *i.e.* the public interest, when performing their contracts. This societal view on the matter was left behind in the second half of the twentieth century, when the Netherlands saw both welfare and individualisation growing. Although still scrutinising contracts as to their being just, the *Hoge Raad* (Supreme Court) no longer based its judgments purely on the public interest. The parties' mutual interests and expectations were deemed more important now, and the former paternalist approach had changed into a fraternalist one. From then on, contracting

8 See, e.g., M.B.M. Loos, 'Volledige harmonisatie van het Europese consumentenrecht: voorzichtigheid geboden!', *Tijdschrift voor Consumentenrecht & handelspraktijken* 7 (2009) 2, pp. 33–36; H.N. Schelhaas, 'Volledige harmonisatie: goed voor de Europese consument?', *Nederlands tijdschrift voor burgerlijk recht* 26 (2009) 2, p. 35; J.M. Smits, 'Full harmonization of consumer contract law? A critique of the draft directive on consumer rights', *European Review of Private Law* 18 (2010) 1, pp. 5–14.

9 J.H. Nieuwenhuis, 'Paternalisme, fraternalisme, egoïsme. Een kleine catechismus van het contractenrecht', *Nederlands juristenblad* 84 (2009) 35, pp. 2254–2263; A.L.M. Keirse, 'Fraternalisme en trouw aan het gegeven woord', *Contracteren* 8 (2009) 4, pp. 105–109.

10 S. Stijns, *Verbintenissenrecht. Boek 1*, Bruges: die Keure 2005, p. 37 ff.

11 S. Stijns, *Verbintenissenrecht. Boek 1*, Bruges: die Keure 2005, p. 43 ff.

parties have to take into account the justified expectations of the opposing party, thus leading to a kind of good faith in the performance of the contract.[12]

On the European level, the contemporary focus on protection of the weaker party can be perceived as well. The huge body of consumer law illustrates this well enough. As the span of protective rules has grown steadily, scholars have come to perceive contract law as no longer being built on the principle of party autonomy. Rather, there are voices that argue we should see the principle of good faith as the basis of all contract law.[13] Lurger even argues that we see the development of a new principle of European contract law: the principle of regard and fairness.[14] German law has been an important forerunner in this development, as its contract law underwent a profound moralisation in the periods following the two World Wars.[15]

What does this have to do with the waves of contract law? Everything. It shows how contract law's history alternately attaches importance to either the principle of party autonomy or the principle of contractual good faith.[16] Whereas the period of time showing 'paternalism' was very much marked by government interference in people's private dealings, 'fraternalism' can be perceived as an effort to return to the strict freedom of contract, albeit curtailed by notions as 'weaker party protection' and 'restoring the contractual equilibrium', if need be by way of courts testing contract terms of their own motion. In this respect it may be argued that although the awareness of the existence of 'weak parties' has led to the development of many duties of care in contractual relationships, these duties are essentially directed at re-establishing the equality of the parties and thus their capability to act freely according to their will. In future, we may see a further return to private autonomy. Indeed, whereas consumer law was traditionally issued in the form of minimum-harmonisation directives – thus leaving room for the Member States to

12 A.L.M. Keirse, 'Epiloog. Het contractenrecht van morgen: de uitzonderingen op het beginsel van de partijautonomie gepromoveerd tot regel', in: I. Samoy (ed.), *Evolutie van de basisbeginselen van het contractenrecht*, Antwerp/Oxford: Intersentia 2010, pp. 263–268.

13 A.L.M. Keirse, 'Epiloog. Het contractenrecht van morgen: de uitzonderingen op het beginsel van de partijautonomie gepromoveerd tot regel', in: I. Samoy (ed.), *Evolutie van de basisbeginselen van het contractenrecht*, Antwerp/Oxford: Intersentia 2010, pp. 263–268; E.H. Hondius, 'De zwakke partij in het contractenrecht; over de verandering van paradigmata van het privaatrecht', in: T. Hartlief & C.J.J.M. Stolker, *Contractsvrijheid*, Deventer: Kluwer 1999, pp. 387–393; B. Filippo, 'Wanneer moet paternalisme worden verkozen boven autonomie in het contractenrecht? Beschouwingen over een goede balans, mede aan de hand van het huurbeschermingsrecht', in: W.H. van Boom, M.L. Tuil & W. Dijkshoorn (eds.), *Autonomie en paternalisme in het privaatrecht*, The Hague: Boom Juridische Uitgevers 2008, pp. 9–10; cf. J.B.M. Vranken, 'Over partijautonomie, contractsvrijheid en de grondslag van gebondenheid in het verbintenissenrecht', in: J.M. Barendrecht, M.A.B. Chao-Duivis & H.A.W. Vermeulen (eds.), *Beginselen van contractenrecht*, Deventer: Tjeenk Willink 2000, pp. 145–155.

14 B. Lurger, 'The "social" side of contract law and the new principle of regard and fairness', in: A.S. Hartkamp, M.W. Hesselink, E.H. Hondius, C. Mak, C.E. du Perron (eds.), *Towards a European Civil Code*, Alphen aan den Rijn: Kluwer Law International 2011, pp. 353–386.

15 O. Lando, 'Is good faith an over-arching general clause in the Principles of European Contract Law?', *European Review of Private Law* 15 (2007) 6, pp. 844–848.

16 A.L.M. Keirse, 'Golfbewegingen in het verbintenissenrecht', J.H.A. Lokin, J.M. Milo, C.H. van Rhee, *Tweehonderd jaren codificatie van het privaatrecht in Nederland. Opstellen over (de geschiedenis van) het privaatrecht naar aanleiding van het tweede eeuwfeest van het Wetboek Napoleon Ingerigt voor het Koningrijk Holland*, Groningen: Chimaira 2010, p. 124.

provide further reaching protection of the consumer than necessary – new directives are in the form of maximum harmonisation. The reason for doing so can be found in the EU's shift of focus from weaker-party protection to the development of the internal market.[17] Contract law does clearly not evolve in a straight line. Rather, its development consists out of waves, not always going in the same direction and often recurring to old solutions.

2.3. *Waves in tort law*

As regards tort law many scholars seem to believe that its history shows an ever-growing basis for liability. Developments in Dutch case law and European legislation, such as the strict liability regime in the 1986 Product Liability Directive,[18] the expansion of duties of care – which not only took place in contract law but in tort law as well –, the introduction of the precautionary principle in specific areas of tort law, and the evolvement of proportional liability seem to support this view.

Nevertheless, all these developments must be perceived as constituting part of just one wave in the history of tort law.[19] When zooming out, we can see how Dutch court judgments between 1838 – when the old Civil Code was introduced – and 1860/1870 already showed a growing readiness to apply tort law in order to award damages to the injured party.[20] The time period of 1870 to 1910, however, marks the return to a much more strict approach, awarding damages only in case of a breach of statute.[21] The current growth of tort law only started in 1919, when the *Hoge Raad* gave its judgment in *Lindenbaum / Cohen*.[22] From that time onwards, tort law was recognised to apply not only in case of the infringement of a person's subjective right or of a statutory obligation, but also in case the defendant acted in breach of an unwritten rule of law.

An interesting example is the Dutch development of immaterial damages.[23] Nowadays this growing area of tort law is perceived as a feature of the contemporary 'emotionalisation' of tort law. Nevertheless, it should be brought back to mind that the old Roman-Dutch

17 See, e.g., M.B.M. Loos, 'Volledige harmonisatie van het Europese consumentenrecht: voorzichtigheid geboden!', *Tijdschrift voor Consumentenrecht & handelspraktijken* 7 (2009) 2, pp. 33–36; H.N. Schelhaas, 'Volledige harmonisatie: goed voor de Europese consument?', *Nederlands tijdschrift voor burgerlijk recht* 26 (2009) 2, p. 35; J.M. Smits, 'Full harmonization of consumer contract law? A critique of the draft directive on consumer rights', *European Review of Private Law* 18 (2010) 1, pp. 5–14.

18 Council Directive 85/374/EEC of 25 July 1985 on the approximation of the laws, regulations and administrative provisions of the Member States concerning liability for defective products.

19 A.L.M. Keirse, 'Golfbewegingen in het verbintenissenrecht', J.H.A. Lokin, J.M. Milo, C.H. van Rhee, *Tweehonderd jaren codificatie van het privaatrecht in Nederland. Opstellen over (de geschiedenis van) het privaatrecht naar aanleiding van het tweede eeuwfeest van het Wetboek Napoleon Ingerigt voor het Koningrijk Holland*, Groningen: Chimaira 2010, pp. 124–127.

20 G.E. van Maanen, 'Stroomtreinen en aansprakelijkheid', *Weekblad voor privaatrecht, notariaat en registratie* (5743) 1985, p. 412.

21 E.g. HR 10-06-1910, *Weekblad van het Recht* 9038 (Zutphense juffrouw).

22 HR 31-01-1919, *Nederlandse Jurisprudentie* 1919, 161 (Lindenbaum / Cohen).

23 A.L.M. Keirse, 'Golfbewegingen in het verbintenissenrecht', J.H.A. Lokin, J.M. Milo, C.H. van Rhee, *Tweehonderd jaren codificatie van het privaatrecht in Nederland. Opstellen over (de geschiedenis van) het privaatrecht naar aanleiding van het tweede eeuwfeest van het Wetboek Napoleon Ingerigt voor het Koningrijk Holland*, Groningen: Chimaira 2010, p. 126.

law, and also the law of the Civil Code of 1809 under the French king Louis Napoleon (the brother of the French emperor Napoleon Bonaparte), already recognised immaterial damages. From 1811 onwards (introduction of the French Civil Code in the Netherlands) Dutch law did not recognise this kind of damages any longer, until 1943[24] marked the starting point of a new development towards immaterial damages. Cleary, we should not think too readily of our law as better than before. Often, contemporary developments have occurred before, and therefore are not as special as we may think.

A closer look at the doctrine of contributory negligence again shows us how historical insights present the current state of the law in a totally new light.[25] Often this doctrine is perceived as constituting a widening of civil liability, but history suggests otherwise. From Roman times onward a finding of contributory negligence meant that the tortfeasor was freed from all liability. The eighteenth century, however, marked a change in this all-or-nothing attitude, resulting in a shift towards a proportional solution. Instead of being liable for nothing, the tortfeasor was now liable for a part – proportional to the contributory negligence of the plaintiff. The resulting expansion of tort law eventually led to a situation in which voices were heard in favour of a complete abolition of the idea of contributory negligence: the tortfeasor would then always be liable for the full amount of the damages. Against this background the current 'renaissance' of contributory negligence must be seen as a development in the opposite direction. Whilst other parts of tort law do show a growing responsibility for the tortfeasor, the doctrine of contributory negligence serves as a counterweight that raises the responsibility of the victim.[26] Rather than being an expansion of tort law, it functions as a limit on liability, and thus constitutes a wave in the opposite direction.

A similar insight can be arrived at when looking at the doctrine of proportional liability. Just like contributory negligence, this doctrine is often conceived of as being part of the ever-growing influence of tort law. The doctrine makes it possible, namely, to hold the defendant partially liable in case the evidence of causality proves to be difficult. One can, however, also argue the opposite: without the doctrine of proportional liability it would be possible to hold the tortfeasor liable for the totality of the harm instead of only a (proportional) part. Such an argument is well defendable when in response to problems regarding the proof of causality the requirements for such proof are released – an effect that the so-called *omkeringsregel* could have. In certain cases, this rule lays down a presumption that the existence of a causal relationship is proven – requiring instead the defendant to suggest reasons why that presumption is not justified in the

24 HR 21-05-1943, *Nederlandse Jurisprudentie* 1943, 455 (Van Kreuningen/Bessem).

25 A.L.M. Keirse, 'Golfbewegingen in het verbintenissenrecht', J.H.A. Lokin, J.M. Milo, C.H. van Rhee, *Tweehonderd jaren codificatie van het privaatrecht in Nederland. Opstellen over (de geschiedenis van) het privaatrecht naar aanleiding van het tweede eeuwfeest van het Wetboek Napoleon Ingerigt voor het Koningrijk Holland*, Groningen: Chimaira 2010, p. 127; see A.L.M. Keirse, *Schadebeperkingsplicht. Over eigen schuld aan de omvang van de schade*, Groningen: Kluwer 2003, p. 23 ff.; E.G.D. van Dongen, *Contributory negligence. A historical and comparative study*, Leiden: Brill 2014.

26 A.L.M. Keirse, *Schadebeperkingsplicht. Over eigen schuld aan de omvang van de schade*, Deventer: Kluwer 2003, p. 36.

circumstances of the case.[27] Thus diminishing the need to prove a causal link between the defendant's act and the plaintiff's harm, the rule can lead to full liability in cases where application of the doctrine of proportional liability would only allow for a partial liability. Seen in this way, the doctrine of contributory negligence casts doubts on the idea of a linear progress of tort law towards ever more liability.

This paragraph makes clear the importance of legal history. If scholars would make more use of it in their analyses of contemporary law, this would prevent them from falling into the trap of seeing the development of law as a linear progress instead of a continuing process of waves. The examples given above all lead to this conclusion. Only by using legal history can we get a truly deeper understanding of the position we are in now.[28]

3. On the contents of this book

All contributors to this book have chosen a theme that transgresses the distinction between contract law and tort law, thereby delving into issues that play a role in both fields of law. Placing these issues in the frame of 35 years of legal development, their contributions can be seen as an illustration of the wave-like character of legal history.

Królikowska starts the discussion with an examination of the growing influence of EU law on the interrelationship between domestic contract law and tort law. She does so by focusing on the issue of concurrence of claims under both fields of law. After treating the various rules of EU Member States on the relationship between the actions in contract and in tort, she discusses various examples of EU legislation in order to see whether and to what extent the EU interferes in the national rules. Interestingly, the EU seems to circumvent the matter and leave it to the Member States whether a plaintiff can only sue in contract or in tort as well: the instruments of EU law are generally directed at only one of them while leaving the other one untouched. In the – now withdrawn – proposal for a Regulation on Common European Sales Law[29] and in the Draft Common Frame of Reference the matter is addressed, but according to Królikowska the solutions are disappointingly unclear.

Lazić continues the discussion with the procedural position of the 'weaker party' in private international law. In so doing, she shows how the developments in contract law discussed above are still relevant for EU legislation today. The focus of her contribution lies on the changes brought about by the adoption of the Brussels Ibis Regulation (also known as: Brussels I Regulation (recast)), which has replaced the old Brussels I Regulation. Discussing the Regulation's scope of application *ratione personae*, the issue of tacit prorogation of jurisdiction, the revised rules on recognition and enforcement of

27 W.D.H. Asser, *Mr. C. Assers Handleiding tot de beoefening van het Nederlands Burgerlijk Recht. Procesrecht. 3. Bewijs*, Deventer: Kluwer 2013, no. 302.

28 See, for instance, J.M. Milo, 'Hang naar heden. Over het verleden in het geldende recht', *Ars Aequi* 66 (2017), pp. 240–249.

29 Proposal for a Regulation on a Common European Sales Law (COM (2011) 635 final), available at http://eur-lex.europa.eu/LexUriServ/LexUriServ.do?uri=COM:2011:0635:FIN:en:PDF (last visited on 6 June 2017). The withdrawal of the proposal was announced by the Juncker Commission in *Commission Work Programme 2015, A New Start*, Strasbourg, 16 December 2014, COM(2014) 910 final, Annex 2, no. 60.

judgments, and the new rule on *lis alibi pendens*, Lazić argues that the revised Regulation further enhances the protection of the weaker party in insurance, consumer and labour disputes. According to her, it provides an example of how other legal instruments in the field of private international law and civil procedure should be revised as well.

Jansen and Somers then shift the focus to human rights. They dedicate their contribution to the influence of the principle of equality on the Belgian law of obligations. Providing an overview of the current state of Belgian law, they address the issue of horizontal effect and the ambivalent case law of on the one hand the Court of Cassation, on the other hand the Constitutional Court. Following that, the role of the principle of equality in the coherency of legislation and case law is discussed. Throughout the contribution it becomes clear how the Belgian law of obligations is more and more pervaded by the principle of equality, only being free from it in case other constitutional rights are at stake. This contribution is a helpful account of the problems we encounter in the process of constitutionalisation of private law.

Voet then takes on the issue of new forms of dispute resolution, by reflecting on the current state of collective redress in Europe. As this doctrine originates from the common law, Voet's discussion of the civil-law adoption of several forms of collective redress illustrates the recurring use of old solutions for new problems. In particular, he focuses on the efforts of the EU to harmonise the law on this point via the Injunctions Directive and the Recommendation on common principles for injunctive and compensatory collective redress mechanisms. Notwithstanding these efforts, most Member States keep following their own rules on collective redress, thus hampering the harmonisation process, whilst private litigants generally do not choose for the 'class-action' possibilities their jurisdictions provide. The latter can be explained by failures in procedural design of class-action regimes on the one hand and fundamental policy choices on the other hand. Perceiving an erosion of the old public-private distinction and the development of alternative and new approaches to mass-harm cases, Voet proposes to integrate all developments in one 'multi-layered framework of regulation, lawmaking and law application'.

Hage then addresses the problem of 'new risks' by focusing on the growing role of artificial intelligence in our society. In his discussion he argues how this changing role can influence legal thinking in the area of the law of obligations. Analysing the concepts of 'responsibility', 'attribution' and 'capacity' in order to scrutinise the idea of 'liability', he argues that human beings are actually quite similar to autonomous agents. Putting aside the old anthropocentric perspective it becomes clear that there are no fundamental objections to holding autonomous agents responsible for acts. The question is not so much whether attribution is true or truthful, but whether it is desirable or useful. Leaving aside the options to attribute events to autonomous agents on the basis of explanatory or predictive power, Hage chooses to focus on purpose: why are people, and why could autonomous agents be liable for their actions? Hage unmasks attribution of responsibility on the basis of desert as a normative practice which does not give clear guidelines as when to attribute and when not to, and consequently prefers the view that attribution must be seen as desirable in order to influence the future for the best. Hage's call to abandon our anthropocentric perspective thus challenges us to rethink the principles on which private law is built.

Finally, *Okany* brings us largely outside the domain of private law. In her paper, she focuses on the question of whether a state can be held legally responsible for wrongful actions committed by a non-governmental entity on the basis that the entity committed them while performing governmental functions on behalf of the State. She argues that this question should be answered affirmatively, and bases her argument on the analogous application of private law concepts. To this end, she argues that a general principle of international law has developed, which brings about that for liability purposes the State should remain responsible and liable towards victims irrespective of whether public interest functions (such as rail transportation, water supply, social security, health care, prisons and immigration control) have been decentralised or privatised. This extended state liability constitutes one of public international law's responses to the increasing decentralisation and privatisation of such public interest functions. She argues that this 'extended liability' under public international law in fact shows a close analogy to the concepts of vicarious liability, strict liability and the non-delegable duty of care in tort law. In doing so, she shows us that the former dogma of 'The King can do no wrong' clearly no longer applies. Although this observation suggests a clear intellectual breach with older notions of state liability, Okany's paper shows how it were arguments of *policy* that paved the way for public international law's contemporary approach to the subject. As these arguments are generally greatly influenced by the particular time frame in which they are made, the development described by Okany fits well in the argument made earlier in this introduction, being just one wave in the overall development of law.[30] This view is supported when zooming out to a more historical perspective, which suggests that modern developments could be seen as a return towards earlier forms of state liability – where in the Low Countries the *Grote Raad van Mechelen* – the predecessor of both the Dutch *Hoge Raad* and the Belgian *Hof van Cassatie* – was competent to hear cases relating to dealings with the lord or the governor, and decided cases against both cities and staff for (what nowadays would be considered) tortuous actions causing damage.[31] The laws of European states show a movement from state immunity to a regime of public authority liability of increasing extent, discarding former limitations of liability and embracing liability of wider scope.[32] However, contradictory tendencies can be evident at the same point of time and retrenchments have occurred in some countries in consequence of concern that public authority liability may have extended too far.[33] State liability, therefore, is subject to the same non-linear development as other parts of the law.

30 See A.L.M. Keirse & R. Ortlep, '*Policy*-argumenten in het overheidsaansprakelijkheidsrecht: een rechtsvergelijkend perspectief', *Overheid & Aansprakelijkheid* 16 (2017) 2, pp. 3-14.

31 See H.J.T.M. van Roosmalen, *Overheidsaansprakelijkheid in Engeland en Nederland* (Ph.D. thesis Leiden), The Hague: Sdu Uitgevers 2007, p. 30.

32 A.W. Bradley & J. Bell, 'Governmental Liability; A Preliminary Assessment', in A.W. Bradley & J. Bell (eds.), *Governmental Liability; A Comparative Survey*, London: BIICL 1991, p. 15; K. Oliphant (ed.), *The Liability of Public Authorities in Comparative Perspective*, Cambridge: Intersentia 2016, p. 852.

33 See for more details and references: K. Oliphant (ed.), *The Liability of Public Authorities in Comparative Perspective*, Cambridge: Intersentia 2016, p. 884; A.L.M. Keirse & R. Ortlep, '*Policy*-argumenten in het overheidsaansprakelijkheidsrecht: een rechtsvergelijkend perspectief', *Overheid & Aansprakelijkheid* 16 (2017) 2, p. 12 ff.

Katarzyna
Królikowska*

CONCURRENCE OF CLAIMS IN DAMAGES AND EU LAW

1. Introduction

The development of gradual harmonization and unification of private law by the European Union leads from selective, product-related directives to more comprehensive and directly effective regulations. For a long time, European law showed no tendency towards comprehensiveness and systematic responsibility for general private law. Adopting a maximum harmonization approach for directives and regulations developed to unify some areas of private law revealed that creating uniform legal framework conditions for private law transactions can only be achieved if a coherent, functioning private law system is available or created. It is clear that before going further some fundamental questions of private law have to be analysed and answered at the European level. Otherwise, the process of covering more areas of national private laws by uniform rules will stop.

In my opinion, one of the reasons for the current deadlock in harmonization of national laws by the EU is the still unsolved question of the approach that the Union sought to adopt towards the relationship of the contractual and tortious liabilities and claims arising out of them under national jurisdictions. The EU private law legislation concentrates very much on harmonizing and unifying contact law, but monetary payments made by the liable party in order to make up for any losses that result from the breach of contract may also be grounded on tort, especially on national product and services liability regimes.

The purpose of this paper is to highlight the importance for the European legislator of the existing concurrent liabilities in damages under national laws. I argue that the EU legislators (EU institutions and the Court of Justice of the European Union) should be more aware of the legal reality of free concurrence of claims available to the claimants under many jurisdictions. Otherwise, there will always be unwished side-effect of national implementations and concurrence of EU-based law with purely national remedies. Due to the complexity of the topic and different scopes of contractual and tortious regulations, an improper approach to the existing concurrence of liabilities leads to the failures in the process of harmonization of the private law in Europe.

* Dr Katarzyna Królikowska, Faculty of Law and Administration, Warsaw University, post-doctoral researcher at the Centre for the Study of European Contract Law (University of Amsterdam), email: k.krolikowska@wpia.uw.edu.pl.

Neglecting this topic in selecting consumer directives results in claims stemming from EU-based national rules that can be easily overruled by concurring claims based on non-harmonized national laws. In preparing more comprehensive instruments, including the European Civil Code, solving this general question seems to be crucial for the further development of uniform solutions for the internal market.

To cope with the complexity of national solutions to the question of concurrence between liabilities in contract and tort, a comprehensive approach was suggested in the literature. This approach is similar to the approach taken by any national legislator when it embarks upon codification of private law. Before drafting of the European Civil Code or any more comprehensive legal instrument in European private law, the list of policy questions regarding the main fundamental issues should be answered.[1] At the top of the list of 50 proposed political questions on European contract law which should be submitted, we can find the most general question on whether contractual relationships should be exclusively dealt with by contractual liability or whether concurring liability (in contract, tort, and restitution) should be allowed.

The problem of concurrence of liabilities/actions has been discussed from the comparative law perspective,[2] regarding the areas of the application of tort law, its boundaries with contract law, the organization of the elements of tortious liability in terms of general clauses in the continental civil codes and the more specific torts of the common law. The problems resulting from differences on the interaction of tort law (or more broadly non-contractual liability law) with contract law in European systems of private law have been analyzed with the special purpose of identifying real or likely obstacles to the smooth functioning of the internal market in contract and commercial practice.[3] The first proposals were directed at the development of basic principles of concurrence of actions from the law of obligations, relating specifically to pure economic loss and other areas of law. The research revealed that, in practice, the rule of absolute free concurrence of claims does not exist and that the content of the rule on concurrence is very strictly connected with the scope of the national contract and tort laws.

1 MW Hesselink, 'The Politics of a European Civil Code', (2004) 6 *European Law Journal* vol. 10, 694, 697. Questions presented in the Annex to the article contains questions adopted by the Dutch legislator in the recodification of Dutch private law. There are another general questions connected with the discussed issue. Question 41 reads as follows: How many types and levels of abstraction should the instrument have, what should be regarded as a general part of EU instrument in private law: general law of obligations including non-contractual liability or general contract law? This question is important for the location of a potential rule on the concurrence of liabilities and remedies. Question 2 concerned the problem of the general duty of good faith and fair dealing and their scope: should a general duty of good faith only supplement or co-shape contractual and legal obligations? Should it be permitted to limit or exclude obligations in certain cases? If so, should the duty of good faith and fair dealing be extended towards pre-contractual relationships (contractual or tortious) or post-contractual relationships (regulated by unjustified enrichment)?

2 Ch von Bar, *The Common European Law of Torts: The Core Areas of Tort Law, Its Approximation in Europe, and Its Accommodation in the Legal System*, vol I, Clarendon Press, Oxford 1998, pp 446–448.

3 Ch von Bar and U Drobnig (eds.), *The Interaction of Contract Law and Tort and Property Law in Europe. A Comparative Study*, Sellier, Munich 2004.

2. National approaches to concurrence of claims in damages

It is not my task to present different national solutions adopted to deal with the fact that, in some circumstances, breaching a contract may additionally constitute a civil wrong (breach of a general duty) which can create alternative rights/remedies in damages. It is sufficient to say that in every European legal order there exists a field of free concurrence of claims, although its location and scope may vary between jurisdictions.

Concurrence of claims in damages is solved and regulated not by a legal statutory provision but by case law (judge-made law, judiciary) in almost every European country except for Poland.[4] In almost all jurisdictions, the problem was left to the judiciary and legal doctrine that established binding meta-rule on concurrence.[5] Regardless of the profound division between division of powers and the tradition of common law and civil law, the issue of concurrent liabilities is always solved either by a binding leading case (precedent) or by an established group of cases. The rules established may be very different, though, but there is always one clear and imperative rule in that matter in a given jurisdiction.[6]

From the theoretical point of view, there can be different solutions to the problem. The law can prescribe that only one liability is to be applied exclusively (*non-cumul des responsabilités*). The opposing principle of free concurrence of contractual and non-contractual claims (*cumul des responsabilités*) is never absolute. When the law allows concurrence of claims based on contractual and non-contractual liability but prescribes that the claimant must make a choice and select before the court only one of the remedies being in competition, then multiple rules could be applied to the same legal facts and the claimant may choose which rules he or she wishes to invoke before the court. In some jurisdictions the court is competent to choose the liability and to decide the case on contract or tort law, regardless of the will of the claimant, acting in favour of the claimant or in line with a public policy.

Modern civil codes are built upon the foundations and systematic approach of Roman law. It is true that the Romans clearly differentiated between the law of tort and the law of contract but concurrent liability was not an issue in Roman law. The law of contract and the law of torts were separate domains with narrow scopes. The law specified the rights and duties of the parties in each category. Both contained a casuistic lists of several delicts and types of contracts and prescribed different sets of remedies (actions). The law of contract was a more recent branch of law and social history is a movement from status to contract.[7] Initially, obligations were classified as arising under two separate headings

4 In Polish private law, Art. 443 of the Polish Civil Code of 1964 allows an alternative concurrence of claims in contract and tort. Pursuant to it, the circumstance that an action or omission which causes damage constitutes non-performance or improper performance of an earlier obligation does not preclude a claim for remedy of damage based on tort unless something else follows from the substance of the earlier obligation. This provision is subject to judicial interpretation.

5 T Weir, 'Complex Liabilities' in *Encyclopedia of Comparative Law*, vol XI, part 2, Dordrecht-Boston-Lancaster-Tübingen 1986, p 25.

6 W Czachórski, 'Le problème du cumul de la responsabilité contractuelle et délictuelle' in *Rapports généraux Au VI-ième Congrès de droit comparé à Hamburg 1962*, Brussels 1964, p 357.

7 H Maine, *Ancient Law*, John Murray 1897, chapter 10, p 170.

ex delicto and *ex contractu* (Institutes of Gaius). Further, the obligation could arise under the four further categories of *ex delicto, ex contractu, quasi ex delicto* and *quasi ex contractu* (Institutes of Justinian). Any recoverable damage could be connected with only one form of action, so in many situations the legal protection was not available where there was no action available or acceptable under the Roman law.

A general tendency towards contract and delict was adopted in establishing modern codifications in the XIXth century. The provisions of civil codes on the law of obligations distinguished two highly important areas: law of contract and law of delict, both having rather narrow scopes of application at the beginning. The mutual relation of the two civil liabilities was uncertain and unclear. With the passage of time, each liability expanded its scope of application, creating a common field where concurrent liabilities and remedies overlap.[8] Although there are many disparities, contractual and delictual liability do not differ fundamentally, and the contractual and delictual standard of social conduct show many similarities in all legal systems in Europe (the common law tradition as represented by English law, the civil law tradition as represented by the French law system and the German law, and the Dutch law system as an example of new 'mixed' legislation).[9]

It should be noted that modern codifications are based on the revolutionary concepts of party autonomy, general freedom of contract and broad freedom to contract,[10] which in broad strokes reflect the classification and general concept of Roman law[11] but in detail often introduced new or even opposite innovations.

The principle of the freedom of contract has led to the strict hierarchy of obligations with the absolute supremacy of contract law in some jurisdictions. After strong debates, the principle of '*non-cumul des responsabilités contractuelle et délictuelle*' was established in France, Spain,[12] Belgium, and Estonia. The principle of '*non cumul*' excludes resorting to non-contractual grounds if there is a contract between the parties. The leading principle states that the contracting parties cannot bring before a court an alternative delictual claim or a separate delictual claim. Blocking concurrent action in tort lasts 'as long as the facts from which the delictual liability would otherwise arise are governed by one of the contract's obligations'.[13]

Constitutional dimensions of codified private law (both contract and property law) were reflected in the body of law. The French Civil Code contained numerous provisions concerning contracts and only six provisions on delictual liability. Therefore, old French doctrine declared the essential nature of the will of the contracting parties. This is reflected in the famous saying that the intentions of the parties, whatever the form of the will's expression, is the justification not only of the binding force of contract in private

8 R Schulze and F Zoll, *The Law of Obligations in Europe: a New Wave of Codifications*, 2013, p 1.

9 M van Rossum, 'Concurrency of contractual and delictual liability in a European perspective' (1995) 4 *European Review of Private Law*, 527, 540.

10 V Ranouil, *L'Autonomie de la volonté: naissance et évolution d'un concept*, Presses Universitaires de France, Paris 1980, p 71.

11 R Zimmermann, *The Law of Obligations. Roman Foundations of the Civilian Tradition*, Juta 1990, p 506.

12 Ch von Bar, above n 2, pp 431–439.

13 J Bell, S Boyron and S Whittaker, *Principles of French Law*, 2nd ed, Oxford University Press 2008, p 328.

law but also its essential element, allowing the parties free shaping of the content of the contractual relationship. Concluding a contract means, under French interpretation of the structure and spirit of the Code, that the parties have also generally chosen to be bound by the terms of their contract and the legal mandatory and semi-imperative (dispositive) rules of the law of contracts only. Because of the 'implied' exclusion of the law of tort, it cannot govern the rights and remedies.

The other reason for the absolute supremacy of contractual liability[14] is the very broad coverage by contract law of the factual situations in real life. This is possible thanks to the very broad and contract-friendly interpretation by the courts of the facts in the individual case. The courts find contractual relationships in circumstances which would never be declared a basis for contractual liability in any other jurisdiction. Moreover, under French law, the rule of privity of contract is also very much relaxed (abandoned) and French courts construe the contractual liability against third parties broadly in the chain of contracts,[15] thus expanding the scope of contract law. Under Article 1121 and Article 1165 of the French Civil Code, a third party who benefits or would benefit under a contract may enforce its claims. For instance, producers are liable in contract on that ground to both immediate and subsequent purchasers of products. Under Article 1792 of the French Civil Code, builders of buildings are liable also to future purchasers.

The broad scope of contract law is reflected in the scope of implied duties and damages recoverable. There are some obligations implied in the binding contract,[16] which results in the development of contractual *obligations de sécurité* in French contract law, which expands the scope of contract law liability as compared to other jurisdictions.[17] Lastly, an important justification for the '*non cumul*' principle is that a few statutory provisions on delicts are constructed and interpreted so widely that maintaining a prohibition on concurrence seems necessary. Otherwise, contracting parties would be always able to switch to one of the many available tort claims.[18] Non-contractual strict liability and gardien liability makes the scope of tortious (delictual) duties very broad, as well as the notion of damage recoverable ('*dommage*'), covering common law damage of pure economic loss.[19]

The principle of party autonomy in private law has led to the opposite *cumul* rule in other jurisdictions. According to German, Austrian, Polish or Italian law, the buyer in

14 Ibid. p 328, J S Borghetti, 'Strict Liability in Tort and the Boundaries of Tort Law' in H Koziol and U Magnus (eds), *Essays in Honour of Jaap Spier*, Jan Sramek Verlag 2016, pp 20–34, C M Sharkey, 'Tort Liability for Pure Economic Loss: A Perspective from the United States and Some Comparative European Insights' (2016) 7 *Journal of European Tort Law* vol 3, 237, 239. Exceptions to the *non-cumul* rule are very rare, see G Viney, *Introduction à la responsabilité*, 3rd ed in J Ghestin (ed) *Traité de droit civil*, Librairie générale de droit et de jurisprudence 2008, no. 48–56–1. A reform proposal (*the Avant-projet de réforme*) created an exception to the *non-cumul* rule for those who suffer personal injury.

15 S Whittaker, 'Privity of Contract and the Law of Tort: the French Experience' (1995) 15 *Oxford Journal of Legal Studies* 327, 337.

16 L-J Constantinesco, 'Die Persönlichkeitsrechte Und ihr Schutz im französischen Recht' (1960) *Archiv für die Civilistische Praxis*, 320, 344.

17 Ch von Bar, above n 12, pp 468–470.

18 M van Rossum, above n 9.

19 M Bussani and V V Palmer, 'Between Contract and Tort: Pure Economic Loss in Europe' in N Cohen and E McEndrick (eds), *Comparative Remedies for Breach of Contract*, Hart Publishing, Oxford and Portland, Oregon 2005, 189.

the sales contract may found his/her claims both on the contract and on extra-contractual, non-contractual basis. In the Netherlands the courts developed the principle of concurrence and, although the 1838 Old Dutch Civil Code was based on the French concepts, the Dutch interpretation of the French code and institutions like freedom of contract and party autonomy led to a different approach.

These systems typically allow concurrent liabilities in a situation where one party to the contract acts in breach of contract and his or her conduct also (additionally) fulfils the definition and requirements of a tort. In such circumstances, a claimant may sue in contract or in tort. Under Dutch and Polish law, the coexistence of contractual and delictual liability in damages is possible only in the case of an unlawful act arising independently of the breach of contract.

There are, however, some specific exceptions to the general rule on concurrence. The common area of application and concurrence of actions encompasses restricted tortious liability being in competition with a broad law of contract.[20] The broad right to a concurrent action is balanced out by narrow tort rules. German tort law provisions do not generally permit recovery of pure economic loss caused by negligence. Damage (*Schaden*) is primarily personal injury or damage to property. Moreover, under German and Austrian law it is possible to limit to some degree or to modify the alternative claim/remedy in tort, due to the leading principle of '*einwirkende Anspruchskonkurrenz*'. This provides that the contractual relationship existing between the parties and all relating legal provisions can impose restrictions upon what can be recovered in tort; if a higher degree of culpability is required for contractual liability, the same degree can be required for the available tort claim.[21]

In England too, the courts have generally accepted concurrent liability. The main area in which concurrent liability for the breach of contract and the tort of negligence may arise is in a case where a contractual term is violated.[22] In English law, only some kinds of tort may be in concurrence with contractual remedies. This is due to the fact that not all torts, negligence for instance, may be available in case of a breach of contract.[23] In common law, liabilities of a professional tradesman, supplier or seller can arise in contract, in tort, under special act regulating the behaviour or quality of goods and services, or in equity for breach of fiduciary duty. The source of the liability depends on the circumstances of each case and there may be overlapping or concurrent liabilities. What is more, some contracts, such as contracts for services (*Astley v Austrust Ltd*),[24] contain an implied promise of the provider to exercise reasonable care and skill. This

20 Ch von Bar, above n 12, pp 419–422, 464–467.

21 B Markensis, H Unberath and A Johnston, *German Law of Contract*, 2nd ed, Hart Publishing, Oxford and Portland, Oregon 2006, p 768.

22 M van Rossum, above n 9, p 539.

23 Another interesting issue is the emergence of new torts. Tortious liability for breach of a duty of good faith and fair dealing was established due to the creative use of torts. Moreover, some American courts have recognised a new *prima facie* tort, described in s.870 of Restatement (Second) of Torts which resembles general basis for tortious liability in civilian systems of private: one who intentionally causes injury to another is subject to liability to the other for that injury, if his or her conduct is generally culpable and not justifiable under the circumstances. See J O'Donovan, *Lender Liability*, Sweet &Maxwell, London 2005, p 30.

24 [1999] 161 C.L.R. 155.

implied duty exists concurrently with the common law duty of care in tort, unless the parties agree to limit or exclude the tortious remedy (*Henderson*). In the absence of such a limitation or exclusion, a claimant may seek a remedy in contract or in tort, although the legal consequences of these claims may be different – because of the different operations of the limitation periods, the defendant's duty to mitigate damages in contract and the claimant's liability for contributory negligence in tort.[25]

In England, a contracting party's ability to bring concurrent actions in tort and contract is still a matter of some uncertainty.

In a leading precedent, *Henderson v Merrett Syndicates Ltd*,[26] the House of Lords recognised that a duty of care in tort can co-exist with obligations arising under a contract in so far as this form of concurrent liability is not contrary to the terms of the contract between the parties: 'the claimant may be entitled to take advantage of the remedy which is most advantageous to him, subject only to ascertaining whether the tortious duty is so inconsistent with the applicable contract that, in accordance with ordinary principle, the parties must be taken to have agreed that the tortious remedy is to be limited or excluded'. On the other hand, in *Tai Hing Cotton Mill Ltd v Lu Chong Hing Bank Ltd*,[27] the Privy Council saw no advantage in searching for a liability in tort where the parties are in a contractual relationship, particularly in a commercial relationship. The court preferred contractual analysis. In *Robinson v PE Jones (Contractors) Limited*, the Court of Appeal rejected the notion of concurrent remedies and interpreted the *Henderson* case narrowly. This points to the acceptance of the hegemony of contractual liability in common law.[28]

3. Analysis of EU law

Concurrence of claims should be taken into account while drafting and implementing EU secondary laws, as well as during interpretation by the CJEU and member governments adopting national laws implementing EU secondary law. In this chapter, I examine how EU legal instruments deal with the question of concurrence of liabilities within the law of obligations, since differing alternative remedies are available to the claimant at the national level.

3.1. Neutrality of EU-based consumer law directives

Directives are the main regulatory instrument for the EU in private law matters. Provisions in directives become binding on private parties only from the time as the national legislator has transposed them into domestic law.Successful implementation meets the goals and policy of the directive and must be followed by the duty to interpret domestic law in line with the purpose, goals and policy of a directive.

At least some directives may cover remedies in both contract and tort, available in case of the breach of contract, but national legislators or national courts may ignore it.

25 *Hawkins v Clayton* [1988] 164 C.L.R. 539 at 583.

26 [1995] 2 A.C. 145 at 193–194.

27 [1986] A.C. 80, at 107.

28 A Cockrell, 'The hegemony of contract' (1998) 115 *SALJ*, 268.

The question is how to protect a private party to whom rights (remedy in tort or contract) have been made sufficiently clear and unconditionally conferred in a directive when the Member State transposes the directive in an *insufficient* way.

From a practitioner's perspective, the regulation of the remedies to which one of the parties can resort if the other party does not meet obligations stemming from the sales contract is very important.

The harmonization of tort law resulting from the Product Liability Directive is not total, and could not be total. Under the Directive, a producer shall be liable only for two kinds of *damage* as Article 9 PLD reads. Namely, damage caused by death or by personal injuries and damage to the property other than the defective product. What is more, there are many matters concerning generally defective products which are not covered by the Directive and are dealt with exclusively under national tort law. Pure economic losses are excluded. Loss of use as consequential damage is not recoverable. EU product liability does not cover non-material damage, since it relates only to 'material' damage. According to Article 9 par 3 PLD, the Directive shall be without prejudice to national provisions relating to non-material damage and does not cover compensation for pain and suffering and other non-material damages payable under national laws. The law of Member States determines the definition and scope of non-material damage in tort and in contract.

3.1.1. Consumer Rights Directive

The Consumer Rights Directive[29] does not provide any EU-based remedies to consumers and leaves it to the Member States to regulate issues and remedies related to the non-performance or improper performance of a consumer contract.

The purpose of the CRD is to approximate only certain aspects of the laws of the Member States concerning contracts concluded between consumers and traders. It regulates only specific rights that consumers have in European law when concluding contracts. In fact, it covers only selected issues of contract law, i.e. consumer pre-contractual information rights and a right of withdrawal from the contract due to non-performance of that special duties.[30] General contract law aspects are not regulated in this Directive, for the Directive shall not affect national general contract law (Art. 3 par 5 CRD). Therefore, it does not harmonize national provisions on liability for non-performance or improper performance of the contract, except for the rule that the consumer shall not incur any liability as a consequence of the exercise of the right of withdrawal from those contracts (Art. 14 par 5 CRD) and the reimbursement of costs in case of withdrawal from distance contracts and off-premises contracts.

29 Directive 2011/83/EU of the European Parliament and of the Council of 25 October 2011 on consumer rights [2011] OJ L304/64.

30 Only to those instruments the minimum level of harmonization applies. According to Art. 4 CRD, Member States shall not maintain or introduce, in their national law, provisions diverging from those laid down in this Directive, including more or less stringent provisions to ensure a different level of consumer protection, but the Directive shall not prevent from offering consumers contractual arrangements which go beyond the protection provided for in this Directive (Art. 3 par 6 CRD).

3.1.2. Consumer Sales Directive

Although the Consumer Sales Directive[31] was adopted to approximate the laws of the Member States on the sale of consumer goods and associated guarantees, it does not govern all issues concerning the liability of the seller but only certain aspects of it. The Directive regulates a limited number of topics, including certain remedies available to the consumer, with the purpose of ensuring within their scope a uniform minimum level of consumer protection in the context of the internal market (Art. 1 par 1 CSD).

It is clear that the EU legislator acknowledged the possibility of free concurrence of claims and liabilities under national laws and did not manage (or want) to regulate it, leaving the issue to the applicable national private law rules. The wording of the preamble to the Directive explains that the EU legislator found himself not yet competent to regulate, modify or harmonize national contractual and non-contractual remedies in case of breach of a consumer sale contract, nor the relationship between them, as expressed in a national rule on concurrence of contractual and tortious claims. The rationale behind that approach is explained in Recital 6 of the Directive, which states that because the main difficulties encountered by consumers at that time and the main source of disputes with sellers concerned the non-conformity of goods with the contract, it was appropriate to approximate by the Directive only national legislation in this respect, 'without *impinging on* provisions and principles of national law relating to contractual and non-contractual liability'. According to Article 8 par 1 CSD, the rights resulting from the Directive (and introduced into national contract law) shall be exercised without prejudice to other rights which the consumer may invoke under the national rules governing contractual or non-contractual liability. In addition, pursuant to Article 18 par 4 CSD added in 2011, in the event of the termination of the contract the consumer may have recourse to other remedies provided by national law.

In other words, neither contractual nor tortious compensation claims for damages are regulated or addressed by the Directive. National rules of contract and tort law concerning claims in damages are not subject to the minimum harmonization obligation,[32] since the minimum standard harmonization concerns only the topics covered by the Directive. On the other hand, the EU legislator takes into account that the national law may regulate free choice on the side of the consumer between national contractual or non-contractual remedies in damages. The Directive does not regulate whether there is or must be any hierarchy between harmonized consumer-sale-contractual claims and non-harmonized tortious claims. What is more, the Directive does not contain any provision which establishes a claim for damages for lack of conformity, let alone one that would indicate whether such claim would have to be based on contract law or on tort law.

[31] Directive 1999/44/EC of the European Parliament and of the Council of 25 May 1999 on certain aspects of the sale of consumer goods and associated guarantees [1999] OJ L171/12.

[32] Within the field covered by this Directive Member States may adopt or maintain in force more stringent provisions to ensure a higher level of consumer protection (Art. 8 par 2 CSD).

Consequently, the Directive includes uniform provisions on some typical contractual remedies which are connected with the execution of a contract,[33] prescribing in the case of a lack of conformity a certain hierarchy of contractual remedies. The preference is given to the right to cure the lack of conformity by first awarding the remedy of specific performance and only as a second tier the right to terminate the contract. The Consumer Sales Directive is drafted for consumer sales, but based on the CISG for professional sales.[34] The purpose of the Directive was to introduce similar regulations[35] and, indeed, implementation of this Directive changed the set of remedies to which buyers are entitled, as well as national terms which are to be implied into contracts of sale concluded between a professional seller and a consumer buyer.[36]

However, the claim for damages, not only in tort, but also in contract, remains outside the harmonizing scope of the Directive. The duty of the Member States to bring into force the laws necessary to comply with the Directive (Art. 11 par 1 CSD) does not extend to all contractual remedies, but is limited only to those resulting from it. As a consequence, only contractual remedies listed in the Directive are subject to the time limits set in its Article 5; only contractual cure remedies resulting from it cannot be directly or indirectly waived or restricted by any contractual terms or agreements with the seller in favour of the consumer (according to Art. 7 par 1 CSD such terms and agreements shall not be binding on the consumer). In my opinion, there is a reason for that. Minimal harmonization of contractual remedies does not require taking steps to harmonize the complex and politically dangerous field of damages.

3.1.3. Services Directive

National laws on liability of providers for services[37] have not been harmonized at the European level yet.[38]

[33] In the case of a lack of conformity, the consumer shall be entitled to have the goods brought into conformity free of charge by repair or replacement; in the first place, the consumer may require the seller to repair the goods or to replace them, unless this is impossible or disproportionate (Art. 3 par 3 CSD) or the seller has not completed the remedy within a reasonable time (Art. 3 par 5 CSD), to have an appropriate reduction made in the price, which is a kind of partial termination, to have the contract rescinded with regard to those goods (Art. 3 par 2 CSD) but only if the lack of conformity is not minor (Art. 3 par 6 CSD). The Consumer Rights Directive of 2011 added another harmonized remedy of reimbursement of all sums paid under the contract upon termination of the contract (Art. 18 par 3 CRD).

[34] U Magnus, 'The CISG's Impact on European Legislation' in F. Ferrari (ed), *The 1980 Uniform Sales Law, Old Issues Revisited in the Light of Recent Experiences*, Sellier, Munich 2003, pp 132–134. According to the Author, it is 'the most prominent example of the influence of the CISG on European legislation'.

[35] B van Zelst, *The Politics of European Sales Law*, diss. UvA 2008, p 188.

[36] MC Bianca and S Grundmann (eds.), *EU Sales Directive. Commentary*, Intersentia, Antwerp 2002.

[37] See comparative reports gathered in U Magnus and HW Micklitz (eds), *Liability for the Safety of Services*, Nomos 2006. Some national laws, e.g. Spanish and Finnish consumer protection law, take regulatory approach to both defective products and defective services.

[38] It seems that the only successful harmonization instrument concerning (tortious) liability for services remains the Convention on the Liability of Hotel-Keepers Concerning the Property of their Guests of 1962 that entered into force in 1979. It covers a very narrow field of services liability which

The proposal for a directive on liability for supplied services[39] was rejected in 1994. Just as the Product Liability Directive, the proposal aimed at regulating only 'tortious' national liability of the suppliers[40] due to the character of the protected interests (health, personal injury, property damage). It did not contain any hint as to the relationship with potentially concurring contractual claims, nor with other independent claims within the field of non-contractual liability. Nevertheless, one of the most important reasons for the rejection of the proposal was the fact that the supply of services is closely interrelated with contractual relationships, making an exclusively non-contractual approach 'less convincing'.[41] Moreover, since defective services are not defective products, suppliers of services are not producers of goods in the meaning of the Product Liability Directive.[42] Similar treatment of both is not justified because there are fundamental differences between products and services which render the rationale of product liability inapplicable. Unlike services, products are produced in one centralized process, and in accordance with general specifications. As a consequence, corporate control over production of products is highly centralized. Services, on the other hand, are less standardized and subject to a centralized control, tend to be more tailor-made and more specific.[43]

Adopted to cover national contract laws, the Services Directive[44] applies to services supplied by providers established in a Member State. Unfortunately, its scope of regulation is very narrow. It does not address the liability aspects, neither of contractual nor tortious remedies. The Directive introduces only a harmonized national right of a service recipient to some pre-contractual information on the provider and his services (Art. 22 SD), leaving even the liability for non-compliance with that duty outside the regulatory content of the Directive. It is also stressed explicitly, that the Directive does not concern rules of private international law governing the law applicable to contractual

is regarded rather as tortious or at least extra-contractual liability. The Convention was prepared within the Council of Europe and remains outside the EU but European countries are the contracting parties to it.

39 Proposal for a directive on the liability of suppliers of services, COM(90) 482 final. The work on the proposal began shortly after passing the directive on product liability, but it did not succeed. The draft closely followed the model of liability for defective products, with one significant exception. It required that the damage must be caused by *implied fault* committed in the performance of the service because the burden of proving the absence of fault was on the service supplier.

40 The proposal sought to harmonize the national rules on non-contractual liability for services of suppliers of services that should be liable for 1) damage resulting from injury to health and personal injury and 2) damage to the physical integrity of movable or immovable property.

41 G Brüggemeier, *Tort Law in the European Union*, Kluwer International 2015, p 193.

42 Case C-495/10, *Dutrueux*, ECLI:EU:C:2011:869, correcting the consequences of solving by ECJ a dispute arising out of defective medical service under product liability directive in Case C-203/99, *Veedfald*, ECLI:EU:C:2001:258. The Restatement (Third) of Torts explicitly excludes services from the scope of the US product liability regime.

43 R Hunter and L Bergkamp, 'Should Europe's Product Liability Regime Be Expanded? Comments on the European Commission's Green Paper on Product Liability', (2001) 17 *Product Safety & Liability Reporter* vol. 29, p 413.

44 Directive 2006/123/EC of the European Parliament and of the Council of 12 December 2006 on services in the internal market [2006] OJ L378/36.

and non-contractual obligations, including those which guarantee that consumers benefit from the protection granted to them by the consumer protection rules laid down in the consumer legislation in force in the Member State (Art. 3 par 2 SD).

However, the EU legislator acknowledges that, under some national laws, service providers may be held liable concurrently both in contract or in tort. The Member States may introduce in their national laws the legal obligation of providers – whose services present a direct and particular risk to the health or safety of the recipient or a third person, or to the financial security of the recipient – to subscribe to professional liability insurance appropriate to the nature and extent of the risk, or to provide a guarantee or similar arrangement which is equivalent or essentially comparable as regards its purpose (Art. 23 par 1 SD). This provision states that, under national law, service providers may be obliged to deliver appropriate insurance to the consumer that would cover damages usually associated with tortious claims (health or safety of the recipient or a third person), or with both tortious and contractual claims (financial security of the recipient). Indirectly, overlap of liabilities is taken into account while the attitude to the kind of provider's liability is neutral even at the stage of pre-contractual relations.

3.1.4. The Travel Package Directive of 1990

Both the Travel Package Directive of 1990[45] and the new directive of 2015 address the harmonization of the national laws relating to the liability for damages. The 1990 TPD was adopted as a sector service directive and one can find some traces of the approach taken in the unsuccessful general directive on defective services.[46] Both directives also share the influence of the CISG.[47]

The 1990 TPD tackles liability of an organiser and a retailer of travel services packages. It is said to regulate liability for the proper performance of obligations, in particular for the damage resulting for the consumer from failure to perform or improper performance of the contract. However, it does not in fact establish its own comprehensive set of EU-based remedies available to the parties of a contract. Instead, it gives a broad discretion to the Member States as regards transposition. Therefore, 'significant divergences between the laws of the Member' still remain,[48] in particular concerning the basis and scope of liability and the solution to the question of concurring contractual and tortious claims, which was the rationale for adopting the new 2015 TPD.

45 Council Directive 90/314/EEC of 13 June 1990 on package travel, package holidays and package tours [1990] OJ L158/59.

46 Pursuant to its Recital 22, the 1990 TPD regulates liability for the proper performance of the obligations, for the damage resulting for the consumer from failure to perform or improper performance of the contract, unless the *defects in the performance* of the contract are attributable.

47 U Magnus, above n 34, pp 142–143.

48 Recital 4 of the new Travel Package Directive of 2015. In many countries the implementation took place in form of a separate statute making the regulation of the liability of organizers a true legal transplant to 'recipient' country of unknown nature. It also raises doubts on the contractual or also tortious character of liability in damages that should be harmonized.

It seems that the Directive is focused on harmonizing only contractual responsibilities of a professional party in the case of improper performance of the package contract.[49] However, it contains one important provision which refers to the problem of liability and damage of the organizer. Under Article 5 par 2 of the 1990 TPD, the Member States are obliged to adopt the necessary national laws to ensure that the organiser and the retailer are *liable*, unless the failure to perform or improper performance is not attributable under the requirements set in the Directive. At this point, the Directive does not distinguish between contractual or tortious liability, even if the harmonization of liability addresses *damage* resulting for the consumer from the failure to perform or the improper performance of the contract, which focuses of the breach of the contractual obligation.

In my view, the regulation of liability can be interpreted more broadly as also encompassing tortious liability in damages, if the national rule of concurrence allows free choice by the claimant. Where free concurrence of claims is safeguarded for the injured party, damage resulting from the failure to perform or from the improper performance of the contract can cover both contractual and tortious damage. In other words, pursuant to Art. 5 there must be effective liability of the organizer under national law in case of non-performance of travel services, but it is up to national law to establish whether the organizer's liability is in contract only, or can be established in both.

The abovementioned understanding of the Directive is strengthened by the second rule relating directly to the liability of the organizer for personal injury which in many jurisdictions is connected more frequently with tortious claims in damages. Pursuant to Article 5 par 2 of the 1990 TPD, in the matter of damage other than personal injury resulting from the non-performance or improper performance of the services involved in the package, the Member States may allow compensation to be limited under the contract and such limitation shall not be unreasonable. It means that the organizer may introduce to the contract some limitations as to his or her liability both in contract and in tort; and, that he or she is not allowed to introduce them in the matter of personal injury resulting from the non-performance or improper performance of the services involved in the package. Here, the EU legislator acknowledges that under national laws damages resulting from the non-performance of some travel contracts can be recoverable in contract or in tort, if a national rule on concurrence of liabilities and remedies allows free choice of alternative claims by the injured party. Article 5 only allows that the compensation (sum of money paid) can be limited under the contract with the consumer. The binding agreement of the parties may limit the scope of both contractual and tortious damages other than personal injury.

In other words, Article 5 TPD allows to claim, under national laws, for material and non-material damages both in contract and in tort, provided that national rules allow

49 The scope and amount of compensation differs depending on whether a significant proportion of the service contracted for is not or is going to be not provided. The organizer may not be liable if he or she makes suitable alternative arrangements for the continuation of the package with compensation for the difference between the services offered and supplied, or he or she should compensate the consumer and take care of him or her if it is impossible to make such arrangements or if they were nor accepted by the consumer for good reasons (Art. 4 par 7 of 1990 TPD).

free choice of the claimant of one of the concurring remedies. As a result, also the CJEU judgement in the *Simone Leitner* case[50] must be read broadly. The justification for the broad interpretation of national law in light of Article 5 of the 1990 TPD and the *Leitner* case can be traced back to the wording and purpose of the Directive. The CJEU explained that the scope of damages recoverable by the travellers from the organizer for non-performance of the contract encompasses material as well as any kind of non-material damage that the consumer experienced and suffered. At the same time, this famous case is the best example of the wide coverage of national law by the two requirements embodied in Article 5 of the 1990 TPD, since the claim raised in the proceedings before the Austrian court against the travel organizer was based on tortious provisions on compensation for pain and suffering (*Schmerzensgeld*). By the same token, the court referring the question to the preliminary ruling was deciding the case not in contract liability in damages but in tort liability, asking whether limitations as to the scope of damages in tort were in line with the Directive.

As a consequence, the 1990 TPD cannot be described as a contract law directive only. Its goal is to approximate the laws relating to packages sold or offered for sale (Art. 1 of the 1990 TPD) and the Member States are obliged to bring into force measures necessary to comply with the Directive. Its implementation into national law is therefore based on the scope of national contract and tort laws and the national leading rules concerning the concurrence of contractual and tortious rights/remedies. Article 5 of the 1990 TPD leaves it to the Member States to determine what remedies should be granted to consumers who have purchased package travel in case of non-performance or improper performance of the contract. In the field covered by its provisions, Member States may adopt more stringent provisions, but only with the purpose to protect the consumers (Art. 8 of the 1990 TPD). It is for the Member States to determine whether such more stringent provisions are introduced or maintained and if so, whether these belong to the law of contract or to the law of tort.

3.1.5. The Travel Package Directive of 2015

By contrast, the new Travel Package Directive[51] constitutes a step backward in EU law development in the field of regulating liability of the organizer of a package contract.

The Directive harmonizes national rules concerning the responsibility of the organizer for the performance of the package contract. There is a certain set and hierarchy of remedies that must be available under harmonized national travel law (termination of the contract, price reduction, compensation for damages)[52] in three situations: the

50 C-168/00, *Leitner*, ECLI:EU:C:2002:163.

51 Directive (EU) 2015/2302 of the European Parliament and of the Council of 25 November 2015 on package travel and linked travel arrangements [2015] OJ L326/1.

52 Implementing *Leitner* judgment, travellers should be entitled to many remedies and/or compensation for damages that should also cover non-material damage such as compensation for loss of enjoyment of the trip or holiday because of substantial problems in the performance of the relevant travel services (Recital 34 of the Directive).

breach of contract that substantially affects the performance of the package,[53] a breach that means that a significant proportion of the travel services cannot be provided as agreed[54] and any other (minor) lack of conformity.[55] The Directive covers only the special contractual remedies available, including the claim for compensation in damages and its place in the hierarchy of contractual remedies.[56] Only those special measures must be adopted in the national laws ensuring compliance with its norms. Moreover, only the provisions on contractual measures were given imperative nature. Travellers may not waive the rights conferred on them by the national measures transposing this Directive (Art. 23 par 2 of the 2015 TPD), neither voluntarily nor by adhering to standard contract terms; and also, any contractual arrangement or any statement by the traveller which directly or indirectly waives or restricts the rights conferred on travellers by the Directive (or rather by the national law implementing the Directive) is not binding on the traveller (Art. 23 par 3 of the 2015 TPD).

On the other hand, any potential liability of the organizer in tort is not regulated by this purely 'contract law directive'. The reason for that is, in my opinion, the new method of harmonization of national private law based on the maximum harmonization level. Unless otherwise provided for in the Directive, Member States shall not maintain or introduce, in their national law, any provisions diverging from those laid down in the Directive, including more or less stringent provisions which would ensure a different level of traveller protection (Art. 4 of the 2015 TPD).

So many disparities and differences between national private law regimes concerning the scope of liabilities in damages and the existence of the national rule on concurrence are the reasons why the EU legislator decided not to regulate the complex issue of

53 Pursuant to Art. 13 par 6 of the 2015 TPD, where a lack of conformity is very serious, i.e. *substantially affects* the performance of the package, and the organiser has failed to remedy it within a reasonable period set by the traveller, the traveller may terminate the package travel contract and request price reduction and/or compensation for damages. The traveller shall be entitled to receive appropriate compensation from the organiser *for any damage* which the traveller sustains as a *result of any lack of conformity*, as set out in Art. 14 par 2 of the 2015 TPD and in line with further requirements set out in Art. 14 par 3 of the 2015 TPD. Pursuant to Art. 14 par 6 of the TPD, the limitation period for introducing those claims shall be not less than two years.

54 According to Art. 13 par 5 of the 2015 TPD, where a significant proportion of the travel services cannot be provided as agreed in the package travel contract, the organiser shall offer alternative arrangements for the continuation of the package. Pursuant to Art. 13 par 6 of the 2015 TPD, if the traveller rejects the proposed alternative arrangements in accordance with the Directive or if it is impossible to make alternative arrangements, he or she is entitled to price reduction and/or compensation for damages without terminating the package travel contract. The other requirements are the same.

55 If the organizer does not remedy (any other) lack of conformity, the traveller may remedy the lack of conformity himself and request *reimbursement* of the necessary expenses or the traveller is entitled to an appropriate *price reduction* for any period during which there was lack of conformity, or the traveller shall be entitled to receive appropriate *compensation* from the organiser *for any damage* which the traveller sustains as a *result of any lack of conformity*, as set out in Art. 14 par 2 and 3 of the 2015 TPD.

56 It was appropriate to set out specific rules on remedies in the case of the lack of conformity in the performance of the package travel contract because the 1990 Directive gave too broad discretion to the Member States as regards transposition which caused fragmentation, significant divergences between the laws of the Member States, higher costs for business and obstacles for those wishing to operate cross-border, as Recitals 4 and 34 read.

concurrent tortious liability of the organizer for improper performance or non-performance of the contracts subject to the Directive. It is still too early for one uniform regulation of that issue, regardless whether it would be done by the regulation or a directive based on the maximum harmonization approach. As a consequence, Article 2 par 3 of the 2015 TPD provides that this Directive does not affect national general contract law, insofar as general contract law aspects are not regulated. Without any doubt, the solution to the potential overlap between the laws of contract and tort is a matter of general contract law. What is more, the Directive should be implemented without prejudice to national contract law for those aspects that are not regulated by it (as its Recital 20 clearly states). Additionally, the Directive should not affect the rights of travellers to present claims both under this Directive *and* under other relevant Union legislation or international conventions and to address claims to the organiser, the carrier or any other liable party.[57]

It is doubtful whether the adopted method of regulation, leaving potential alternative concurrent liability of the organizer in tort under some national laws behind, serves the objectives of the new Directive. Its purpose is the achievement of a high level of consumer protection as uniform as possible by approximating the laws of the Member States in respect to contracts between travellers and traders (Recital 51 of the Directive). Disparities in the rules protecting travellers in different Members States act as a disincentive to buying packages and linked travel arrangements in another Member State and, likewise, a disincentive for organizers and retailers in one Member State to sell such services in another Member State (Recital 6 of the Directive).

3.1.6. Digital Directives of 2016

The European Commission has tabled two proposals for new directives, one pertaining to contracts for the supply of digital content,[58] the other regarding online and other distance sales of goods.[59] In both, the EU legislator interferes with areas that have so far been the exclusive domain of national civil law (and not even dealt with in the Consumer Sales Directive), such as determining adequate levels of damages or the more detailed consequences of termination of the contract.

With the two proposals of digital directives, the Commission no longer strives for complete EU rules in the area of sales law. Instead, it now intends to introduce maximum harmonization, but limited to some areas of contract law. The EU refuses to become a traditional civil law legislator. Instead, it goes back to regulating certain spheres, but not

57 In order to avoid overcompensation, compensation or price reduction granted under this Directive and the compensation or price reduction granted under other relevant Union legislation or international conventions should be deducted from each other (Recital 36 of the Directive).

58 Commission Proposal for a Directive of the European Parliament and of the Council on certain aspects concerning contracts for the supply of digital content, COM(2015) 364 final (hereinafter: Digital Content Directive Proposal).

59 Commission Proposal for a Directive of the European Parliament and of the Council on certain aspects concerning contracts for the online and other distance sales of goods, COM(2015) 365 final (hereinafter: Online Sales Directive Proposal).

all aspects of complex private relationships.[60] Although areas covered by the directives are subject to the full maximum harmonization, with regard to digital content the Member States remain free to call on national legislatures to lay down the detailed conditions for the exercise of the *right to damages*.[61] Article 9 of the Online and Distance Sale of Goods Proposal deals with the contractual remedies for lack of conformity of goods; however, the proposal does not contain a remedy for compensation,[62] leaving the right to claim damages to national law.[63] According to Article 1 par 4 of the Directive Proposal, the Directive shall not affect national 'general contract laws'. This wording of the proposal raises questions: Does that mean that a *special* contract rule on remedy in damages is excluded, thanks to the maximum harmonization character of the Directive? Are *tortious* damages available, being outside the scope of the Directive?

Additionally Article 14 par 1 of the Digital Content Directive Proposal states that the supplier shall be liable to the consumer for any economic damage to the digital environment of the consumer caused by a lack of conformity with the contract or a failure to supply the digital content, but the Member States shall lay down detailed rules for the exercise of the right to damages. This means that national rights and obligations, as well as the remedies for consumers, may vary between Member States, since the Directive will not affect national laws to the extent that the topics concerned are not regulated by this Directive. Member States should also remain free to provide rules for the detailed conditions for the exercise of rights, such as the *right to damages* to the extent not covered by the Directive. As follows from Recital 44, consumers should be entitled to compensation for damages caused to the consumer's digital environment by a lack of conformity with the contract or a failure to supply the digital content. However, it should be for Member States to lay down the detailed conditions for the exercise of the right to damages.

It seems that neither proposal creates uniform rules across the EU. Instead, they result in sets of European and national rules that might differ greatly from one country to another.

3.1.7. Unfair Consumer Terms Directive

The Unfair Consumer Terms Directive[64] was not meant to directly harmonize the content of the national rules on the relation of liabilities in contract and tort. The purpose of the Directive is to approximate the laws of the Member States, but only those relating to unfair terms in some contracts, namely in contracts concluded between a seller or supplier (a professional party) and a consumer (Art. 1 par 1 UCTD). Neither the relation between contractual claims and claims stemming from any other non-contractual

[60] A critical analysis of both proposals presents M Lehmann, 'A Question of Coherence. The Proposals on EU Contract Rules on Digital Content and Online Sales', (2016) 23 *Maastricht Journal*, 752, 774.

[61] Recital 44 and Article 14(2) of the Digital Content Directive Proposal.

[62] In the case of a lack of conformity with the contract, the consumer shall be entitled to have the goods brought into conformity by the seller, free of charge, by repair or replacement, or to a proportionate reduction of the price, or to terminate the contract.

[63] See the Explanatory Memorandum to the Online and Distance Sale of Goods Proposal, p. 3.

[64] Council Directive 93/13/EEC of 5 April 1993 on unfair terms in consumer contracts [1993] OJ L95/29.

liability in private law, nor the effects of the concluded standard terms contract on the existence and possible scope of the remedies available under harmonized national private law is the effect of the Directive.

Only a contractual term, for instance regulating liability of the parties to a consumer contract that has not been individually negotiated can be declared as unfair, if it is contrary to the requirement of good faith, or if it causes a significant imbalance in the parties' rights and obligations arising under the contract, to the detriment of the consumer (Art. 3 par 1 UCTD). This means that statutory provisions or judge-made law (both EU-based and not harmonized) rules on liability in damages or on concurrence of claims/remedies in damages cannot be controlled by courts, nor declared by courts as an unfair abusive term as Article 1 par. 2 UCTD confirms.

However, the scope of the Directive covers the effects (or rather avoidance) of the concluded standard term contract provisions in an indirect way when the pre-arranged standard terms contain some express provisions on the exclusion or limitation of the seller's or supplier's liability in case of a breach of contract. In general, the unfairness of any contractual term on liability may be assessed, taking into account the nature of the goods or services for which the contract was concluded and by referring, at the time of conclusion of the contract, to all the circumstances attending the conclusion of the contract and to all the other terms of the contract or of another contract on which it is dependent (Art. 4 par 1 UCTD).

It should be noted that among the terms which may be regarded as unfair (and are listed in the Annex to the Directive as clear examples of contractual unfairness) one can find standard terms relating to liability in damages. According to the European legislator, there are three potentially abusive terms relating to the seller's or supplier's liability in consumer standard term contracts. They are listed as a minimum standard, since the Directive introduces the *minimum* harmonization rule at this point and the scope of these terms may be the subject of amplification or more restrictive editing by the Member States in their national laws.

First, a term excluding or limiting the *legal liability* of a seller or supplier in the event of the death of a consumer or personal injury to the consumer resulting from an act or omission of that seller or supplier was listed. Because under national private laws this kind of damage/injury (death or personal injury) is typically covered by tortious or non-contractual liability rules and most claimants ground their claims in tort/delict, this standard term refers mostly to the contractual exclusion or limitation of the liability in tort, in particular liability in damages. Although it can also refer to the exclusion or limitation to liability in damages in contract.

Second, abusive can be a term inappropriately excluding or limiting the *legal rights* of the consumer against the seller or supplier in the event of total or partial non-performance or improper performance of any of the contractual obligations. Again, this event refers to the different degrees of the breach of contract (improper performance, partial or total non-performance) for which the contractual remedies laid down in national laws outside the scope of the harmonization by the UCTD, including remedy in damages, are available. Nevertheless, this example can be interpreted as also covering *legal rights* grounded in tortious or non-contractual liability, if they are available concurrently or alternatively under the national private law regime. The rationale for this is that the

EU-based national law on standard terms must be integrated into national private law, governed by non-harmonized general national rules, relating in particular to the concurrence of claims/remedies available in contract and tort in the case of the breach of contract. In other words, standard terms in a consumer contract excluding or limiting liability in tort, in particular liability in damages, are also potentially unfair and void.

Third, also a term excluding or hindering unduly the consumer's right to take *legal action* or exercise any other *legal remedy* is listed as potentially abusive. This example refers to the contractual provision, included into standard terms, on the limitation of the procedural actions/remedies which under national law are available to the consumer as grounded in the existing substantive right, such as a claim in damages in contract or – if the national rule on concurrence so allows – in tort. If there is an overlap of contractual and tortious claims in the given jurisdiction, this standard term provision can limit the choice of the consumer relating to the use of a procedural right to bring an action before a court either in contract or in tort or concurring actions in damages.

In other words, if in a given jurisdiction free concurrence is possible and based on the free choice of the consumer, he or she cannot be deprived of the right to raise before the court one of the available concurring claims against the seller or supplier. Consequently, one-sided limitation by the seller or supplier of such possibility is to be regarded as abusive. Such a term must be individually negotiated with the consumers and they should agree voluntarily to such terms.

It is clear from the above that the Directive is neutral as to the discussed issue on the existence and content of the national rule on the concurrence of contractual and tortious claims in damages. The EU legislator does not analyse whether the national solution on the concurrence is just and fair or reasonable. Once it is available, it must be taken into account while concluding pre-drawn contracts with consumers being regarded as a weaker party to the contract in the internal market. Article 4 par 1 USTD states that the assessment of unfairness of a contractual term on liability (located in standard terms) must take into account not only the nature of the goods or services for which the contract was concluded but also all the circumstances attending the conclusion of the contract and all the other terms of the contract or of another contract on which it is dependent. The 'other terms of contract… on which it is dependent' contain also those terms of contract with constitute a part of contractual relationship as mandatory provisions of statutory law or judge-made law.

3.1.8. Conclusion

The analysis of selected EU law directives leads to the conclusion that they do not intervene nor regulate the possible tortious liability of the seller, supplier or trader, nor tortious claims that may be available for consumers or travellers in the case of non-performance or improper performance of a consumer contract. Except for Art. 5 of the 1990 TPD, the harmonization of national provisions on professional liability was conducted in contract only. The Directives cover only a total or partial set of contractual remedies available to the consumer.

Therefore, the question of possible concurrent claims in damages in tort is solved by the court solely under national rules on concurrence of liabilities in damages. The rules on concurrence are not modified by the fact that alternative national claims are grounded on EU-based and non-harmonized national laws, respectively. The European origin of national provisions implementing the abovementioned directives is not relevant for the issue of concurrence (except for Art. 5 of the 1990 TD which acknowledges possibility of concurrent tortious claims), since the existence of overlap between the laws of tort and contract, as well as the solution to the problem of concurrence under general private law, fall outside the scope and spirit of the directives. Moreover, there should not be established an opposite rule. Neither the purpose of the directive nor the duty to bring interpretation of national provisions in line with the directive could be the basis for an EU-based rule excluding any alternative non-contractual claims in tort. There is no possibility to create an EU *non-cumul* rule stemming from the spirit of the fragmented directives or from the silence of the EU legislation on the topic.

As a consequence, there is no room to create either an EU concurrence-friendly rule or EU *non-cumul* rule on exclusion of any non-contractual national claims in situations of improper performance covered by the directives. So far, there is also no need to apply the *Marleasing* doctrine of interpretation of national law in line with the directives. In case a national court denied the concurrent claim as being disallowed under national law because of a wrong interpretation of a directive, the private party could not base the claim directly on the directive, since under the *Marshall* doctrine there is no horizontal direct effect of directives.[65] Directives have direct effect only between the Union and the Member States and private parties are bound only by the national legislative act by which the directive has been transposed into national law.

There is no need and no reason to apply the obligation of the Member State to interpret national law in line with the directive, as established in *Marleasing*.[66] This horizontal indirect effect of directives is another reaction to the absence of horizontal direct effect of directives, and means that national courts are obliged to interpret domestic law in the light of the directive, regardless whether it was implemented or unimplemented (fully). The national court is required to interpret national law, regardless of whether it is passed before or after the directive, in the light of the wording and purpose of the directive to preclude a *result contrary* to its objective. According to some commentators, conform interpretation of national private law is another type of transposing the EU law ground of liability into the respective national law system of remedies and causes of action allowing compensation.[67]

65 Case 152/84, *Marshall*, ECLI:EU:C:1986:84, Case C-91/92, *Faccini Dori*, ECLI:EU:C:1994:29, Case C-192/94, *El Corte Inglés*, ECLI:EU:C:1996:88, Joined Cases C-397–403/01, *Pfeiffer and Others*, ECLI:EU:C:2004:584.

66 Case C-106/89, *Marleasing*, ECLI:EU:C:1990:395. This interpretative obligations is deduced from the Member States' legal duty to take all measures necessary to ensure compatibility with EU law, pursuant to Art. 4 par 3 TEU.

67 For general remarks see K Havu, 'Horizontal Liability for Damages in EU Law – The Changing Relationship of EU and National Law', (2012) 18 *European Legal Journal*, 407, 408, N Reich, 'Horizontal Liability in EC Law: Hybridization of Remedies for Compensation in Case of Breaches of EC Rights', (2007) 44 *Common Market Law Review*, 705 ff. In the last article one can find very interesting proposal for a general ground for EU breach-of-law liability to be introduced in the law of delict/torts of each Member State as a breach of a protective statute.

When a directive has been transposed in due time but incorrectly, the liability *British Telecommunications* regime applies[68] which is a modification of the *Francovich* type of responsibility.[69] The Member State can be made responsible and liable for depriving its residents from a right conferred to them through a directive. The most important ground of liability entails the violation of a provision of EU law which confers rights to private parties, i.e. it must have a protective effect towards legitimate private interests. This kind of liability should be available in case the state, while implementing a directive erroneously interprets its scope as too narrow and implements it improperly. There is only one requirement: to trigger state liability a sufficiently serious breach has to be established; the seriousness depending on the degree of clarity and precision of the directive provisions. What is more, another problem arises, namely that of no real sanction. The majority of actions for damages against improper legislative acts has been unsuccessful.[70] Neither judges nor courts can be sued even for manifest breaches which take place in the following situations:[71] 1) the national court fails to apply a clear and precise provision of EU law, 2) the national court fails to abide by well-established ECJ case law, 3) the national court refuses to make an obviously indicated reference for preliminary ruling, 4) the national court makes a reference but commits a flagrant error in applying the ruling of the ECJ.

Because the current wording and purpose of the consumer directives do not allow the creation of one uniform EU rule (whatever its content) on the relationship of remedies provided for in the 'contract law directives' and potentially alternative national claims in tort, the national courts cannot fail to fulfil the duty to apply the *Marleasing* doctrine while deciding cases in which the problem of concurrence arises.[72]

68 Case C-392/93, *British Telecommunications*, ECLI:EU:C:1996:131.

69 Joined Cases 6/90 and 9/90, *Francovich*, CLI:EU:C:1991:428. The right to rely on the directive before the national court under *Francovich* covers only failures of Member States to transpose EU directives properly and in time. The liability regime in *Francovich* requires four conditions to be fulfilled: no transposition of a directive within the prescribed period, conferral of rights on private parties by the directive in an unconditional and precise manner, the beneficial private party must incur damage, there must be a causal link between the breach and the damage sustained by the private party.

70 For England and Germany see T Lock, 'Is Private Enforcement of EU Law through State Liability a Myth?', (2012) 49 *Common Market Law Review*, 1675, 1675.

71 Case C-173/03, *Traghetti*, ECLI:EU:C:2006:391. See also T Tridimas, *General Principles of EU Law*, Oxford University Press 2005, p 526.

72 The state is generally not liable for judiciary, unless it is a failure of a national court of last instance. That kind of failure might give rise to *Köbler* liability of a Member State which is states' liability for their judicial bodies of last instance, rather for gross malfunctioning of the institution judiciary. See Case C-224/01, *Köbler*, ECLI:EU:C:2003:513. But one must remember that 'It is one thing to have a principle of liability to ensure the application and effectiveness of EU but it is quite another to see what it achieves in practice. In fact, the case law of the ECJ itself calls into question the effectiveness of the rules of liability for breach of EU law', C van Dam, *European Tort Law*, 2 ed, Oxford University Press 2013, p 50.

3.2. *The proposal for the common European sales law regulation*

The proposal for the Common European Sales Law Regulation[73] was based on the assumption that the best option for introducing uniform rules in private law in Europe is harmonization by adopting a regulation on contract or private law, establishing a more comprehensive regime than directives and covering all questions from the formation of the contract to the remedies for non-performance.[74] Unfortunately, the project that was cancelled[75] in February 2015 was focused only on the contractual liability of the seller. It concentrated only on contractual damages (Art. 159 on the right to damages)[76] meaning a sum of money to which a person may be entitled as compensation for loss, injury or damage (Art. 2 point g CESL). The buyer's contractual remedies in Art. 106(1) CESL like the seller's remedies in Art. 131(1) CESL reflected international standards.

The EU legislator decided that all the matters of non-contractual liability that were not addressed in the Common European Sales Law should be governed by the pre-existing rules of the national law, remaining outside the Common European Sales Law. These issues include, among others, the law of torts as CESL did not govern any matters outside the remit of contract law. According to Article 4 par 2 CESL, only issues within the scope of the instrument but not expressly settled by it were to be settled in accordance with the objectives and the principles underlying it and all its provisions, *without recourse* to the national law that would be applicable in the absence of an agreement to use the CESL or any other law. This means that, to prevent legal uncertainty, questions of contractual liability not expressly regulated but nevertheless 'covered' by the provisions of the CESL had to be settled within the CESL principles and that the otherwise applicable law did not apply. The problem discussed in the literature was how such different domestic traditions might influence the uniform application of the CESL adopted as a contract by the parties.[77]

In my opinion, while analysing whether the concurrence of the contractual claims based on CESL and tortious claims based on national laws would be possible, the legal nature of the CESL must be taken into account. Regulation as a legislative instrument aims to replace the national private law. The solution to the problem of potential concurrence of national claims in tort and remedies grounded on CESL was influenced

73 European Commission Proposal for a Regulation of the European Parliament and of the Council on a Common Sales Law, Brussels, 11.10.2011, COM(2011) 635 final.

74 M Lehmann, 'A Question of Coherence. The Proposals on EU Contract Rules on Digital Content and Online Sales', (2016) 23 *Maastricht Journal*, 752, 773.

75 The CESL was withdrawn in 2015 due to disagreements between national governments over the proposal which means a temporary stagnation in the process of unification of European contact and sales law.

76 The proposed CESL Regulation listed the buyer's and the seller's remedies in the case of non-performance of an obligation by the other party (Articles 106, 131, 157). Remedies which were not incompatible might be cumulated.

77 S Vogenauer, 'The DCFR and the CESL as Models for Law Reform' in G Dannemann and S Vogenauer (eds), *The Common European Sales Law in Context. Interactions with English and German Law*, Oxford University Press 2013, p 824.

by the answer to the general question of the role and legal nature of the CESL regulation once a sales contract under CESL would be concluded.

Opting into the Common European Sales Law could amount to a choice of law under Article 3 of the Rome I Regulation. In that case, the question of whether to make a choice of law and to which system would remain relevant for issues being outside the scope of the instrument, in particular for the law of torts and the rule on the issue whether there is concurrence between contractual and non-contractual liabilities and whether the claims can be brought together; all these issues would be decided by the applicable national law.[78] On the other hand, the CESL was prepared to harmonize the national contract laws by creating within each Member State's national law a 'second contract law regime for contracts within its scope' and not by requiring amendments to the existing national contract laws (as the proposed Recital 9 of CESL clearly states). In that case, as a second contract regime within the same national law of a Member State, it would only become applicable, as a matter of national law, once given national law would be indicated as the law governing the contract. However, it was not entirely clear how a European sales law would become a 'second national regime' or rather, an optional instrument referred to as a 28th regime.

Under Dutch law it was noticed that the concurrence between the CESL and national private law may give rise to many 'classic' problems of concurrence. The problems of concurrence of claims governed by the CESL and grounded on national private law could be coordinated by using the leading national doctrine on concurrence.[79] Nevertheless, the legal form of a regulation would establish the relationship of priority of the regulation over national private law. The totality and maximum approach of the CESL regulation has led some commentators to introduce some limitations as to the free concurrence of alternative tortious claims. 'The uniformity of results which the CESL... seeks to achieve throughout the EU would require the CESL... rules to be exclusive in a particular area'. The principles of *effet utile* and subsidiarity will decide 'whether parallel regimes of an entirely different nature, in particular tort and property, must be tolerated'.[80]

Nevertheless, the CESL did not give any indication as to what the relationship of the remedies provided by the CESL ('contractual liability') was to other claims based on national law, particularly to tortious/delictual liability. The analysis of the remedial system under the proposal for a Regulation on a Common European Sales Law contains some suggestions for possible amendments, focusing in particular on the delivery of

78 MW Hesselink, 'How to opt into the Common European Sales Law? Brief Comments on the Commission's Proposal for a Regulation', (2011) 15 *Centre for the Study of European Contract Law Working Paper Series*, p 1.

79 R de Graaff, *Something old, something new, something borrowed, something blue? Applying the doctrine of concurrence on European sales law and international air law*, LLM thesis, Leiden University 2013, p 29. I agree that applying Dutch solution to the problem would only rarely lead to real escape into the law of torts because Dutch rule on concurrence states that application of tort law is excluded when it is frustrating the purpose of a contract norm, here the right or obligation based on the CESL provisions.

80 J Wendehorst in R Schulze (ed), *Common European Sales Law (CESL). Commentary*, Nomos Verlagsgesellschaft, Baden-Baden 2012, p 70.

goods not conforming to the contract.[81] At this point, the CESL might disappoint because of this lack of a clear solution to the problem of concurrence or expressed exclusion of potential concurrence of remedies available under national laws. The same sales contract might be subject to different findings depending on which is the national law applying outside the ambit of the CESL. From this point of view, lack of any hint on the applicability and scope of concurrent tortious claims based on the national laws seems to be inconsistent with the grounding idea of the CESL and more precisely with the leading assumption of a uniform law which was drafted exactly to avoid different results of cases tried in different Member States.

3.3. General approach in the Draft Common Frame of Reference

In 2004 the Commission launched a project to develop a Common Frame of Reference (CFR) for European Contract Law which was euphemistically described as a 'tool box' for the development of European contract law.[82] In order to achieve a more coherent European contract law,[83] the academic non-binding collection of model rules was adopted which contains a set of definitions, general principles and model rules in the field of private law. The DCFR originates in an initiative of European legal scholars and remains as an academic text.[84] Its structure looks remarkably similar to the Principles of European Contract Law.

Principles (rules of a more general nature), definitions (suggestions for the development of a uniform European terminology) and model rules (soft law rules that might be used as a model for EU legislation) have been adopted for the comprehensive regulation of the future contract law. The future legal effect of the Common Frame of Reference may range from a non-binding legislative document or restatement of common principles to the foundation for an optional instrument in European contract law. Therefore, the CFR was intended to provide a structure and guideline for the development of a whole harmonised European private law but has a specific focus on contract law.

81 B Piltz, *The proposal for a Regulation on a Common European Sales Law: provisions on remedies. Note*, Directorate General for Internal Policies, European Parliament 2012, p 7. Another interesting inconsistency in the text of the CESL is the unclear catalogue of the 'contractual' remedies the buyer had in a sales contract and in a contract for the supply of digital content. Art. 106 CESL seemed to give only a résumé of the remedies and not an exhaustive list of them, since mandatory provision of Art. 2(2) CESL, not permitting any modifications by the parties, established liability 'for any loss' caused to the other party. The same scope of liability was prescribed in Article 29(1) CESL. There also was no indication as to what is their relation to Art. 106 CESL, Art. 55 CESL and to Chapter 16 CESL.

82 Commission Communication, European Contract Law and the Revision of the Acquis: the Way Forward, COM(2004) 651, p 3.

83 Communication from the Commission to the Council and the European Parliament on European contract law, 11 July 2001, COM(2001) 398 final.

84 Ch von Bar, E Clive, H Schulte-Nölke et al. (eds), *Principles, Definitions and Model Rules of European Private Law, Draft Common Frame of Reference (DCFR), prepared by the Study Group on a European Civil Code and the Research Group on the Existing EC Private Law (Acquis Group), based in part on a revised version of the Principles of European Contract Law*, Sellier, Munich 2009.

The first and most interesting issue here is that in the academic Draft Common Frame of Reference concurrence of claims/remedies in damages is regulated by model rules. This is due to the fact that the DCFR is developed on the basis of comparative studies of EU law and the laws of the Member States and, therefore, has to reflect the underlying values to be found in the existing laws. The rule on concurrence (whether allowing or excluding alternative claims) belongs to these values, although the national solutions are not the same in each system.

The DCFR solution seems to be to mediate between the different national rules on concurrence. It takes a rather balanced position in comparison to so many different answers to the problem in different legal systems. There are differences between the underlying values for concurrence of contractual and tortious claims for compensation in damages in individual jurisdictions. It should be noted that the Principles of European Tort Law prepared in 2005 by the European Group on Tort Law[85] do not tackle the issue of the relationship of tort law to the contractual liability or existing contract between the parties. There is a glimpse in PETL Article 2:102(4), where among protected interests one can find damage to 'contractual relationship', protection of which may be more limited in scope (as well as protection of pure economic interests), in comparison to other protected interests like life, bodily or mental integrity, human dignity and liberty or damages caused by intentional harm that should enjoy the most extensive protection. The DCFR non-contractual liability arising out of damage is liability only for legally relevant damage (DCFR terms of VI.–2:101).[86]

The second interesting issue is that in the academic Draft Common Frame of Reference concurrence of claims/remedies in damages is regulated by the rules relating to non-contractual (tortious) liability, thus establishing the relationship of tortious claims to contractual liability. Non-contractual liability can be concurrent to any other kind of liability but I doubt whether a rule of general free concurrence of different actions seems to be the basic principle in the DCFR.[87]

The analysis must start from the structure of the DCFR. The law of obligations as a whole is covered in Books I-VII. The text and structure of the model rules are organized

85 The Basic norm in Art. 1:101 PETL states that any person to whom damage to another is legally attributed is liable to compensate that damage, and that damage may be attributed in particular to the person whose conduct constituting fault has caused it; or whose abnormally dangerous activity has caused it; or whose auxiliary has caused it within the scope of his functions. PETL distinguishes the following bases of liability: liability based on fault (including liability with a reversal of the burden of proving fault), strict liability and liability for others, as well as remedies in form of damages (pecuniary and non-pecuniary).

86 It means that in the case of potential concurrence of claims, a mere failure to perform a contractual obligation to deliver goods at the correct time or of the correct quality is not legally relevant damage for tortious liability and by the same token not covered by the DCFR rule VI.–2:101. The question of concurrence does not exist where the scope of tort law is narrower than that of contract law. Silence of tort law or lack of compensation of certain damages under tort law (ie under the DCFR rules) does not mean that 'tortious' claims are excluded in case of non-performance of a contractual obligation which would be a solution on the concurrence itself.

87 A G Castermans and R de Graaff, 'The general concept of concurrence applied to European inslovency law' in B Santen and D van Offeren (eds), *Perspectives on International Insolvency Law: A Tribute to Bob Wessels*, Kluwer, Deventer 2014, p 34.

like in a private law codification. The model rules are divided into Books and each Book is subdivided into Chapters or Parts. The DCFR contains contractual and non-contractual parts, as well as general parts common for the two general regimes. Contractual matters are regulated in Book II on 'Contracts and other juridical acts'[88] and Book IV on 'Specific contracts and obligations arising from them'.[89] The non-contractual liabilities are regulated separately in Book VI on 'Non-contractual liability arising out of damage',[90] Book V on 'Benevolent intervention in another's affairs'[91] and Book VII on 'Unjustified enrichment'.[92] There are also two levels in the general part of the law of obligations. Book III on 'Obligations and corresponding rights'[93] relates to both contractual and non-contractual liabilities.[94] The most general part, namely Book I on 'General Provisions'[95] applies to all liabilities. It is subsidiary though and its application is based on the principle *lex specialis derogat legi generali*. Where there is a general rule and a special rule applying to a particular situation within the scope of the general rule, the special rule prevails in any case of conflict (DCFR I.-1:102(5)).

Taking the abovementioned structure into account, I agree that there is a principle of free concurrence of various contractual actions/remedies within the scope of 'DCFR contract law'[96] and a free concurrence of actions stemming from various non-contractual liabilities, including even the concurrence of two or more 'tortious' liabilities.[97] Nevertheless, the relationship of non-contractual liability to contract law is regulated by the two special rules set out in DCFR rule VI.–1:103 on the scope of application of the rules contained in Book VI on Non-contractual liability arising out of damage.

88 DCFR II.-1:101 to II.-9:411. Here, the DCFR incorporates PECL in a partly revised form as many rules are derived from PECL. The key term used here is 'contract' and 'obligation'.

89 DCFR IV.-1:101 to IV.G.-4:107.

90 DCFR VI.-1:101 to VI.-7:105.

91 DCFR V.-1:101 to V.-3:106.

92 DCFR VII.-1:101 to VII.-7:103.

93 DCFR III.-1:101 to III.-7.601.

94 Provisions of Book III are directly applicable to contractual rights and obligations, they also apply to non-contractual rights and obligations. As it was explained in the DCFR, applying this model rules only to contractual rights and obligations would create the gap between contractual and other obligations which does not exist in the laws of Member States. It also would put the coherence of the structure of European private law at risk.

95 DCFR I.-1:101 to I.-1:106.

96 This is expressed by the (DCFR Art. III.-3:102) located in the Book III. Obligations and corresponding rights (DCFR III.-1:101 to III.-7.601) applying to the contract part of the European private law. The basic principle of free concurrence of contractual actions/remedies is a ground for different remedies available for a breach of contract. DCFR II.-1:107(2) located in Book II. Contracts and other juridical acts (DCFR II.-1:101 to II.-9:411) states also that mixed contracts are governed by all (of course contractual) applicable rules, unless this is contrary to the nature and purpose of the contract.

97 According to the DCFR rule VI.–1:103(d), the provisions of the 'tortious' non-contractual liability for damage caused do not affect remedies available on other legal grounds. By the 'other legal grounds' we must understand here another special DCFR rules on special 'tortious' regimes. Within the DCFR we can find special national regimes in rule VI.–2:203(2) on defamation and VI.–2:208(2) on loss caused to a consumer as a result of unfair competition, and rule VI.–3:207 on other types of strict liability under national laws being 'other accountability for the causation of legally relevant damage'.

According to the DCFR rule VI.–1:103(d), the provisions of the 'tortious' non-contractual liability for damage caused to another do not affect *remedies available on other legal grounds*. This rule could be a basis for the conclusion that the DCFR is based on the principle of free concurrence of contractual and non-contractual claims (*cumul des responsabilités*) since it underlies the relationship of the law on non-contractual liability to other areas of private law liability. This rule extends to the legal remedies available. A claim for damages under the law on non-contractual liability can be in competition with a contractual claim to damages. However, the DCFR provisions on non-contractual liability for damages do not apply in so far as their application would contradict *the purpose of other private law rules* (DCFR rule VI.-1:103c). In other words, although the law on non-contractual liability does not oust other bases of claim, it may be ousted by other private law rules (i.e. DCFR rules).

In the explanatory part of the DCFR, we can read that this provision concentrates predominantly on the relationship between the model DCFR rules on contractual and on non-contractual liability. The main purpose of that rule is to regulate the relationship of 'tortious' non-contractual rules to the law of contract and, in a case of potential conflict, to give priority to contract and the content of the contract regulated by contract law provisions. In fact, the solution is based on the principle of exclusion of claims in tort (*non-cumul des responsabilités*). This might be the consequence of the fact that the DCFR is based on the principle of private autonomy.[98] The assumption made by the drafters of the DCFR leads to the conclusion that a contract is the basic legal instrument which enables persons to enjoy the freedom to regulate every aspect of their relations with each other by agreement and contract law, and not by other applicable rules, in particular provisions of tort law. That is why the DCFR provisions on non-contractual liability for damages do not apply insofar as their application would contradict *the purpose of other private law rules* like the general rule of good faith and fair dealing. Moreover, the general duty of good faith and fair dealing, which extends to contract and to every other obligation under the DCFR,[99] may influence also the content and scope of the rule on concurrence.

Only one problem remains. The priority of contract law is unclear as to the scope of *subsidiarity* of non-contractual liability law. DCFR rule VI.-1:103(c) can be subject to the different interpretations based on the values underlying liability regimes. It can become even more unclear when we treat this rule as a model rule for the EU legislator.[100] In the explanatory part of the DCFR we read: 'Should it come to a conflict between the values of contract law and non-contractual liability law in any particular case, whereby contract law

98 H Eidenmüller, F Faust, HCh Grigoleit, N Jansen, G Wagner and R Zimmermann, 'The Common Frame of Reference for European Private Law – Policy Choices and Codification Problems' (2008) 28 *Oxford Journal of Legal Studies*, 659, 660.

99 O Lande, 'Is Good Faith an Over-arching General Clause in the Principles of European Contract Law', (2007) 15 *European Review of Private Law*, 841, 841.

100 The DCFR rules VI.-1:103(c)(d) are said to be an example of the problem to which extent the proposed rules satisfy the requirements of legal certainty and legal clarity, and the criteria of internal consistency and systematic integrity, see H Eidenmüller, F Faust, HCh Grigoleit, N Jansen, G Wagner and R Zimmermann, above n 99, p 659. Generally it is doubtful whether the Draft of CFR reflects and convincingly integrates the legal sources on which it is based.

denies liability which would subsist according to the provisions on non-contractual liability, then it is for the rules of contract law to assert *priority* if that is to be claimed in accord with the objective of the contract law rules'.[101] In other words, the 'contract law' adopted by the EU shall make it clear whether non-contractual liability remedies are excluded or available to the party to the contract. But this is only an interpretation of the rule which clearly states that not the content but the *purpose* of other private law rules must be taken into account in interpreting the solution to the potential concurrence of claims in damages.

Therefore, like the solution adopted in the proposal for a CESL regulation, the approach adopted in the DCFR is also rather disappointing. Such an important and general question should be solved in a clear provision on concurrence and not according to the interpretation of the *purpose* of adopted EU rules of contract law. Is that requirement satisfied when potential application of the 'tortious' liability with the corresponding contract law provision would deprive the latter of its effect? If so, the contract law rules should have priority, leading to the general superiority of contractual remedies and is close to the absolute French exclusion of the claims in tort once a contract is concluded.

4. Conclusions and recommendations

For the concurrence of claims in EU law there are still at least two fields of great importance:

- the interconnections of contract law and the law of delict in the services sector (issues of personal injuries, lost expectations, anti-discrimination issues);
- further harmonization of product liability and the relationship of national liability in contract, in tort negligence and EU-based national law on product liability to EU law on sales and services.

Unfortunately, the temporary failure of the codification of private law by the EU keeps the harmonization and unification of private law in Europe in stagnation. Maximum harmonization consumer directives occurred to be unsuitable tools for harmonization. Product-related directives constitute a fundamental problem of private law in the course of European integration, since they are based on the selective and functional regulatory approach of EU private law which is aimed not at a consistent and fair system of legal relations of private persons, but at the legal systematisation of particular market sectors. Consumer protection poses distinct issues because of its fragmented scope, mandatory nature and social dimension and should not be confused with general contract law reform.[102]

Maybe another approach could be suggested for the complex issue on concurrence. We should reconsider the original conception of a directive.[103] The principle of minimum

[101] Ch Von Bar, E Clive, H Schulte-Nölke et al. (eds), above n 83, p 3005.

[102] G Howells, 'The Scope of European Consumer Law' (2005) 3 *European Review of Contract Law*, 360, 372.

[103] Ch U Schmid, '*Co-ordination problems between European and national private law: a Scenario to be avoided in the Europeanization of Tenancy Law*', p 21, paper available at <www.eui.eu/Documents/DepartmentsCentres/Law/ResearchTeaching/ResearchThemes/EuropeanPrivateLaw/TenancyLawProject/CoordinationProblemsSchmid.pdf> accessed 15.01.2017.

not maximum harmonization enables the national legislator to gradually achieve the goals in line with European instructions. We should remember that creating uniform legal framework conditions for private law transactions can only be achieved if a coherent, functioning private law system is available. Creation of such a system would take more time but could allow the adoption of a better solution to the matter at hand. Therefore, directives might prescribe only the regulatory objectives, while the choice of means would be made at national level.

As to the more comprehensive approach, in the current state of EU law it seems to be impossible to develop one uniform common rule on concurrent contractual and tortious liabilities. Moreover, we have to cope with the observation that it is not plausible to develop a general model relationship of interaction between contract and tort law that can be applied successfully everywhere in Europe.[104] Also, the fundamental question of whether different national rules on concurrence and organization of those rules governing the interplay of possible concurrent contractual and tortious liabilities constitute an obstacle for the internal market and, therefore, must be harmonized or even unified, still seems difficult to answer.[105]

The most comprehensive but disappointing EU model law (DCFR) is based on the functional priority of contract law over tort law. In that way, we have returned to the quite unclear assumption made at the beginning of the work on that instrument. Since the law of contract is integrated into a larger legal environment, including tort law, tortious claims must be brought into consideration, but there is no objective reason why contract law should be given priority over the surrounding areas of law.[106] It is obvious that in the sphere of liability of sellers, suppliers and service providers contract law cannot be considered in isolation from tort law, but it is not clear what the justification would be for adopting the *subsidiary function* of tortious compensation for damages depending solely on the *purpose* of the law of contract. Thus, this approach is not convincing for the future unification of European private law.

104 Ch Von Bar, 'Rechtsvergleichende Beobachtungen zum Ineinendergreifen von Vertrags- Und Deliktsrecht in Europa' in R Schulze (ed), *Compensation of Private Losses. The Evolution of Torts in European Business Law*, Sellier, Munich 2011, pp 201–212.

105 Ibid.

106 Communication on European Contract Law. Joint Response of the Commission on European Contract Law and the Study Group on a European Civil Code, Osnabrück 25.10.01.

Vesna Lazić*

THE PROCEDURAL POSITION OF A 'WEAKER PARTY' IN THE REGULATION BRUSSELS IBIS**

Abstract

This contribution discusses the changes introduced by the revised Regulation regarding cross-border disputes involving a policyholder, the insured or a beneficiary under the insurance agreements, a consumer or an employee. It addresses most important amendments particularly those relating to expanding the Regulation's scope of application ratione personae, adjustments of the rule on tacit prorogation and on the revised rules on enforcement that have bearing on disputes involving parties with a weaker bargaining position.

Keywords: Regulation Brussel Ibis; weaker parties; consumer disputes; insurance contracts; individual contracts of employment; jurisdiction; recognition and enforcement of judgements; *lis pendens*; choice of court agreements

1. Introduction

The jurisdictional and enforcement regime of the Brussels I Regulation[1] contain provisions the purpose of which is to minimise the imbalance and to restore the bargaining position of 'weaker' parties in commercial legal relationships. These provisions intend to ensure that any advantage presumed or achieved by a contracting party with a dominant bargaining position will remain without legal entitlement and effect. Consequently, certain rights obtained in such legal transactions will be unenforceable against a 'weaker party'. To this end rules on jurisdiction and enforcement

* Prof. Dr. Vesna Lazic (email: V.Lazic@asser.nl; V.Lazic@uu.nl) is a Senior Researcher at the T.M.C. Asser Institute, Associate Professor of Private Law, Utrecht University and Professor of European Civil Procedure at the University of Rijeka.

** This paper is earlier published in V. Lazić & S. Stuij (eds.), *Brussels Ibis Regulation: Changes and Challenges of the Renewed Procedural Scheme*, Asser Press/Springer Publishing, 2017, pp. 51–71.

1 Council Regulation (EC) No. 44/2001 of 22 December 2000 on jurisdiction and the recognition and enforcement of judgments in civil and commercial matters, OJ L 12, 16 February 2001, pp. 1–23 (hereinafter: Regulation Brussels I).

are adjusted so as to enhance the position of a weaker party in proceedings before national courts. The provisions aiming at protecting a weaker party relate to disputes arising under insurance contracts, and consumer and labour disputes.[2]

Additionally, a prorogation of jurisdiction is only valid to the extent that it complies with the special rules provided for weaker party disputes. Consequently, the courts in the EU Member States can establish jurisdiction against a weaker party defendant only on the basis of the Regulation. The applicability of national rules on jurisdiction is thereby excluded. In other words, such defendants are 'protected' against national rules on jurisdiction in EU Member States including exorbitant jurisdictional grounds.

The revised Regulation[3] further enhances the level of protection of weaker parties. The present contribution addresses the major changes in that respect.

2. Rules on jurisdiction in the Brussels I Regulation

The provisions aimed at protecting the position of a weaker party in litigation under the Brussels I regime can be summarised as follows:

a) A weaker party – a policyholder, the insured or a beneficiary, consumer or employee – has a choice to bring proceedings against the other party to a contract either in the court of the Member State in which that other party is domiciled or in which it is more convenient to a weaker party (most likely in the country of its own domicile) or which is otherwise closely related to the dispute.
b) Conversely, proceedings may be brought against a weaker party to the contract only in the courts of the Member State in which the 'weaker' party is domiciled.
c) Forum selection clauses in these disputes have limited binding effect against a 'weaker' party. In other words, they may be successfully invoked against a weaker party only if the conditions provided in the relevant provisions of the Regulation are met.[4]

Thus, an insurer domiciled in a Member State may be sued in the Member State of its domicile or in the Member State where the plaintiff is domiciled if an action is brought by a policyholder, the insured or a beneficiary. A co-insurer may be sued in a Member State where proceedings were brought against the leading insurer.[5] With respect to liability insurance or the insurance of immovable property, the insurer may also be sued in the

2 As such these rules prevail over both the general rule in Article 2 and alternative jurisdictional grounds in Articles 5, 6 and 7. See e.g., CJEU Judgment in *FBTO Schadeverzekeringen* of 13 December 2007, Case C-463/06, EU:C:2007:792, Para. 28. On the other hand, the rules on exclusive jurisdiction have prevalence over the jurisdictional rules in Sections 3, 4 and 5. Among the latter rules themselves, the rules on insurance contracts prevail over the rules on jurisdiction in consumer disputes.

3 Regulation (EU) No. 1215/2012 of the European Parliament and of The Council of 12 December 2012 on jurisdiction and the recognition and enforcement of judgments in civil and commercial matters (recast), OJ L 351, 20.12.2012, pp. 1–32, it applies from 10 January 2015 (hereinafter: Brussels Ibis Regulation).

4 This issue is addressed in a greater detail in Section 2.2.1, *infra*.

5 Art. 9(1) Regulation Brussels I.

courts of the place where the harmful event occurred.[6] The same holds true 'if movable and immovable property are covered by the same insurance policy and both are adversely affected by the same contingency'.[7] Also, the insurer may be joined in the proceedings initiated by an injured party against an insured if the law of the court where such proceedings are pending so permits. However, it is only the injured party that is to be protected under Article 11(2) of the Brussels I Regulation and not any statutory assignee. A social security institution cannot be considered to be a weaker party deserving protection in the application of the rules on the international jurisdiction of courts. Therefore, an insurer (a statutory assignee) cannot sue the insurer of an injured party before the courts of its Member State when the insurer is located in another Member State.[8]

On the other hand, the insured, policy holder or beneficiary as a weaker party may be sued only in the courts of the Member State of its domicile. Thus, a weaker party may choose among the possibilities given in Articles 9 and 10 when filing an action against the insurer, whilst it can be sued exclusively in the country of its domicile. The only exception is in the case of direct actions by an injured party against the insurer when the law governing such direct actions provides that the policy holder or the insurer may be joined as a party.[9]

Similarly, when a contract complies with the definition of a 'consumer contract' under Article 15 of the Regulation,[10] a consumer may choose between the *forum rei* and *forum actoris*.[11] Conversely, a consumer may only be sued in the courts of the place where he/she is domiciled (Article 16(2)). As in the case of insurance contracts,[12] the right to bring a counterclaim in the court where the original claim is pending is retained.[13]

Also, an employee may only be sued in the Member State of his/her domicile. The action against an employer may be brought in the courts of the country of its domicile, in the country where the employee habitually carries out or has carried out his work or in the courts where the business which engaged the employee is or was situated, if the employee does not carry out his work in any one country. Accordingly, an employee may choose between the *forum rei* and *forum laboris* – the courts where he habitually carries out his work or the courts of the last place where he carried out his work. If the employee does not habitually carry out his work in any one country, he may choose between the

6 No definition of 'where the harmful event occurred' can be found in the Recast, but it must be assumed that an interpretation similar to that of Art. 7(1)(b)(2) should be applied. See also, Kropholler & von Hein 2011, Art. 10 note 1.

7 Art. 10 Brussels I Regulation.

8 CJEU Judgment in *VorarlbergerGebietskrankenkasse v. WGV-SchwäbischeAllgemeineVersicherungs AG* of 17 September 2009, Case C-347/08, EU:C:2009:561.

9 Arts. 12(1) and 11(3) Brussels I Regulation. See also, Kropholler & von Hein (2011) stating that rhe concept 'matters relating to a contract' must be interpreted broadly in order to include a wide variety of agreements, for example, life insurance policies'.

10 For more particulars, see Section 2.1.2 *infra*.

11 Art. 16(1) Brussels I Regulation. In the CJEU Judgment in *Armin Maletic,Marianne Maletic v. lastminute.com GmbH, TUI Österreich GmbH* of 14 November 2013, Case C-478/12, EU:C:2013:735, the Court stated that Art. 16(1) also applies with respect to jurisdiction in proceedings against 'the contracting partner of the operator with which the consumer concluded that contract and which has its registered office in the Member State in which the consumer is domiciled'.

12 Art. 12(2) Brussels I Regulation.

13 Art. 16(3) Brussels I Regulation.

courts of the employer's domicile and the courts where the business that engaged the employee is or was situated.[14]

In applying the Regulation and its predecessor, the 1968 Brussels Convention, the relevant case law of the Court of Justice of the European Union (CJEU) illustrates that the criterion 'habitually carries out his work' can also be applied when the work is carried out in the performance of a contract of employment in more than one Member State. According to the relevant case law of the CJEU, it is the place where an employee has established the effective centre of his working activities.[15] In order to identify that place, certain relevant circumstances need to be taken into account, such as where the employee spends most of his working time, 'where he has an office where he organises his activities for his employer and to which he returns after each business trip abroad'.[16] In the absence of an office, it will be the place in which the employee carries out the majority of his work.[17] The Court, in its various decisions interpreting jurisdictional grounds, has emphasised the need to guarantee adequate protection to the employee as the weaker of the contracting parties also when the employee carries out his work in more than one contracting state.[18] In other words, such an employee should not be deprived of procedural protection under the Regulation. Only if the effective centre of his working activities cannot be established will the employee have to file the claim against his employer either in the courts of the employer's domicile or the courts where the business that engaged the employee is or was situated. The need to ensure 'more adequate protection for the party who from the socio-economic point of view is regarded as the weaker in the contractual relationship'[19] is reflected not only in private international law instruments that regulate procedural issues, but also in those that unify conflict of law rules.[20]

14 Art. 19 Brussels I Regulation reads: 'An employer domiciled in a Member State may be sued:
1. in the courts of the Member State where he is domiciled; or
2. in another Member State:
   (a) in the courts for the place where the employee habitually carries out his work or in the courts for the last place where he did so, or
   (b) if the employee does not or did not habitually carry out his work in any one country, in the courts for the place where the business which engaged the employee is or was situated.

15 See the CJEU Judgment in *Heiko/Koelzsch* of 15 March 2011, Case C-29/10, EU:C:2011:151.

16 CJEU Judgment in *Petrus Rutten v. Cross Medical Ltd* of 1 December 1995, Case C-383/95, EU:C:1997:7. See also CJEU Judgment in *Mulox IBC Ltd v. Hendrick Geels* of 13 July 1991, Case C-125/92, EU:C:1993:306.

17 CJEU Judgment in *Weber* of 3 April 2014, Case C-37/00, EU:C:2014:12, Para. 42.

18 See e.g., CJEU Judgment in *Petrus Rutten v. Cross Medical Ltd* of 1 December 1995, Case C-383/95, EU:C:1997:7, Para. 22; CJEU Judgment in *Giulia Pugliese v. Finmeccanica SpA, Betriebsteil Alenia Aerospazio* of 10 April 2003, Case C-437/00, EU:C:2003:219, Para. 18.

19 Giuliano and Lagarde 1980, p 1.

20 See e.g., 1980 Convention on the law applicable to contractual obligations, converted into Regulation No. 593/2008 of the European Parliament and of the Council of 17 June 2008 on the law applicable to contractual obligations, OJ L 177, 4 July 2008, pp. 6–16 (Rome I Regulation) in which party autonomy in determining the applicable law is somewhat restricted so as to ensure that the rights and interests of consumers and employees receive maximum protection. With respect to contracts of employment, the objective of the relevant provision of Art. 6 of the Convention is to guarantee adequate protection for the employee. Within that context, the CJEU emphasised that the criterion of the country in which the employee 'habitually carries out his work' must be given a broad interpretation. The subsidiary criterion

The analysis of the rules on jurisdiction illustrates that the Brussels I Regulation departs, to a certain extent, from the general rule contained in Article 2 – domicile of the defendant – in lawsuits against a 'stronger party'.[21] In disputes arising under consumer and insurance contracts, a weaker party is given the possibility to choose between the *forum rei* and *forum actoris* (consumers) and some other fora (the insured). Although following similar lines, a slightly different approach has been adopted in setting out the grounds for jurisdiction in disputes arising from individual employment contracts. A weaker party – an employee – is given the possibility to choose between fora closely related to the individual contract of employment. In particular, he/she can file the claim in the courts where he/she habitually carries out his/her work. However, differently from insurance and consumer contracts, the choice does not expressly include the *forum actoris*, even though in practice the place where an employee habitually carries out his work and his domicile will most frequently be in the same country. Outside the context of 'weaker party disputes', the domicile of the plaintiff, as well as the nationality of a claimant, is generally considered to be an exorbitant jurisdictional ground – i.e., a criterion that, according to internationally accepted standards, does not justify assuming jurisdiction against a defendant domiciled abroad.

2.1. *Brussels Ibis Regulation – Consequences for weaker party disputes*

The Brussels Ibis Regulation applies as of 10 January 2015. It introduces changes in a number of areas.[22] Among the changes which are relevant to the issues discussed in the present contribution, extending the territorial (or formal) scope of application in disputes involving weaker parties has to be mentioned. Besides, a number of new provisions are inserted either to ensure a greater degree of protection for weaker parties or to clarify the existing regulatory scheme aimed at the protection of such parties.

2.1.1. Scope of application

In the Commission's Proposal the universal application of jurisdictional rules and their extension to disputes involving third party defendants was suggested.[23] The so-called

– the place of business through which the employee was engaged – can determine the applicable law only in cases where the court cannot determine the place where the employee habitually carries out his work. See e.g., CJEU Judgment in *Heiko Koelzsch v. Luxembourg of* 15 March 2011, Case C-29/10, EU:C:2011:151, Para. 44 and CJEU Judgment in *Jan Voogsgeerd v. Navimer SA* of 15 December 2011, Case C-384/10, EU:C:2011:842. For more particulars on the topic, including the commentaries on the relevant case law, see van Hoek 2011, pp. 650–658; van den Eeckhout 2014, pp. 3–8; Even 2013, pp 13–24; Laagland 2012, pp 63–78; Derks 2011, pp. 8–11; Boonstra 2014.

21 The domicile of the defendant is the main rule under the Regulation and is a generally accepted standard for international jurisdiction (*actor sequitur forum rei*).

22 The amendments relate to the provisional measures, the *lis pendens* rule and choice of court clauses, expanding the territorial scope of application, and some new provisions intended to ensure a further protection of weaker parties. With respect to the enforcement of judgments, the exequatur is no longer required, but the public policy exception has been retained among the grounds for refusing recognition and enforcement.

23 For detailed comments on the proposal for universal jurisdiction, see J. Weber 2011, pp. 620 et seq.

'universal scope' would result in the abolition of the dual regime of jurisdictional rules in cross-border cases within the European Union. Consequently, no exorbitant jurisdictional grounds could be relied upon in cases involving defendants from outside the European Union. The idea of universal application has not been accepted in the Recast Regulation. Yet its territorial (personal or formal) scope of application has been somewhat extended. In principle, the Regulation still applies only if the defendant is domiciled in an EU Member State. The exceptions in cases of choice of court agreements and exclusive jurisdiction have been retained. The scope of application in cases of prorogation of jurisdiction has thereby been expanded even further, so that the domicile of the parties has become irrelevant. Consequently, the provision of Article 25 (the current Article 23 of Regulation 44/2001) will apply in all cases where the jurisdiction of a court in an EU Member State has been agreed upon.[24] Choice of court agreements providing for the jurisdiction of a court of a third state will still be governed by national rules.

Additionally, the territorial scope is expanded in the Recast Regulation so as to include certain 'weaker' party disputes, notably consumer and labour law disputes. The provision of Article 6(1) of the Recast Regulation (the current Article 4 of the Brussels I Regulation) reads as follows:

> '1. If the defendant is not domiciled in a Member State, the jurisdiction of the courts of each Member State shall, subject to Articles 18(1), 21(2) and Articles 24 and 25, be determined by the law of that Member State.'

The reference to Articles 24 and 25 relates to exclusive jurisdiction and a prorogation of jurisdiction respectively (the current Articles 22 and 23). The provisions of Articles 18 and 21 relate to disputes involving consumers and employees.

Thus, a court in a Member State may establish its jurisdiction on the basis of the jurisdictional rules of the Brussels Ibis Regulation in all disputes involving a consumer or an employee regardless of the domicile of the other party. The provision of Article 6(1) refers only to consumer (Article 1(1)) and labour disputes (Article 21(2)), but there is no reference to insurance contracts. Consequently, the jurisdictional rules contained in Section 3 relating to insurance contracts only apply if a defendant is domiciled in an EU Member State.[25] The relevant provisions on jurisdiction in Article 18[26] relating to

[24] Under Art. 25 of the Brussels Ibis Regulation it is no longer required that one of the parties to the agreement on jurisdiction is domiciled in an EU Member State. Under the current regime of Art. 23 of Brussels I, for its applicability it is required that a court of an EU Member State is agreed upon and that one of the parties is domiciled in a Member State. Under the revised Art. 25 it applies to prorogation clauses providing for the jurisdiction of a court in a Member State regardless of the domicile of the parties.

[25] For more particulars on the territorial scope of application of the Recast Regulation, see Lazić in Bodiroga-Vukobrat et al. 2013, pp. 184–188.

[26] Art. 18 of the Brussels Ibis Regulation reads as follows:

'1. A consumer may bring proceedings against the other party to a contract either in the courts of the Member State in which that party is domiciled or, *regardless of the domicile of the other party*, in the courts for the place where the consumer is domiciled.

consumer contracts (Article 16 of the Brussels I Regulation) and Article 21[27] relating to contracts of employment (Article 19 of the Brussels I Regulation) have been adjusted so as to reflect the changes introduced to the territorial scope of application in Article 6 of the Recast. Accordingly, the new regulatory scheme further enhances the protection of consumers and employees. In particular, such 'weaker parties' may rely on the rules on international jurisdiction in disputes against professionals and employees domiciled outside the European Union. On the other hand, the Regulation continues to apply only to claims against consumers and employees domiciled in the EU Member States. Such a conclusion follows from the fact that Article 6 refers only to Article 18 paragraph 1[28] and Article 21 paragraph 2 respectively.

2.1.2. Revised provision on tacit prorogation

Besides the scope of application and relevant rules on jurisdiction in disputes involving consumers and employees, there is a further amendment to the provision on the tacit prorogation of jurisdiction. It has been amended so as to better accommodate the interests of 'weaker' parties. Under the current regime of Brussels I, if a defendant enters an appearance, a court in an EU Member State in principle does not examine *ex officio* whether or not it has jurisdiction under the Regulation. The exception is an obligation to examine whether a court in another state has exclusive jurisdiction according to Article 22. This follows from the current text of Article 24 of Brussels I which relates to tacit prorogation,[29] as well as from Article 25.[30]

The jurisdictional rules in disputes involving weaker parties are not mentioned in Article 24 of Brussels I Regulation. Yet a violation of the jurisdictional grounds in

2. Proceedings may be brought against a consumer by the other party to the contract only in the courts of the Member State in which the consumer is domiciled.
3. This Article shall not affect the right to bring a counter-claim in the court in which, in accordance with this Section, the original claim is pending.' (emphasis added).

27 Art. 21(1) of the Brussels Ibis Regulation reads as follows:
'1. An employer domiciled in a Member State may be sued:
(a) In the courts of the Member State in which he is domiciled; or
(b) In another Member State:
(i) in the courts for the place where or from where the employee habitually carries out his work or in the courts for the last place where he did so, or
(ii) if the employee does not or did not habitually carry out his work in any one country, in the courts for the place where the business which engaged the employee is or was situated.
2. An employer not domiciled in a Member State may be sued in a court of a Member State in accordance with point (b) of paragraph 1.' (emphasis added).

28 Art. 18(1) determines jurisdiction when a professional is the defendant, see the text *supra* note 51.

29 Art. 24 of Brussels I Regulation reads as follows:
'Apart from jurisdiction derived from other provisions of this Regulation, a court of a Member State before which a defendant enters an appearance shall have jurisdiction. This rule shall not apply where appearance was entered to contest the jurisdiction, or where another court has exclusive jurisdiction by virtue of Article 22.'

30 Where a court of a Member State is seised of a claim which is principally concerned with a matter over which the courts of another Member State have exclusive jurisdiction by virtue of Article 22, it shall declare of its own motion that it has no jurisdiction.

disputes arising out of insurance contracts and consumer disputes, as well as the rules on exclusive jurisdiction, presents a valid ground to refuse the enforcement of the judgment under Article 35(1) of the Brussels I Regulation. Considering that the provision on tacit prorogation in Article 24 of Brussels I Regulation does not refer to disputes involving weaker parties, the CJEU has held that the court seised could validly assume jurisdiction in such disputes if a weaker party enters an appearance without contesting jurisdiction.[31] It reasoned, inter alia, that 'although in the fields concerned by Sections 3 to 5 of Chapter II of that regulation the aim of the rules on jurisdiction is to offer the weaker party stronger protection (...), the jurisdiction determined by those sections cannot be imposed on that party'.[32] One could expect that a weaker party should be put in a position to be fully aware of the effects of submitting his/her defence as to the substance and that the court seised should therefore determine *ex officio* what is the intention of entering an appearance. However, the Court held that '[s]uch an obligation could not be imposed other than by the introduction into Brussels I Regulation of an express rule to that effect'.[33]

Thereby the protection intended to be ensured in Article 35(1) is somewhat undermined, as the 'violation' of the jurisdictional rules referred to therein would not qualify as a ground for refusing the enforcement of the judgment even if a weaker party was unaware of the protection of its procedural position provided under the Regulation. The newly introduced provision in Article 26(2) of the Recast Regulation remedies such a result and improves the positions of weaker parties. It reads as follows:

> 'In matters referred to in Sections 3, 4 and 5 (...) where the policyholder, the insured, the injured party of a beneficiary of the insurance contract, the consumer or the employee is the defendant, the court, before assuming jurisdiction under paragraph 1, shall ensure that the defendant is informed of his right to contest the jurisdiction and of the consequences of entering or not entering an appearance.'

Thus, the court seised is under an obligation to inform a 'weaker' party defendant i.e., a policy holder/an insured/injured party/a beneficiary of the insurance contract, a

31 See CJEU Judgment in *Česká podnikatelská pojišťovna as, Vienna Insurance Group v. Michal Bilas* of 20 May 2010, Case C-111/09, EU:C:2013:165, where the Court held that 'Article 24 (...) must be interpreted as meaning that the court seised, where the rules in Section 3 of Chapter II of that regulation were not complied with, must declare itself to have jurisdiction where the defendant enters an appearance and does not contest that court's jurisdiction, since entering an appearance in that way amounts to a tacit prorogation of jurisdiction.'

32 Ibid., Para. 30. Majority took the view that the holding expressed in this judgement was not only valid for insurance contracts, but would also apply to consumer contracts and individual contracts of employment. See, e.g., Magnus/Mankowski/ Alfonso-Luis/Calvo Caravaca/Javier Carrascosa Gonzales, (2016) Art. 26, p. 678, para. 24.

33 Ibid. With respect to a dispute against consumers, when interpreting the Consumer Directive, the CJEU on various occasions held that that the courts were to examine *ex officio* whether a dispute settlement clause, including forum-selection clauses, had to be considered as unfair contractual terms. See e.g., the CJEU Judgment in *Pannon GSM Zrt.* of 4 June 2009, Case C-243/08, EU:C:2009:350. For more particulars, see Section 2.2.3, *infra*.

consumer or an employee of the consequences of entering an appearance. Such additional protection for a weaker party is to be met with approval.[34]

The provision of Article 24 of Brussels I Regulation has remained unchanged and is contained in Article 26(1) of the Brussels Ibis Regulation. In accordance with paragraph 1 of this provision, a weaker party will be 'protected' as any other party domiciled in one Member State sued in a court of another Member State that does not enter an appearance. In such a case, the court seised is required to declare *ex officio* its lack of competence if it cannot establish its jurisdiction based on the provisions of the Regulation. When a defendant does enter an appearance the court seised is only required to examine jurisdiction on its own motion when the courts of another Member State have exclusive jurisdiction under the Regulation. As already explained, according to the new regulatory scheme of the Brussels Ibis Regulation, the court will have to warn a weaker party about the need to contest jurisdiction and the consequences of its failure to do so. A failure to inform a weaker party under Article 26(2) should present a reason to refuse the enforcement of a judgment according to Article 45 Regulation Brussels Ibis.[35]

The further amendments affecting the regulatory scheme on the prorogation of jurisdiction are discussed *infra* under 1.1.3.

2.1.3. Limited binding nature of choice of court agreements under the Brussels Ibis Regulation

The idea of limiting the effectiveness of choice of court agreements has been retained in the revised Regulation. In fact, no changes have been introduced regarding the provisions specifically regulating the validity of forum-selection clauses with respect to weaker party disputes. Yet some alterations to the general provision on prorogation of jurisdiction in Article 25 (ex Article 23 of the Regulation Brussels I), as well as changes to the *lis alibi pendens* rule in Article 29 (ex Article 27) may have some bearing on the regulation of forum-selection clauses in disputes involving weaker parties. The analysis of the changes introduced is preceded by an outline of the regulatory scheme under the Brussels I Regulation.

2.1.3.1. Choice of court agreements under the Brussels I Regulation

Prorogation of jurisdiction is dealt with in Article 23 of the Brussels I Regulation. In particular, the definition of the 'written form requirement' is provided in Paragraphs 1 and 2. The issue of substantive validity is to be determined on the basis of the applicable

34 See also, Hays 2013, p. 4; Lazić 2013, p. 12.

35 *Contra*, Magnus/Mankowski/Calvo Caravaca & Carrascosa Gonzalez (2016), p. 682, para 35, referring to Nuyts, La refonte du règlement Bruxelles I, RCDIP 2013, 1, 60. The authors, however, give no reason or argumentation in support of such a view. Others merely conclude that Article 26(2) neither expressly no impliedly provides which consequences follow from a breach of the obligation by a court to inform a weaker party of the right to contest jurisdiction, but offer no suggestion on how to interpret and apply the changes introduced. Magnus/Mankowski/Mankowski/Peter Nielsen, Brussels Ibis Regulation (2016) Art. 19, para. 49.

national law. In accordance with Article 23(5), a jurisdiction agreement concluded in violation of the provisions of Articles 13, 17 and 21 will have no legal force. These provisions define the conditions for the validity of prorogation agreements in insurance, consumer and labour law disputes respectively. In the same vein, no effect will be given to agreements purporting to exclude the jurisdiction of the courts having exclusive jurisdiction under Article 22.[36]

Only an insured person, a consumer and an employee are protected by the rules restricting the effectiveness of jurisdiction agreements. No other category of 'weaker parties' is protected by the provision on the prorogation of jurisdiction under the Regulation, even though some other parties such as commercial agents, distributors and franchisees also have a weaker bargaining position.[37] The same was true of claims arising out of maintenance which had been within the substantive scope of application of Brussels I before the Maintenance Regulation came into force. The latter permits the prorogation of jurisdiction in Article 4, but only in favour of the courts in a Member State which either has a close connection with the parties and their relationship[38] or the courts which are otherwise competent to hear certain closely related disputes.[39]

The special regime on the restricted effectiveness of prorogation agreements in disputes involving insured persons, consumers and employees can be summarised as follows:

(a) Jurisdiction agreements entered into after a dispute(s) has arisen may successfully be relied upon by both parties. Thus, there are no restrictions on the binding nature and enforceability of such agreements in disputes relating to insurance, consumer and individual contracts of employment.[40]

(b) Prorogation of jurisdiction stipulated before a dispute has arisen may successfully be invoked by a weaker party if it gives the possibility to a weaker party to sue in courts other than those indicated in the relevant Sections 3, 4 and 5.[41] However, against a weaker party such an agreement either cannot be enforced at all[42] or has binding effect only if the parties have agreed on the jurisdiction of courts in a particular Member State connected to the dispute as determined under the relevant provisions of the Regulation.[43]

36 Some authors have argued that such an agreement will be invalid as far as international jurisdiction is concerned, but may still be valid as an agreement on local jurisdiction within a Member State, if such agreements would be valid and permitted under the relevant national law. See Magnus and Mankowski 2012, p. 497.

37 Compare ibid., referring to a principal-agent relationship.

38 The courts in a Member State of the habitual residence or nationality of either party, Art. 4(1)(a) and (b).

39 According to Art. 4(1)(c), in disputes concerning maintenance obligations between spouses or former spouses the parties may agree on the jurisdiction of the court which has jurisdiction in matrimonial matters or the court in a Member State of their last common habitual residence for a period of at least one year. Besides, according to Art. 4(3) of the Maintenance Regulation the provision on the choice of court agreements 'shall not apply in a dispute relating to a maintenance obligation towards a child under the age of 18'.

40 Arts. 13(1), 17(1) and 21(1) of Brussels I Regulation.

41 Arts. 13(2), 17(2) and 21(2) of Brussels I Regulation.

42 This is the case relating to individual contracts of employment.

43 Arts. 13(3)-(5) and 17(3) of the Brussels I Regulation.

Thus, an agreement on jurisdiction entered into after a dispute has arisen is enforceable against both an employee and an employer. An agreement on jurisdiction entered into before a dispute has arisen may be relied upon by an employee, when such an agreement allows the employee to sue in courts other than the courts specified in Section 5. However, it cannot be successfully invoked against him.[44]

In a similar vein, choice of court agreements involving consumers entered into after a dispute has arisen are binding upon both parties (Article 17(1) Brussels I Regulation). Jurisdictional clauses entered into before a dispute has arisen are binding if relied upon by a consumer, allowing the consumer to bring proceedings in courts other than those specified in Section 4 (Article 17(2) of the Brussels I Regulation).[45] Both parties may successfully invoke an agreement which provides for the jurisdiction of courts in the EU Member State of their common domicile or habitual residence at the moment of contracting, if such an agreement is permitted under the law of that Member State.[46] Thus, when the parties (or one of them) change their domicile or habitual residence from the moment of the conclusion of the contract, a forum-selection clause providing for the jurisdiction of the courts of the parties' common domicile or habitual residence may be successfully invoked against a consumer, subject to the condition that such a choice is permitted under the law of the Member State of the chosen court.

As to matters relating to insurance, jurisdiction agreements entered into before a dispute(s) has arisen is binding upon an insurer if it permits an insured to institute proceedings in courts other than those mentioned in Section 3. Against the ensured such an agreement will be binding under the conditions provided for in Article 13(3)-(5). Thus, it will be enforceable against a weaker party if it provides for the jurisdiction of the courts in the Member State of the parties' common domicile or habitual residence even though a harmful event occurred abroad, if such an agreement is not contrary to the law of that state.[47] Also, such an agreement will be enforceable in cases of compulsory insurance or insurance related to immovable property in a Member State against a policy holder who is not domiciled in a Member State or if a contract of insurance covers one or more risks set out in the Regulation.[48] Just as in the case of employment and consumer contracts, choice of court agreements entered into after a dispute has arisen will be binding against both parties.

44 Art. 21 of the Brussels I Regulation.

45 Art. 17(2) of the Brussels I Regulation provides that such a clause is enforceable if it allows the consumer to bring proceedings in courts other than those indicated in this Section.

46 Art. 17(3) of the Brussels I Regulation provides that provisions on jurisdiction under that Section may only be departed from by an agreement 'which is entered into by the consumer and the other party to the contract, both of whom are at the time of conclusion of the contract domiciled or habitually resident in the same Member State, and which confers jurisdiction on the courts of that Member State, provided that such an agreement is not contrary to the law of that Member State'.

47 Such an agreement confers jurisdiction on the courts in a Member State which is closely connected with both parties. See also, Kropholler and von Hein 2011, Art. 13, nos. 3 and 4.

48 Art. 13(3)-(5) and Art. 14 of the Brussels I Regulation. For more particulars on jurisdiction in insurance contracts, see Vassilakakis 2014, pp. 1079 et seq.

2.1.3.2. Choice of court agreements in the Brussels Ibis Regulation

The provisions relating to choice of court agreements in insurance, consumer and labour law contracts have remained unchanged in the Brussels Ibis Regulation. Yet it introduces a number of amendments to the prorogation of jurisdiction in Article 25 (Article 23 of Brussels I). First of all, the applicability of this provision is extended so that it is no longer required that one of the parties to the agreement on jurisdiction is domiciled in an EU Member State. Under the current regime of Brussels I, for Article 23 to apply it is required that a court of an EU Member State is agreed upon and that one of the parties is domiciled in a Member State. Under the revised Article 25, it applies to prorogation clauses providing for the jurisdiction of a court in a Member State regardless of the domicile of the parties. Forum-selection agreements providing for the jurisdiction of a court of a third state are accordingly governed by national rules. As to 'weaker party' disputes, expanding the scope of application with respect to choice of court agreement will have consequences regarding insurance contracts and to some extent with respect to individual employment and consumer contracts, even though the personal scope of application is extended in the Brussels Ibis Regulation as already explained.[49]

Another amendment is a conflict of law rule for the substantive validity of prorogation agreements. According to the newly introduced rule, the law of the Member State of the chosen court will govern the substantive validity of such agreements.[50] The relevant decisions of the CJEU illustrate that the same law will also apply with respect to the interpretation of the choice of court agreement, its renewal or succession into a forum-selection agreement.[51] Recital (20) of the Brussels Ibis Regulation clearly states that the reference to the law of the Member State of the chosen court includes the conflict of law rules of that state. Such a solution under the Brussels Ibis Regulation is a major shortcoming of the newly introduced rule on the choice of law for the substantive validity of prorogation agreements. This provision does not present a true uniform private international law rule. Instead, it merely refers to the national conflict of law rules of the Member State whose court has been chosen. Consequently, there is no uniform conflict of law rule within the EU for the law applicable to the substantive validity of jurisdiction agreements.[52] This provision will also apply to the prorogation of jurisdiction in weaker party disputes.

49 See Section 2.2, *supra*.

50 Art. 25(1) provides that a court or the courts of a Member State designated by an agreement between the parties shall have jurisdiction 'unless the agreement is null and void as to its substantive validity under the law of that Member State'.

51 Under Art. 23 of the Brussels I Regulation these issues are to be dealt with in accordance with the national substantive law determined by national conflict of law rules. See e.g., the CJEU Judgment in *Benincasa* of 3 July 1997, Case C-269/95, EU:C:1997:337, Para. 31; CJEU Judgment in *Iveco Fiat* of 11 November 1986, Case C-313/85, EU:C:1986:423, Paras. 7–8; CJEU Judgment in *Coreck Maritime* of 9 November 2000, Case C-387/98, EU:C:2000:606, Para. 24.

52 On the criticism relating to the provision on the substantive validity of forum-selection clauses, see Lazić 2013, p. 16. With respect to comments on the Proposal, see Heinze 2011, p. 8, electronic copy available at <http://ssrn.com/abstract=1804111> (last visited 8 October 2014); Camilleri 2011, p. 298. But see Beaumont and Yüksel, in K. Boele-Woelki et al. (eds.) 2010, pp. 563–577. At p. 575–577, in their

The most important change is the revision of the *lis pendens* rule so as to depart from the 'priority rule' expressed in Article 27 of the Brussels I Regulation. According to this provision, the court of a Member State seised of a matter involving the same cause of action and between the same parties shall of its own motion stay its proceedings until the court first seised has established its jurisdiction. With a view of enhancing the efficiency of choice of court agreements and combating 'torpedo actions',[53] the Brussels Ibis Regulation provides for an exception to this rule when there is a prorogation of jurisdiction. In such a case, any court seised other than the court designated in an exclusive choice of court agreement shall stay the proceedings until the court seised on the basis of the agreement declares its lack of jurisdiction.[54] Accordingly, the designated court will have priority 'to decide on the validity of the agreement and on the extent to which the agreement applies to the dispute pending before it',[55] even if a court of another Member State has been seised first. The court chosen in the agreement can proceed regardless of whether or not the non-designated court has decided to stay proceedings.

However, the rule on the priority of the chosen court is deviated from in some, but not in all cases involving 'weaker parties'. Thus, Article 31(4) of the Brussels Ibis Regulation provides that the priority rule in favour of the chosen court does not apply when a 'weaker party' is a claimant and the choice of court agreement is invalid under the provisions of the Regulation. Such wording implies that the new 'priority rule' does not apply when a prorogation clause is invoked by an insurer, an employer or a professional. Conversely, if a forum-selection clause is invoked by a weaker party, then a court before which a 'stronger party' has initiated proceedings will be bound by a new 'priority in favour of the chosen court' rule. Accordingly, the provision of Article 31(4) implies no changes with respect to weaker party disputes. It merely ensures that the new rule will not affect the jurisdictional rules of the Regulation intended to protect the procedural position of a weaker party, including those on the prorogation of jurisdiction. Thus, the court seised of a matter by a 'weaker party', and not the chosen court, will be competent to rule whether a forum-selection clause is valid and enforceable under the Regulation.

The possibility to determine the jurisdiction of a court by an agreement between the persons involved in a dispute may be restricted in other private international law instruments to an even greater extent. This is the case with respect to disputes concerning maintenance obligations, and even more so in matters of inheritance and family law. Thus, the possibility to choose a competent court is limited in different ways in the Maintenance Regulation.[56] First, it is limited by the requirement of a 'link' between the

comments to the Proposal the authors favour the solutions in both the 2005 Hague Convention and the changes suggested to be introduced in Art. 23, including *renvoi*.

53 'Torpedo actions' or the 'Italian torpedo' refers to actions instituted before a non-chosen court in order to postpone filing an action before the court designated in a forum-selection clause. In accordance with the current priority rule in Article 27, the latter must stay its proceedings until the court fist seised has decided on its jurisdiction. For more particulars, see Lazić 2013, pp. 5–27.

54 Art. 31(2) of the Brussels Ibis Regulation.

55 Recital (22) of the Brussels Ibis Regulation.

56 Council Regulation (EC) No. 4/2009, *supra* note 5.

dispute, the parties and the chosen court (Article 4(1)(a) ad (b)). Besides, there is no possibility to choose the competent court in disputes relating to maintenance obligations towards minors.[57] These legal sources remain outside the scope of the present contribution and accordingly are not further discussed.

2.1.3.3. Relevance of other EU legal sources and the case law of the CJEU for the limited binding nature of choice of court agreements

The procedural position of a weaker party is not only protected in EU private international law instruments. Other legal sources, such as directives, may indirectly serve the same purpose even though they are primarily aimed at the approximation of substantive law. This is particularly so as far as Council Directive 93/13/EEC of 5 April 1993 on unfair terms in consumer contracts is concerned. In order to protect the procedural position of a weaker party, the effectiveness of dispute resolution clauses – a prorogation of jurisdiction entered into before a dispute has arisen[58] – may be further restricted. The main reason is that such agreements in transactions involving 'weak parties' are in principle not freely negotiated. Usually they are part of the general terms and conditions or rather standard contracts drafted by business parties which consumers automatically adhere to. A weaker party – a consumer – is left with no choice but to accept such a clause if he/she wishes to enter into a particular legal transaction ('take it or leave it'). The same holds true for employees and insurance policy holders or beneficiaries under contracts of insurance.

When interpreting Directive 93/13/EEC, the CJEU firmly supports the protection of the procedural position of a consumer.[59] Thus, the Court has held that the national courts of the Member States have the power and obligation to examine of their own motion the unfairness of a contractual term conferring jurisdiction on the courts within the meaning of Article 3(1) of the Directive.[60] In its decision of 4 June 2009 (*Pannon GSM Zrt. V. Erzsébet Sustikné Győrfi)* the Court held, inter alia, that 'Article 6(1) of Council Directive 93/13/EEC of 5 April 1993, on unfair terms in consumer contracts, must be interpreted as meaning that an unfair contract term is not binding on the consumer, and it is not necessary, in that regard, for that consumer to have successfully contested the validity of such a term beforehand.' More importantly, the Court has held

[57] In Regulation (EU) No. 650/2012, there is a rather exceptional possibility for the parties in the matter of succession to agree on jurisdiction: if the deceased has made a choice for the applicable law all the parties in the succession can agree that the courts in this country would be competent to rule on all matters in succession. Although it should generally be distinguished from the prorogation of jurisdiction in civil and commercial matters, the regulatory scheme of Council Regulation (EC) No. 2201/2003, Art. 12 also provides for a limited possibility to deviate from the jurisdictional rules in matters of parental responsibility.

[58] The same holds true for arbitration clauses.

[59] For the debate on the case law of the CJEU and whether the CJEU in interpreting these Directives overemphasises consumer interests, see Trstenjak and Beysen 2011, pp. 95–124.

[60] CJEU Judgment in *Pannon GSM Zrt. V. Erzsébet Sustikné Győrfi* of June 2009, Case C-243/08, EU:C:2009:350; see also the CJEU Judgment in the joined cases *Océano Grupo Editorial and Salvat Editores* of 27 June 2000, Cases C-240/98 to C-244/98, EU:C:2000:346, Paras. 21–24.

that a national court is 'required to examine, of its own motion, the unfairness of a contractual term'. Where such a term has been found to be unfair, the national court must not apply it. The same duty exists when the national court ascertains its own territorial jurisdiction.

When determining whether a contractual term is to be categorised as unfair within the meaning of Article 3(1) of Directive 93/13 it has held that a contractual term which was drafted in advance by a professional and was not subject to individual negotiations conferring jurisdiction on a court of the professional's principal place of business satisfies the criteria to be qualified as unfair for the purposes of the application of the Directive.[61]

3. Procedural position of a weaker party – Rules on the recognition and enforcement of judgments

In principle, when deciding on the recognition and enforcement of a judgment rendered by a court of an EU Member State, the courts are not permitted to examine whether or not jurisdiction was properly ascertained. Yet, in exceptional circumstances it is possible to review a decision as to jurisdiction even though such a possibility is very much restricted.[62] The jurisdiction may be the subject of a review pursuant to Article 35 of the Brussels I Regulation, with respect to exclusive jurisdiction, jurisdiction in insurance and consumer disputes and Article 72. If a court violates these rules the judgment rendered may be refused recognition and enforcement in another Member State.

It should be noted that Section 5 relating to disputes arising out of employment contracts are not mentioned. The rationale behind this is that it would be contrary to the interest of an employee considering that the employee is the claimant in the vast majority of cases.[63] Yet, employees are treated differently and less favourably than consumers and insured/policy holders. As rightly emphasised in the literature, it 'generates a split between the rules on jurisdiction on the one hand and the rules on recognition on the other hand'.[64]

61 CJEU Judgment in the joined cases *Océano Grupo Editorial and Salvat Editores* of 27 June 2000, C-240/98 to C-244/98, EU:C:2000:346, Paras. 21–24. The same line of reasoning may be applied with regard to arbitration agreements. In Art. 3(3) of the Directive reference is made to the Annex which provides for an indicative and non-exhaustive list of the terms which may be regarded as unfair. The Annex expressly refers to arbitration agreements as follows: '(q) excluding or hindering the consumer's right to take legal action or exercise any other legal remedy, particularly by requiring the consumer to take disputes exclusively to arbitration not covered by legal provisions, unduly restricting the evidence available to him or imposing on him a burden of proof which, according to the applicable law, should lie with another party to the contract'. On the interpretation of the Directive with respect to arbitration clauses in consumer contracts, see the CJEU Judgment in *Asturcom Telecomunicaciones SL* of 6 October 2009, Case C-40/08, EU:C:2009:615 and CJEUJudgment in *Elisa María Mostaza Claro v. Centro Móvil Milenium SL* of 26 October 2006, Case C-168/05, EU:C:2006:675. See also, CJEU Judgment in *Katalin Sebestyén v. Zsolt Csaba Kővári, OTP Bank, OTP Faktoring Követeléskezelő Zrt, Raiffeisen Bank Zrt* of 3 April 2014, Case C-342/13, EU:C:2014:1857.

62 Leyton and Mercer 2004, para 26.086.

63 Commission Proposal, COM(1999) 348 final, p. 25.

64 Magnus and Mankowski 2012, p. 711. In general, for criticism on this point in the Brussels I Regulation, see also, Geimer and Schütze 2010, Art. 35, n. 14.

The changes introduced in this respect in the Brussels Ibis Regulation should be met with approval as they enhance the level of protection for weaker parties. The revised version deviates slightly from the regulatory scheme of the Brussels I Regulation, where grounds for refusal were contained in separate provisions in Article 34 and 35. Instead, all the grounds in Brussels Ibs Regulation are consolidated in Article 45. Just as under the Brussels I Regulation, in Paragraph 3 it provides that, as a matter of principle, the jurisdiction of the court of origin may not be reviewed, except under the circumstances referred to in Paragraph (1)(e). The latter refers to exclusive jurisdiction,[65] as well as disputes in insurance, consumer and employment matters, 'where the policy holder, the insured, a beneficiary of the insurance contract, the injured party, the consumer or the employer was the defendant'. Thus, employment contracts are now placed on the same footing as other transactions involving 'weaker' parties. Besides, the position of a 'weaker' party is protected to a greater extent in the revised Regulation, considering that a violation of jurisdictional grounds may only be an obstacle to recognition if a weaker party was a defendant in the dispute. Conversely, a 'stronger' party will not be able to invoke a violation of the rules on jurisdiction in Sections 3, 4 or 5 in the enforcement proceedings initiated by a 'weaker' party. Such a legal regulation represents a valuable improvement and clarification with respect to grounds to refuse recognition or enforcement.

4. Concluding remarks

Legal instruments on private international law and especially those relating to international jurisdiction and more generally civil procedure illustrate that the EU legislator attaches great importance to the protection of the procedural position of a party with a weaker position in a legal relationship. In particular, the rules on jurisdiction, as well as on the recognition and enforcement of judgments contained in the Brussels I Regulation are meant to ensure that procedural justice is preserved for certain categories of 'weaker parties'– employees, consumers and insurance policy holders or other beneficiaries of insurance contracts.

Such protection of the procedural position of weaker parties is even further enhanced in the revised Regulation. This is particularly achieved by useful adaptations to the relevant provisions relating to tacit prorogation and grounds to refuse recognition and enforcement. The latter have been adjusted so as to expressly include violations of the jurisdictional rules in disputes arising under contracts of employment. It is also clearly stated that a violation of the jurisdictional rules presents a reason for refusing enforcement or recognition only if this is relied upon by a weaker party. Besides, the scope of application *ratione personae* of the revised Regulation is widened so that consumers and employees may rely on the privileged jurisdictional rules regardless of the domicile of the other party. Finally, the revised rule on *lis alibi pendens* reversing the priority in deciding on jurisdiction in case of prorogation of jurisdiction does not apply when weaker parties are claimants.

[65] Art. 45(1)(e)(ii).

Regrettably the same approach and level of protection for weaker parties is not maintained in other legal instruments unifying the rules of private international law and civil procedure on the EU level. Thus, some EU Regulations do refer to consumers in connection with the rules on jurisdiction, but decisions on jurisdiction in cases involving consumers cannot be 'controlled' in a Member State of the enforcement.[66] More importantly, the recently revised Regulation on Small Claims[67] makes a passing reference to consumers in Recitals (2) and (3), but just like its predecessor contains no provisions which would aim at protecting the procedural position of consumers.

66 Regulation (EC) No. 805/2004 of the European Parliament and of the Council of 21 April 2004 creating a European Enforcement Order for uncontested claims, OJ L 143, 30 April 2004, pp. 5–39 and Regulation (EC) No. 1896/2006 of the European Parliament and of the Council of 12 December 2006 creating a European order for payment procedure, OJ L 399, 30 December 2006, pp. 1–32.

67 Regulation (EC) No 861/2007 of the European Parliament and of the Council of 11 July 2007establishing a European Small Claims Procedure as amended in Regulation (EU) 2015/2421 of the European Parliament and of the Council of 16 December 2015 amending Regulation (EC) No 861/2007 establishing a European Small Claims Procedure and Regulation (EC) No 1896/2006 creating a European order for payment procedure OJ of 24 December 2015, OJ L 341 of 24 December 2015, p. 1, which will apply as from 14 July 2017.

References

Beaumont P, Yüksel B, (2010) The Validity of Choice of Court Agreements under the Brussels I Regulation and the Hague Choice of Court Agreements Convention', in K. Boele-Woelki et al. (eds.), *Convergence and Divergence in Private International Law*, 2010, pp. 563–577. At p. 575–577

Boele-Woelki K et al. (eds.), (2010) Convergence and Divergence in Private International Law. *Journal:563–577. At:575–577*

Boonstra K, (2014) EVO/Rome I beoogt law shopping te voorkomen, maar niet om cherry picking te bevorderen. Tijdschrift voor Recht en Arbeid 6/7(58): *pages*

Camilleri SP (2011) Article 23: Formal Validity, Material Validity or both? Journal of Private International Law 7(2): 298

Derks CBG, (2011) Toepasselijk recht: hoe gewoon is de gewone werkplek in de internationale arbeidsverhouding? Arbeidsrecht Maandblad voor de praktijk 45:8–11

Van den Eeckhout V (2014) De ontsnappingsclausule van art. 6 lid 2 EVO. Hoe bijzonder is de zaak Schlecker? Tijdschrift Recht en Arbeid 31(4):3–8

Even Z (2013) Het toepasselijk recht op arbeidsovereenkomsten. Artikel 6 EVO en 8 Rome I steeds verder ontrafeld. Nederlands Internationaal Privaatrecht 1:13–24

Geimer, R., Schütze, R.A., Geimer, E. et al., *Europäisches Zivilverfahrensrecht* (C.H. Beck, Munchen, 2010), Kommentar Art. 35, n. 14

Giuliani M, Lagarde P (1980) Report on the Convention on the law applicable to contractual obligations. OJ C 282:1

Hays P, (2013) Notes on the European Union's Brussels-I "Recast" Regulation – An American Perspective. The European Legal Forum 1:4

Heinze Ch (2011) Choice of Court Agreements, Coordination of Proceedings and Provisional Measures in the Reform of the Brussels I Regulation. Max Planck Private Law Research Paper 11(5):8. <http://ssrn.com/abstract=1804111>. Last visited 8 October 2014

Hoek van, AAH (2011) Heiko Koelzsch tegen Groothertogdom Luxemburg. *Ars Aequi ...*:650–658

Kropholler,J., and Hein,J., *Europäisches Zivilprozessrecht: Kommentar zu EuGVO, Lugano-Übereinkommen 2007, EuVTVO, EuMVVO und EuGFVO* (Frankfurt am Main: Recht und Wirtschaft, 2011).

Laagland FG (2012) Grenzeloze problemen bij grensoverschrijdende arbeid. Arbeidsrechtelijke Annotaties 11(3):63–78

Lazić V (2013) The Revised *Lis pendens* rule in the Brussels Jurisdiction Regulation. Review of European Law 2:5–27

Lazić V (2013) 'Enhancing the Efficiency of Dispute Settlement Clauses in the European Union. In: Bodiroga-Vukobrat N et al. (eds.) Legal Culture in Transition – Supranational and International Law Before National Courts, Logos Verlag Berlin, 2013, pp 184–188

Leyton, A. and Mercer, H., *European Civil Practice* (2nd revised edn, Sweet & Maxwell, 2004), Para. 26.086.

Magnus U, Mankowski P, Calvo Caravaca A-L & Carrascosa Gonzalez J., (2016) in Magnus U and Mankowski P (eds.) Brussels Ibis Regulation, Munich: Sellier, 2016.

Magnus U, Mankowski P, Nielsen P, (2016) in Magnus U and Mankowski P (eds.) Brussels Ibis Regulation, Munich: Sellier, 2016.

Magnus U, Mankowski P, Nielsen PA (2012), European Commentaries on Private International Law, *Brussels I Regulation* 2nd Revised Edition, 2012.

Magnus U, Mankowski P (2012), European Commentaries on Private International Law, *Brussels I Regulation* 2nd Revised Edition, 2012.

Trstenjak V, Beysen F (2011) European Consumer Protection Law: *Curia Semper Dabit Remedium*? CML Rev 48:95–124

Vassilakakis E (2014) International Jurisdiction in Insurance Matters under Regulation Brussels I. *In Essays in honour of Spyridon VI. Vrellis*, pp. 1079 *et seq*

Weber J (2011) Universal Jurisdiction in Third States in the Reform of the Brussels I Regulation. Rabels Zeitschrift 75:620 et seq.

Sanne Jansen
Stefan Somers*

THE PRINCIPLE OF EQUALITY AS A CATALYST: THE INCREASING INFLUENCE OF THE PRINCIPLE OF EQUALITY ON THE BELGIAN LAW OF OBLIGATIONS

1. Introduction

1. During the last decades, the role of human rights in the European legal system has expanded. This is especially true for the principle of equality and non-discrimination in Belgium. Not only has this principle led to the rise of non-discrimination law, it has also been used by the Constitutional Court – by using a very broad interpretation of the principle of equality – as an instrument to broaden its competences. Consequently, all legal branches are affected by this 'constitutionalisation'-process. This is also the case for the Belgian law of obligations.

2. In 1981, this evolution was only in its infancy. The first anti-discrimination law had been adopted that year, but it did not yet have the broad scope of application that it would receive later on.[1] It was only gradually that anti-discrimination law became relevant for the law of obligations.[2] Similarly, the Constitutional Court[3] has been established in 1984 but only started to have influence on the law of obligations in 1995 when it found some prescription rules in the field of tort law to be in violation with the constitutional

* Sanne Jansen is a postdoctoral researcher and B.A.E.F. fellow at the Yale and Columbia Law School and a KU Leuven research fellow, Institute for the Law of Obligations. Stefan Somers is a postdoctoral researcher and B.A.E.F. fellow at the Columbia Law School and assistant professor of the law of obligations at the VUB.

1 Law of 30 July 1981 'tot bestraffing van bepaalde door racisme of xenofobie ingegeven daden', *BS* 8 August 1981.

2 S Stijns and S Jansen, 'Actuele ontwikkelingen inzake de basisbeginselen van het contractenrecht' in S Stijns, V Sagaert, I Samoy *et al.* (eds.), *Verbintenissenrecht, Themis*, die Keure, Bruges 2012, pp 1–50; S Stijns and S Jansen, 'De basisbeginselen van het contractenrecht: kroniek van de recentste evoluties', (2013) *TBBR*, pp 2–30. See also more general for private law: S Jansen, 'De invloed van het Europese antidiscriminatierecht op privaatrechtelijke verhoudingen' in I Samoy, V Sagaert and E Terryn (eds), *Invloed van het Europese recht op het Belgische privaatrecht*, Intersentia, Antwerp 2012, pp 145–206.

3 Which at that time was called the *'Cour d'arbitrage/Arbitragehof'*. The Name of the Court changed to 'Cour Constitutionnelle/Grondwettelijk Hof' or 'Constitutional Court'. In function of uniformity and readability, we will always use the term Constitutional Court in the context of this contribution.

principle of equality.[4] Some scholars at that time were surprised by this 'sudden' influence of the principle of equality on the law of obligations.[5] Nevertheless, it has become more and more common that the compatibility of rules of the law of obligations with the principle of equality is tested before the Constitutional Court.[6]

3. In this contribution we will discuss the increasing influence of the principle of equality and non-discrimination in the Belgian law of obligations[7] since the adoption of the first anti-discrimination law in 1981 and the establishment of the Constitutional Court in 1984. In order to do so, we will make a distinction based on the different addressees to whom the principle of equality is aimed: government and citizens. Indeed, the principle of equality is aimed at citizens who make contracts in the sense that it forbids them to discriminate one another. The government, on the other hand, has to take the principle of equality into account when it makes laws or delivers judgments with regard to the law of obligations. Rules cannot be drafted in such a way so that they treat different tort victims or contracting parties in a similar situation in a discriminatory way.

2. Principle of equality and horizontal relationships (citizen to citizen)

4. In this first part we will discuss the effect of the principle of equality in horizontal relationships, between the contractual parties themselves and in the tortfeasor-victim relation. Especially in (pre-)contractual relations, the freedom to contract[8] can be restricted

4 Constitutional Court 21 March 1995, no. 25/95. See also: X Thunis and A Deleu, 'Prescription et discrimination en droit Belge' in P Jourdain and P Wéry (eds), *La prescription extinctive. Etudes de droit comparé*, Bruylant, Brussels 2010, pp 704 and 780.

5 P Traest, 'De verjaring van de burgerlijke vordering voortspruitend uit een misdrijf: de geschiedenis en de onzekere toekomst' (note under Arbitragehof 21 March 1995), (1994–95) *RW* 1324, 1325 and H Bocken, 'Gelijkheid in aansprakelijkheid – De rechtspraak van het Arbitragehof en de ontwikkeling van het aansprakelijkheidsrecht' in *De herziening van de bevrijdende verjaring door de wet van 10 juni 1998; De gelijkheid hersteld?*, Kluwer, Antwerp 1999, p 5.

6 In the field of tort law this has been demonstrated by: S Somers, 'Bijzondere aansprakelijkheidsregimes en het gelijkheidsbeginsel', (2015) *TPR* 1, pp 1–70 and S Somers, 'Special liability regimes and human rights under Belgian law and the European Convention on Human rights', (2014) *Journal of European Tort Law* 310, 310–338.

7 This contribution will focus on tort law and general contract law, including – when relevant – some special contracts such as tenancy contracts, lease contracts, sales contracts, and service contracts. See for a contribution about discrimination in special contracts: C Cauffman, 'Discriminatie bij bijzondere overeenkomsten', (2006–07) *RW* 287, 287–304. We will not discuss (extensively) the influence of the principle of non-discrimination in insurance contract law and labour contract law, although some references can be made.

8 See e.g. about the tension between freedom of contract and the prohibition to discriminate: N Bernard, 'Les lois anti-discrimination et le secteur du logement (privé et social)' in C Bayart, S Sottiaux and S Van Drooghenbroeck (eds), *De nieuwe federale antidiscriminatiewetten,* die Keure, Bruges 2008, pp 808–809; M Dambre, 'De wet bestrijding discriminatie en het huurrecht' in M De Vos and E Brems (eds), *De Wet bestrijding discriminatie,* Intersentia, Antwerp 2004, pp 322 *et seq*; A De Boeck, 'Doorwerking van het gelijkheidsbeginsel in het contractenrecht. De contractsvrijheid in het nauw gedreven?' in *Vrijheid en gelijkheid. De horizontale werking van het gelijkheidsbeginsel en de nieuwe antidiscriminatiewet*, Maklu, Antwerp 2003, pp 416 *et seq.*; J Kusters, 'Discriminatie ten opzichte van

by the principle of equality. All aspects of the freedom to contract will be affected: 1) the freedom to choose whether to contract or not; 2) one's ability to freely choose with whom to contract, and 3) to determine the content of the contract.[9] Two legal instruments must be closely examined in this respect: the federal antidiscrimination laws of 10 May 2007[10] and the antidiscrimination decree of 10 July 2008.[11, 12] Those laws are meant to implement the European antidiscrimination directives.[13] Secondly we will also take into account the influence of Articles 10 and 11 of the constitution in horizontal relations.[14]

2.1. *Antidiscrimination laws in the law of obligations: from 1981 until present*

2.1.1. Historical background of the antidiscrimination laws

5. The first law that forbade discrimination in the Belgian legal order was the antiracism law of 30 July 1981.[15] At that time, it had not yet the broad scope of application that it

allochtonen op de private huurmarkt' in *Vrijheid en gelijkheid. De horizontale werking van het gelijkheidsbeginsel en de nieuwe antidiscriminatiewet,* Maklu, Antwerp 2003, pp 546 *et seq.*; S Stijns and S Jansen, 'De basisbeginselen van het contractenrecht: kroniek van de recentste evoluties', (2013) *TBBR* 2, no. 17 *et seq.*; K Vanderschot, 'De bestrijding van discriminatie in het gemeen contractenrecht' in S Stijns and P Wéry (eds), *Antidiscriminatiewet en contracten,* die Keure, Bruges 2006, pp 47 *et seq.*; A Van Oevelen and C Cauffman, 'Contractvrijheid, contractweigering en antidiscriminatie' in *Bijzondere overeenkomsten, XXXIVe Postuniversitaire Cyclus Willy Delva,* Kluwer, Mechelen 2008, pp 441–443.

9 See also extensively: S Stijns and S Jansen, 'De basisbeginselen van het contractenrecht: kroniek van de recentste evoluties', (2013) *TBBR* 2, 2–30.

10 Law of 10 May 2007 'ter bestrijding van discriminatie tussen mannen en vrouwen', *BS* 30 May 2007 (hereafter: the gender law); Law of 10 May 2007 'ter bestrijding van bepaalde vormen van discriminatie', *BS* 30 May 2007 (hereafter: the general antidiscrimination law). The Law of 10 May 2007 changes (again) the Law of 30 July 1981 'tot bestraffing van bepaalde door racisme of xenophobie ingegeven daden' (hereafter: anti-racism law).

11 Flemish decree of 10 July 2008 'houdende een kader voor het Vlaamse gelijkekansen- en gelijkebehandelingsbeleid', *BS* 23 September 2008.

12 Although we will touch upon the principle of non-discrimination in some specific contracts (see also *supra*, footnote 7), we will not treat special legislation with regard to specific non-discrimination rules in specific contracts such as e.g. Article 7 and 10 of the Law of 20 February 1991 'Regels betreffende de huurovereenkomsten met betrekking tot de hoofdverblijfplaats van de huurder in het bijzonder', *BS* 22 February 1991, 3468; Article VII.69 and VII.126 Wetboek van economisch recht (WER) (about consumer credit and consumer mortgages)... See also: C Cauffman, 'Discriminatie bij bijzondere overeenkomsten', (2006–07) *RW* 287, no. 39, 61, 67 and 68.

13 See for a general overview of the implemented directives and their relation to the antidiscrimination laws: S Jansen, 'De invloed van het Europese antidiscriminatierecht op privaatrechtelijke verhoudingen' in I Samoy, V Sagaert and E Terryn (eds), *Invloed van het Europese recht op het Belgische privaatrecht,* Intersentia, Antwerp 2012, p 187, footnote 210.

14 We will not treat the principle of equality in EU law and with regard to the European Convention of Human Rights. See also: S Jansen, 'De invloed van het Europese antidiscriminatierecht op privaatrechtelijke verhoudingen' in I Samoy, V Sagaert and E Terryn (eds), *Invloed van het Europese recht op het Belgische privaatrecht,* Intersentia, Antwerp 2012, pp 150–173.

15 Law of 30 July 1981 'tot bestraffing van bepaalde door racisme of xenofobie ingegeven daden', *BS* 8 August 1981, 9928. See also about its antecedents and origins: D De Prins, S Sottiaux and J Vrielink, *Handboek Discriminatierecht,* Kluwer, Mechelen 2005, pp 291 *et seq.*

would receive later on. The law has mainly been introduced to fulfil Belgium's obligations to implement the UN Convention on the Elimination of All Forms of Racial Discrimination.[16] The law has been modified several times.[17] Important changes have been introduced in 1994, 2003 and 2007 (see *infra*). Important for this contribution is that Article 2 of this law prohibits and criminalizes discrimination based on race, skin colour, origin or national or ethnic descend in case of delivering goods and services on a publicly accessible place. This means that racial discrimination is forbidden in case of delivery of publicly available goods and services, implying a prohibition of racial discrimination in those contractual relations.

6. In 1993 another important law established the Centre for Equality of Chances and the Fight Against Racism.[18] Its competences were at the time, amongst others, to carry out research, to advise the government and other institutions, to advise individuals with regard to their rights and obligations, to introduce legal proceedings with regard to the law of 30 July 1981, and to provide information.[19]

7. Then, the law of 12 April 1994[20] broadened the scope of application of the antiracism law. This change was necessary because of the low impact of the antiracism law up until then.[21] The law raised the criminal sanctions and defined the concept of 'discrimination' and the discrimination grounds.[22] Important about this definition is that it referred to the prohibition of discrimination in 'social life',[23] and not only to 'public life', as is the case in the previously mentioned UN-convention of 1966 (*supra* no. 5). This means that the prohibition is not only applicable in vertical but also in horizontal relations, between citizens themselves.[24] Furthermore, it left out the words 'publicity' and 'publicly'[25] in a way that it enhanced the prohibition and criminalisation of discrimination in the private

16 See the International Convention on the Elimination of All Forms of Racial Discrimination, New York, 7 March 1966. See also the Law of 9 July 1975 'houdende goedkeuring van het Internationaal Verdrag inzake de uitbanning van alle vormen van rassendiscriminatie, opgemaakt te New York op 7 maart 1966', *BS* 11 December 1975.

17 See: www.ejustice.just.fgov.be/cgi_loi/change_lg.pl?language=nl&la=N&cn=1981073035&table_name=wet.

18 Law of 15 February 1993 'tot oprichting van een Centrum voor gelijkheid van kansen en voor racismebestrijding', *BS* 19 February 1993, 3764.

19 Article 3 of the Law of 15 February 1993 (first version).

20 *BS* 14 May 1994.

21 Verslag namens de commissie voor justitie over het Wetsontwerp houdende wijziging van de wet van 30 juli 1981 tot bestraffing van bepaalde door racisme of xenofobie ingegeven daden, no. 1294/3 93/94, p. 3.

22 Verslag namens de commissie voor justitie over het Wetsontwerp houdende wijziging van de wet van 30 juli 1981 tot bestraffing van bepaalde door racisme of xenofobie ingegeven daden, no. 1294/3 93/94, p. 2.

23 See Article 1 of the Law of 12 april 1994.

24 D De Prins, S Sottiaux and J Vrielink, *Handboek Discriminatierecht*, Kluwer, Mechelen 2005, pp 302–303.

25 See also D De Prins, S Sottiaux and J Vrielink, *Handboek Discriminatierecht*, Kluwer, Mechelen 2005, p 352.

sphere and broadened the sanctions in case of discrimination in delivering goods and services.[26] These last specifications broadened the scope of application of the antiracism to contract law and increased the likelihood to deal adequately with and to punish e.g. a discriminatory refusal to contract on the ground of race.

8. The law of 20 January 2003 aimed to strengthen even more the legislation of 1981 against racism.[27] Although after the changes of the law in 1994 the number of judicial decisions applying the antiracism law had increased, the number of convictions was still not in proportion with the number of the complaints.[28] The law also aimed to implement the EU Directive 2000/43/EC of 29 June 2000.[29] This law e.g. broadened the concept of racism, replaced the term 'race' by 'so-called race' and replaced the terms 'descend and nationality' by 'skin colour, national or ethnic descend'.[30] Another change is that not only acts of discrimination or segregation towards one person can be sanctioned, but also towards a group.[31] The law also broadened the tasks of the Centre for Equality of Chances and for the Fight Against Racism by adapting the law of 15 February 1993. The Centre has e.g. been conferred the task to process complaints, to negotiate and to collect and publish statistics and jurisprudence about discrimination.[32]

A bit later, the first so-called 'antidiscrimination law' of 25 February 2003 was adopted.[33, 34] It was mainly introduced to implement two European Directives.[35] It

26 See e.g. Articles 1 and 2 of the Law of 12 April 1994. Verslag namens de commissie voor justitie over het Wetsontwerp houdende wijziging van de wet van 30 juli 1981 tot bestraffing van bepaalde door racisme of xenofobie ingegeven daden, no. 1294/3 93/94, p. 2.

27 Law of 20 January 2003 'tot versterking van de wetgeving tegen het racisme', *BS* 12 February 2003.

28 Verslag namens de commissie voor justitie over het Wetsontwerp tot versterking van de wetgeving tegen racisme, no. 1407/005 01/02, Doc 50, p. 6: free translation 'Between 1981–1989 – a period in which statistics were available, 1266 complaints were filed, of which 987 were classified without consequences. In this period only 43 files have been the subject of a court decision: 16 convictions, 14 acquittals and 4 discontinuations of criminal proceedings'.

29 Council Directive 2000/43/EC of 29 June 2000 implementing the principle of equal treatment between persons irrespective of racial or ethnic origin, [2000] OJ L180, pp 22–26.

30 Verslag namens de commissie voor justitie over het Wetsontwerp tot versterking van de wetgeving tegen racisme, no. 1407/005 01/02, Doc 50, pp 6–7.

31 See changed Article 4 of the Law of 30 July 1981: Verslag namens de commissie voor justitie over het Wetsontwerp tot versterking van de wetgeving tegen racisme, no. 1407/005 01/02, Doc 50, pp 6–7.

32 See changed Article 8 of the Law of 15 February 1993.

33 Law of 25 February 2003 'ter bestrijding van discriminatie en tot wijziging van de wet van 15 februari 1993 ter oprichting van een Centrum voor gelijkheid van kansen en racismebestrijding', *BS* 17 March 2003, *err. BS* 13 May 2003. See for the preparatory works: Verslag namens de commissie voor justitie over het Wetsontwerp ter bestrijding van discriminatie en tot wijziging van de wet van 15 februari 1993 tot oprichting van een Centrum voor gelijkheid van kansen en voor racismebestrijding, 1578/008 01/02, Doc. 50 referring to: Verslag namens de commissie voor justitie over het Wetsontwerp tot versterking van de wetgeving tegen racisme, nr. 1407/005 01/02, Doc 50.

34 See about the antecedents of this law: D De Prins, S Sottiaux and J Vrielink, *Handboek Discriminatierecht*, Kluwer, Mechelen 2005, pp 441 *et seq.*

35 Council Directive 2000/43/EC of 29 June 2000 implementing the principle of equal treatment between persons irrespective of racial or ethnic origin, [2000] OJ L180, pp 22–26 and Council Directive 2000/78/EC of 27 November 2000 establishing a general framework for equal treatment in employment and occupation, [2000] OJ L303, pp 16–22.

prohibited discrimination based on gender, so-called race, skin colour, origin, national or ethnic descend, sexual orientation, marital or civil status, birth, fortune, age, faith or religion, the present or future state of health, disablement or a physical characteristic. The definition of a direct or indirect discrimination was inspired on the definition in the EU Directives. More importantly to our topic: the law prohibited any direct and indirect discrimination in every sector of social life: e.g. the delivery of goods and services to the public[36] and any other economic, social or political activity available to the public.[37] The law entailed criminal and civil sanctions (implying a reversal of the burden of proof). In so far that the existing antiracism law already entailed criminal sanctions, the law of 25 February 2003 only implied that also its civil sanctions are applicable to discrimination on the basis of race, skin colour, origin, and national or ethnic descend.[38]

9. The federal antidiscrimination laws of 10 May 2007 have been introduced after the annulment of a few dispositions of the antidiscrimination law of 2003[39] by the Constitutional Court.[40] This law was annulled partially because of the fact that it provided only for a closed list of discrimination grounds, omitted the grounds of 'language' and 'political views', and contained some criminal provisions that would go against the freedom of expression. Because of this annulment and the obligation to implement the EU directives,[41] the legislator has introduced three antidiscrimination

36 See about the difference between public and private horizontal relations: D De Prins, S Sottiaux and J Vrielink, *Handboek Discriminatierecht*, Kluwer, Mechelen 2005, p 504. See also: A De Boeck, 'Doorwerking van het gelijkheidsbeginsel in het contractenrecht. De contractsvrijheid in het nauw gedreven?' in *Vrijheid en gelijkheid. De horizontale werking van het gelijkheidsbeginsel en de nieuwe antidiscriminatiewet*, Antwerp, Maklu 2003, pp 435–436. See also with regard to discrimination and tenancy law: M Dambre, 'De wet bestrijding discriminatie en het huurrecht' in M De Vos and E Brems (eds), *De Wet bestrijding discriminatie*, Intersentia, Antwerp 2004, pp 325–326; N Van Leuven, 'De Antidiscriminatiewet en de huurovereenkomst' in S Stijns and P Wéry (eds), *Antidiscriminatiewet en contracten*, die Keure, Bruges 2006, p 116.

37 See also about the specification 'available to the public': D De Prins, S Sottiaux and J Vrielink, *Handboek Discriminatierecht*, Kluwer, Mechelen 2005, pp 511–512.

38 See Verslag namens de commissie voor justitie over het Wetsontwerp tot versterking van de wetgeving tegen racisme, no. 1407/005 01/02, Doc 50, p 9.

39 See extensively about the antidiscrimination law of 2003: D De Prins, S Sottiaux and J Vrielink, *Handboek discriminatierecht*, Kluwer, Mechelen 2005, 593p.

40 Constitutional Court 6 October 2004, no. 157/2004. The law of 2003 was partially annulled because of the fact that there was a 'closed' list of discrimination grounds that did not include 'language' and 'political conviction' and because the penal dispositions violated the freedom of expression. See D De Prins and J Vrielink, 'Die Wiederkehr des Gleichen. Het Grondwettelijk Hof en de (federale) discriminatiewetgeving', (2009/10) *TBP* 579, 580.

41 *Antiracism law*: Council Directive 2000/43/EC of 29 June 2000 implementing the principle of equal treatment between persons irrespective of racial or ethnic origin, [2000] OJ L180, pp 22–26; *gender law*: Council Directive 75/117/EEC of 10 February 1975 on the approximation of the laws of the Member States relating to the application of the principle of equal pay for men and women, [1975] OJ L45, pp 19–20; Council Directive 76/207/EEC of 9 February 1976 on the implementation of the principle of equal treatment for men and women as regards access to employment, vocational training and promotion, and working conditions, [1976] OJ L39, pp 40–42, as amended by Directive 2002/73/EC of the European Parliament and the Council, 23 September 2002, amending Council Directive 76/207/EEC on the implementation of the principle of equal treatment for men and women

laws in 2007:[42] the gender law (combating discrimination between men and women), the anti-racism law (combating discrimination based on race, which is incorporated in the law of 30 July 1981) and the general antidiscrimination law (combating discrimination based on other grounds). On 10 July 2008 the antidiscrimination decree has been introduced, framing the Flemish policy on equal chances, to combat discrimination falling within the competences of the Flemish Community. On 20 March 2009 the Flemish government also issued a decree securing the access of public spaces by persons with an assistance dog.[43] We must, for the sake of completeness, also mention a law of 2011 that prohibits to wear garments that (almost) fully cover the face.[44] It is important to bear this last law in mind, when examining the cases about discriminatory refusal to contract on the basis of religion or state of health involving headscarves (see *infra*, no. 17 *et seq.*).

Finally, in 2013 and 2014 the Centre of Equality of Chances and for the Fight Against Racism was dismantled and split up into two institutions: the Federal Centre for

as regards access to employment, vocational training and promotion, and working conditions [2002] OJ L269, pp 15–20; Council Directive 86/378/EEC of 24 July 1986 on the implementation of the principle of equal treatment for men and women in occupational social security schemes, [1986] OJ L225, pp 40–42, amended by Council Directive 96/97/EC of 20 December 1996, amending Directive 86/378/EEC on the implementation of the principle of equal treatment for men and women in occupational social security schemes, [1997] OJ L46, pp 20–24; Council Directive 97/80/EC of 15 December 1997 on the burden of proof in cases of discrimination based on sex, [1998] OJ L14, pp 6–8; see also the recast Directive 2006/54/EC of the European Parliament and Council of 5 July 2006 on the implementation of the principle of equal opportunities and equal treatment of men and women in matters of employment and occupation, [2006] OJ L204, pp 23-36 (this Directive repeals the following Directives: Directive 78/117/EEC, Directive 76/207/EEC, Directive 2002/73/EC, Directive 86/378/EEC, Directive 96/97/EC, Directive 97/80/EC and Directive 98/52/EC); Council Directive 2004/113/EC of 13 December 2004 implementing the principle of equal treatment between men and women in the access to and supply of goods and services, [2004] OJ L373, pp 37–43; Council Directive 86/613/EEC of 11 December 1986 on the application of the principle of equal treatment between men and women engaged in an activity, including agriculture, in a self-employed capacity, and on the protection of self-employed women during pregnancy and motherhood, [1986] OJ L359, pp 56–58 replaced by Directive 2010/41/EU of the European Parliament and the Council of 7 July 2010 on the application of the principle of equal treatment between men and women engaged in an activity in a self-employed capacity and repealing Council Directive 86/613/EEC, [2010] OJ L180, pp 1–6; Council Directive 79/7/EEC of 19 December 1978 on the progressive implementation of the principle of equal treatment for men and women in matters of social security, [1979] OJ L6, pp 24–25; *general antidiscrimination law*: Council Directive 2000/78/EC of 27 November 2000 establishing a general framework for equal treatment in employment and occupation, [2000] PB L303, pp 16–22.

42 See for an extensive overview: J Tojerow, 'La réforme du 10 mai 2007: motifs et orientation' in C Bayart, S Sottiaux and S Van Drooghenbroeck (eds), *De nieuwe federale antidiscriminatiewetten*, die Keure, Bruges 2008, pp 1–30.

43 Decree of 20 March 2009, 'houdende de toegankelijkheid van publieke plaatsen voor personen met een assistentiehond', *BS* 8 May 2009, 35850 amended by the Decree of 28 June 2013, 'houdende de wijziging van diverse bepalingen van het decreet van 20 maart 2009 betreffende de toegankelijkheid van publieke plaatsen voor personen met een assistentiehond', *BS* 19 July 2013, 45502.

44 Law of 1 June 2011, 'Wet tot instelling van een verbod op het dragen van kleding die het gezicht volledig dan wel grotendeels verbergt', *BS* 13 July 2011, 41734.

Migration (as from 2015: Myria) that has been established by the law of 17 August 2013[45] and the Interfederal Centre for Equality of Chances (as from 2015: Unia) that has been established by the law of 19 January 2014.[46] Myria is responsible for the issues of migration, the fundamental rights of foreigners and a dignified treatment. Unia is responsible to fight discrimination by enhancing equality of chances and participation in all societal domains (such as the labour market, housing, education, culture, health, citizenship…). Article 6 of the law of 19 January confirms the competence of Unia to take action in legal proceedings.

2.1.2. Federal antidiscrimination laws of 2007 and antidiscrimination decree of 2008

2.1.2.1. General

10. The new antidiscrimination laws of 2007 and the Flemish antidiscrimination decree of 2008 prohibit e.g. unjustified unequal treatment in relations between individuals. Articles 12 anti-racism law, 19 gender law, 14 general antidiscrimination law, and 15 *juncto* 20 antidiscrimination decree prohibit direct discrimination,[47] indirect discrimination,[48] the order to discriminate, and intimidation. Their scope of application is restricted to their personal and material scope of application (see *infra*). In this context we will mainly frame discrimination in (pre-)contractual relations.

11. The three antidiscrimination laws and the antidiscrimination decree prohibit the above mentioned forms of discrimination based on a 'closed list' of discrimination grounds.[49] Article 3 of the anti-racism law prohibits discrimination on the ground of *nationality, so called 'race', skin colour, origin* or *national* or *ethnic descent.* Article 3 of

45 Law of 17 August 2013 'Wet van 15 februari 1993 tot oprichting van een Centrum voor gelijkheid van kansen en voor racismebestrijding met het oog op de omvorming ervan tot een federaal Centrum voor de analyse van de migratiestromen, de bescherming van de grondrechten van de vreemdelingen en de strijd tegen de mensenhandel', *BS* 5 March 2014, 18455.

46 Law of 19 January 2014 'Wet houdende instemming met het samenwerkingsakkoord van 12 juni 2013 tot oprichting van een interfederaal Centrum voor gelijke kansen en bestrijding van discriminatie en racisme', *BS* 5 March 2014, 18458.

47 Direct discrimination means that a not justified differentiation in treatment is directly based on one of the discrimination grounds.

48 Indirect discrimination means that a not justified differentiation in treatment is based on an apparently neutral provision, standard, or procedure that harms particularly people that are characterized by a certain discrimination ground in comparison with other people.

49 This means that only the grounds that are listed in the law, are protected. The antidiscrimination law of 2003 originally also contained such a closed list of discrimination grounds. This list has been challenged before the Constitutional Court (Constitutional Court, 6 October 2004, no. 157/2004, B14–15). The Court decided to annul the closed list with the motivation that there was a different treatment because a discrimination ground that was not listed among the listed grounds, seemed to be considered less worthy of protection as a discrimination ground that was listed. Hereafter it specified that there was no reasonable justification for a difference in treatment for the grounds '*language*' and '*political conviction*'. This was how old Article 2, §1 of this law got annulled.

the gender law combats discrimination on the ground of *sex*. Article 4 of this law equals sex to *pregnancy, childbirth, motherhood* and *transsexuality*. Article 3 of the general antidiscrimination law prohibits discrimination on the ground of *age, sexual orientation, civil status, birth, wealth, belief, ideology, political convictions, language, current or future state of health, a handicap, a physical or genetic characteristic or social descent*.[50] This closed list was attacked before the Constitutional Court because the list would be in itself discriminatory.[51] In a judgment of the Constitutional Court of 12 February 2009 was decided that the legislator can protect some discrimination grounds, which merit more protection, better than other discrimination grounds.[52] Some discrimination grounds are thus better protected than others. It is also called the 'hierarchy of discrimination grounds'.[53] However, the Constitutional Court recognized in a judgment of 2 April 2009 an additional discrimination ground: 'trade union conviction'.[54] This means that the closed list has been partially abolished and that the Court created an 'opening clause' for not-listed grounds in the closed list.[55] This jurisprudence has been repeated in a judgment of 16 July 2009.[56]

12. A discriminating refusal to contract, discriminatory cancellation and discriminating contractual terms fall within the (wide) material scope of application of our antidiscrimination laws. Indeed, the laws are e.g. applicable to, in the public sector as well as in the private sector, the access and offer of goods and services that are publicly available, additional mechanisms for social security, labour relations, the membership of or the involvement in an employer or employees union or any organisation of which the members exercise a certain profession, amongst others the advantages that those organisations offer, access to and participation in, or any other exercise of an economic,

50 See Article 16, §3, §4 and §5 for a list of the discrimination grounds in the antidiscrimination decree.

51 Constitutional Court 12 February 2009, no. 17/2009, B13 *et seq*.

52 According to the Court the victims of discrimination on another ground than the once listed, enjoy legal protection by calling upon civil responsibility and the possibility to declare discriminating contractual terms null based on Articles 6, 1131 and 1133 of the Civil Code (CC) (because it is contrary to public order). See also D De Prins and J Vrielink, 'Die Wiederkehr des Gleichen. Het Grondwettelijk Hof en de (federale) discriminatiewetgeving', (2009–10) *TBP* 579, 592–593; D De Prins, 'Het Grondwettelijk Hof en de federale discriminatiewetten' in C Bayart, S Sottiaux and S Van Drooghenbroeck (eds), *Actuele topics discriminatierecht*, die Keure, Bruges 2010, p 21.

53 D De Prins, 'Het Grondwettelijk Hof en de federale discriminatiewetten' in C Bayart, S Sottiaux and S Van Drooghenbroeck (eds), *Actuele topics discriminatierecht*, die Keure, Bruges 2010, p 22.

54 Constitutional Court 2 April 2009, no. 64/2009.

55 De Prins proposes three conditions that the Conditional Court should respect as to add a ground to the closed list: 1) a ground has to be important and must appear in international treaties for human rights; 2) such an 'important' ground may not be ruled out explicitly by the parliament and lastly, 3) the existing legislation may not prescribe an equivalent protection compared to the prohibition of discrimination in the general antidiscrimination law: D De Prins, 'Het Grondwettelijk Hof en de federale discriminatiewetten' in C Bayart, S Sottiaux and S Van Drooghenbroeck (eds), *Actuele topics discriminatierecht*, die Keure, Bruges 2010, pp 25–26.

56 Constitutional Court 16 July 2009, no. 123/2009. Also in this case 'trade union conviction' has been added to the 'closed' list. The Court refers directly to the judgment of 2 April 2009, no. 64/2009.

social, cultural or political activity accessible to the public.[57] This scope of application clearly shows that the antidiscrimination laws are applicable in relations between individual persons.[58]

The fact that the discrimination, based on the protected grounds, is prohibited with regard to the access and offer of goods and services that are publicly available and any other exercise of an economic, social, cultural or political activity accessible to the public, is crucial with regard to the protection of the principle of equality in contract law. Moreover, compared to the antidiscrimination law of 2003, the laws of 2007 clearly mention 'the access and offer' of goods and services. The 2003 law only mentioned 'delivery' of goods and services', casting doubt on the applicability of the law in the pre-contractual phase. Nevertheless, there was a consensus in doctrine that this did not mean a restriction to the delivery at the execution phase of the contract, excluding the pre-contractual phase.[59] The 2007 legislation makes it clear that it is applicable in all contractual phases such as the pre-contractual and the execution phase.[60] Similarly to the 2003 law, the 2007 laws only prohibit discrimination in the horizontal 'public' sphere and not in purely private relationships.[61] Indeed, they prohibit discrimination on the

57 Article 5 general antidiscrimination law; Article 6 gender law; Article 5 anti-racism law.

58 See for the antidiscrimination decree Article 20: this list is more focused to the competences of the communities and the regions (such as e.g. education, vocational training...).

59 See with regard to the former antidiscrimination law: M Dambre, 'De wet bestrijding discriminatie en het huurrecht' in M De Vos and E Brems (eds), *De Wet bestrijding discriminatie*, Intersentia, Antwerp 2004, p 325; A De Boeck, 'Doorwerking van het gelijkheidsbeginsel in het contractenrecht. De contractsvrijheid in het nauw gedreven?' in *Vrijheid en gelijkheid. De horizontale werking van het gelijkheidsbeginsel en de nieuwe antidiscriminatiewet*, Maklu, Antwerp 2003, pp 435; C Cauffman, 'Discriminatie bij bijzondere overeenkomsten', (2006–07) *RW* 287, 291. See also Article 3.1(h) Council Directive 2000/43/EC *'access to and supply'*. Comp.: N Van Leuven, 'De Antidiscriminatiewet en de huurovereenkomst' in S Stijns and P Wéry (eds), *Antidiscriminatiewet en contracten*, die Keure, Bruges 2006, pp 117 *et seq.* (is not sure whether or not the whole execution phase is covered).

60 The wide wording of the antidiscrimination laws does not rule this out. See also A Van Oevelen and C Cauffman, 'Contractvrijheid, contractweigering en antidiscriminatie' in *Bijzondere overeenkomsten, XXXIVe Postuniversitaire Cyclus Willy Delva*, Kluwer, Mechelen 2008, p 471. Moreover, one is not only prohibited to discriminate in an offer, but also not in publicity or advertisements. See N Van Leuven, *Contracten en mensenrechten. Een mensenrechtelijke lezing van het contractenrecht*, Intersentia, Antwerp 2009, pp 101 and 102, no. 172 and 173; see also S Stijns and E Swaenepoel, 'De evolutie van de basisbeginselen in het contractenrecht, geïllustreerd aan de hand van het contractueel evenwicht' in I Samoy (ed), *Evolutie van de basisbeginselen van het contractenrecht*, Intersentia, Antwerp 2010, no. 28. In the *Feryn* jugdement (in which an employer has publicly declared not recruiting employees of a certain ethnic origin or race) the Court of Justice of the EU has decided (10 July 2008, no. C-54/07) that this entailed direct discrimination under the 'Racial Equality Directive' 2000/43 of 29 June 2000 implementing the principle of equal treatment between persons irrespective of racial or ethnic origin. Van Leuven derives correctly from this that one cannot discriminate in a rental advertisement or a job offer advertisement.

61 See also A Van Oevelen and C Cauffman, 'Contractvrijheid, contractweigering en antidiscriminatie' in *Bijzondere overeenkomsten, XXXIVe Postuniversitaire Cyclus Willy Delva*, Kluwer, Mechelen 2008, p 471.

protected grounds with regard to the access and offer of services *to the public*[62] and any other exercise of an economic, social or political activity *available to the public.*[63]

13. An *unequal treatment* between individual persons is not automatically prohibited, but it is only forbidden and discriminatory if the difference in treatment cannot be justified. Sottiaux describes the different systems of justification as 'open'[64] or 'closed'[65], and in between, a whole myriad of intermediate systems exist.[66] According to this author, our legal system has chosen in the antidiscrimination legislation the option of an 'intermediate system'. Bayart and Bosmans summarize that there is an open system of justification for indirect differentiations and a mixed system for direct differentiations.[67, 68] If someone e.g. refuses to contract with a person because of his race (*i.e.* a direct differentiation), this can in principle not be justified (completely closed system). Yet, this closed system is subject to exceptions with regard to labour relations. A direct differentiation can be justified by genuine and determining occupational

62 See about the difference between public and private horizontal relations: D De Prins, S Sottiaux and J Vrielink, *Handboek Discriminatierecht*, Kluwer, Mechelen 2005, p 504. See also: A De Boeck, 'Doorwerking van het gelijkheidsbeginsel in het contractenrecht. De contractsvrijheid in het nauw gedreven?' in *Vrijheid en gelijkheid. De horizontale werking van het gelijkheidsbeginsel en de nieuwe antidiscriminatiewet*, Maklu, Antwerp 2003, pp 435–436; C Cauffman, 'Discriminatie bij bijzondere overeenkomsten', (2006–07) *RW* 287, 292. See also with regard to discrimination and tenancy law: M Dambre, 'De wet bestrijding discriminatie en het huurrecht' in M De Vos and E Brems (eds), *De Wet bestrijding discriminatie*, Intersentia, Antwerp 2004, pp 325–326; N Van Leuven, 'De Antidiscriminatiewet en de huurovereenkomst' in S Stijns and P Wéry (eds), *Antidiscriminatiewet en contracten*, die Keure, Bruges 2006, p 116.

63 See also about the specification 'available to the public': D De Prins, S Sottiaux and J Vrielink, *Handboek Discriminatierecht*, Kluwer, Mechelen 2005, pp 511–512; C Cauffman, 'Discriminatie bij bijzondere overeenkomsten', (2006–07) *RW* 287, 293.

64 In an open system the judge can balance case by case the 'discriminating' act or expression and the provided justification and can assess whether the difference in treatment is objectively justified by a legitimate aim and whether or not that the means to obtain that aim are reasonable and necessary.

65 Only certain grounds of justification are allowed such as e.g. genuine and determining occupational requirements (e.g. in labour relations).

66 S Sottiaux, 'De rechtvaardigingsgronden in het federale discriminatierecht' in C Bayart, S Sottiaux and S Van Drooghenbroeck (eds), *De nieuwe federale antidiscriminatiewetten*, die Keure, Bruges 2008, pp 230–231 and 235.

67 C Bayart and I Bosmans, 'De federale antidiscriminatiewetten en arbeidsbetrekkingen in de private sector: algemeen overzicht' in C Bayart, S Sottiaux and S Van Drooghenbroeck (eds), *De nieuwe federale antidiscriminatiewetten*, die Keure, Bruges 2008, pp 654–656.

68 The antidiscrimination laws define the concept of a 'direct differentation' as follows: '*de situatie die zich voordoet wanneer iemand ongunstiger wordt behandeld dan een ander in een vergelijkbare situatie wordt, is of zou worden behandeld op basis van [de discriminatiegrond]*' (the situation in which someone gets (or would be) treated less favourable than someone else in a comparable situation based on [a discriminationground]. The antidiscrimination laws define the concept of indrect differentiation as '*de situatie die zich voordoet wanneer een ogenschijnlijk neutrale bepaling, maatstaf of handelswijze personen [die getroffen zijn door een bepaalde discriminatiegrond], in vergelijking met andere personen bijzonder kan benadelen.*' (the situation in which an apparently neutral provision, standard, or procedure that harms particularly people [that are characterized by a certain discrimination ground] in comparison with other people) See about the difference direct/indirect differentiation: C Bayart and C Deiteren, 'Direct en indirect onderscheid' in C Bayart, S Sottiaux and S Van Drooghenbroeck (eds), *De nieuwe federale antidiscriminatiewetten*, die Keure, Bruges 2008, pp 171–225.

requirements and if the differentiation is to be considered and accepted as a measure of positive action.[69, 70]

14. The antidiscrimination laws contain an extensive list of sanctions, amongst others civil sanctions. Discriminating terms in contracts are void and null (*i.e.* a partial nullity).[71] The victim can also claim a fixed sum of damages or damages for losses actually incurred according to contract or tort law.[72] Furthermore, there is a prohibition of retaliations.[73] The judge can likewise impose a lump sum and/or a prohibitory injunction.[74] To enhance the deterrent effect, the laws prescribe also criminal sanctions.[75] Moreover, the laws regulate the (reversal of the) burden of proof and proof by means of field testing, patterns of unfavourable treatment and statistical information.[76]

An important question that arises is whether in case of a discriminatory refusal to contract, a prohibitory injunction (combined with a lump sum), can be used to force the discriminating

69 See e.g. S Sottiaux, 'De rechtvaardigingsgronden in het federale discriminatierecht' in C Bayart, S Sottiaux and S Van Drooghenbroeck (eds), *De nieuwe federale antidiscriminatiewetten*, die Keure, Bruges 2008, p 248.

70 This example is only valid for the discussed discrimination ground and the referred scope of application; because for every discrimination ground and every scope of application different rules apply with regard to justification.

71 See Article 15 general antidiscrimination law, Article 20 gender law, Article 13 anti-racism law, Article 27 antidiscrimination decree. See for more information about the civil sanctions: J-F Germain and C Eyben, 'Les sanctions civiles. La nullité et les dommages et intérêts forfaitaires' in C Bayart, S Sottiaux and S Van Drooghenbroeck (eds), *De nieuwe federale antidiscriminatiewetten*, die Keure, Bruges 2008, pp 333–360.

72 Article 18 general antidiscrimination law, Article 23 gender law, Article 16 anti-racism law, Article 28 antidiscrimination decree.

73 Articles 16–17 general antidiscrimination law, Articles 21–22 gender law, Articles 14–15 anti-racism law, Articles 37–38 antidiscrimination decree.

74 Articles 19–20 general discrimination law, Articles 24–25 gender law, Articles 17–18 anti-racism law, Articles 29–30 antidiscrimination decree. See about the prohibitory injunction: G Closset-Marchal and S Van Drooghenbroeck, 'L'action en cessation en matière de discrimination' in C Bayart, S Sottiaux and S Van Drooghenbroeck (eds), *De nieuwe federale antidiscriminatiewetten*, die Keure, Bruges, 2008, pp 361–414.

75 With regard to contract law, only discrimination on the ground of nationality, so-called race, origin and national or ethnic descend would be in some situations be punished by criminal sanctions (see Articles 24–25 anti-racism law); See also N Van Leuven, *Contracten en mensenrechten. Een mensenrechtelijke lezing van het contractenrecht*, Intersentia, Antwerp 2009, pp 121–122; See for other criminal provisions: Titel IV general discrimination law, gender law and anti-racism law, Articles 31–35 antidiscrimination decree. See for more information B Blero, 'L'incrimination pénale de la discrimination en question' in C Bayart, S Sottiaux and S Van Drooghenbroeck (eds), *De nieuwe federale antidiscriminatiewetten*, die Keure, Bruges 2008, pp 463–506. See the judgement of Constitutional Court 12 February 2009, no. 17/2009, B.40-B.53 about amongst others the criminal principle of legality. See also D De Prins, 'Het Grondwettelijk Hof en de federale discriminatiewetten' in C Bayart, S Sottiaux and S Van Drooghenbroeck (eds), *Actuele topics discriminatierecht*, die Keure, Bruges 2010, pp 34–35.

76 Titel V general discrimination law, gender law and anti-racism law; Afd. VI antidiscrimination decree. See for more information: J Rorive and V van der Plancke, 'Quels dispositifs pour prouver la discrimination?' in C Bayart, S Sottiaux and S Van Drooghenbroeck (eds), *De nieuwe federale antidiscriminatiewetten*, die Keure, Bruges 2008, pp 415–462.

party to contract effectively (*i.e. 'contractdwang'*). This would mean that the contract is specifically performed, against the will of the discriminating party. Most authors agree that this sanction would be in most cases too far reaching, and would not be in line with the freedom to contract.[77] Moreover, in our opinion, it is important to assess whether the human rights (e.g. Articles 8, 9, 10 or 11 ECHR or Article 1 of the first protocol with the ECHR) of the discriminatory party would be violated if he would be forced to contract. When a judge determines a remedy, he has to take into account the human rights of the involved parties.[78] With this regard, it is important to notice that when assessing the proportionality between the severity of an infringement of a human right and the legitimate aim that is pursued with the infringement, a judge must look whether the legitimate aim can be achieved in a less intrusive manner.[79] Since the aim to protect a victim of discrimination in most cases can be achieved by granting a compensation (and by applying criminal sanctions in order to deter the discriminating party), it seems likely that in most situations, it will not be proportionate to force a discriminating party to contract.

15. Taking into account the personal and material scope of application of the antidiscrimination laws and the antidiscrimination decree, it is prohibited to discriminate in (pre)contractual relations between individual persons. If one concludes a contract, this discriminatory behaviour will often be expressed by a refusal to contract or the inclusion of discriminating contractual terms. The following applications in case law illustrate discriminating practices in the pre-contractual stage, tackled by the antidiscrimination legislation.

2.1.2.2. Applications in lower courts

16. We have seen that the antiracism law has been changed subsequently to enhance its impact in courtrooms (see *supra*, no. 5 *et seq.*). Over the years, it became possible for

77 M Dambre, 'De wet bestrijding discriminatie en het huurrecht' in M De Vos and E Brems (eds), *De Wet bestrijding discriminatie*, Intersentia, Antwerp 2004, pp 342 and 346 (nuances this in case of a landlord with overwhelming market dominance); N Van Leuven, 'De Antidiscriminatiewet en de huurovereenkomst' in S Stijns and P Wéry (eds), *Antidiscriminatiewet en contracten*, die Keure, Bruges 2006, pp 136–137. See also A De Boeck, 'Doorwerking van het gelijkheidsbeginsel in het contractenrecht. De contractsvrijheid in het nauw gedreven?' in *Vrijheid en gelijkheid. De horizontale werking van het gelijkheidsbeginsel en de nieuwe antidiscriminatiewet*, Maklu, Antwerp 2003, pp 437 and 439; C Cauffman, 'Discriminatie bij bijzondere overeenkomsten', (2006–07) *RW* 287, 295–296; K Vanderschot, 'De bestrijding van discriminatie in het gemeen contractenrecht', in S Stijns and P Wéry, *Antidiscriminatiewet en contracten*, die Keure, Bruges 2006, pp 57–58; A Van Oevelen and C Cauffman, 'Contractvrijheid, contractweigering en antidiscriminatie' in *Bijzondere overeenkomsten, XXXIVe Postuniversitaire Cyclus Willy Delva*, Kluwer, Mechelen 2008, pp 477–478. Comp.: J Kusters, 'Discriminatie ten opzichte van allochtonen op de private huurmarkt' in *Vrijheid en gelijkheid. De horizontale werking van het gelijkheidsbeginsel en de nieuwe antidiscriminatiewet*, Maklu, Antwerp 2003, p 567 (addresses the question, but does not answer it).

78 S Somers, *Het buitencontractueel aansprakelijkheidsrecht en de rechten van de mens: kruisbestuiving in een meergelaagde rechtsorde*, Intersentia, Antwerp 2016, pp 557–562.

79 D Harris, M O'Boyle, E bates and C. Buckley, *Law of the European Convention on Human Rights*, Oxford University Press, Oxford 2009, p 348.

citizens to act against each other on the basis of our antidiscrimination legislation. This means that there was a 'horizontalisation' of the principle of equality in our legislation: citizens were prohibited by law to discriminate each other in an increasing range of societal domains. The law of 12 April 1994 e.g. has made an important step in this regard by changing the antiracism law. It left out the word 'publicly' in a way that it enhanced the prohibition and criminalisation of discrimination in the private sphere and broadened the sanctions in case of discrimination in delivering goods and services.[80] The antidiscrimination law of 2003 broadened the material scope by prohibiting also discrimination on other than race-related discrimination grounds, such as: gender, sexual orientation, marital or civil status, birth, fortune, age, faith or religion, the present or future state of health, disablement or a physical characteristic. Moreover, the law prohibits any direct and indirect discrimination in almost every sector of social life. Indeed, the law was applicable to, e.g. the delivery of goods and services that are publicly available, or any other economic, social, cultural or political activity accessible to the public. In sum, this meant a true 'horizontalisation' of our antidiscrimination legislation. This trend was even enhanced by the laws in 2007, broadening the list of discrimination grounds. The result of this horizontalisation is reflected in the case law. Every year, a growing number of cases can be found about the topic of discrimination in the law of obligations. As already been mentioned, most cases involve a discriminatory refusal to contract.

2.1.2.2.1. Discriminatory refusal to contract[81]

17. Discriminatory refusals to contract often happen in the context of *nightlife businesses, the entertainment sector, and the catering industry.* Think about discriminatory refusals to access a dancing, a bar, a restaurant...We will discuss these cases taking into account three themes: discriminatory refusal because of disablement or illness; discriminatory refusal because of religion, discriminatory refusal because of race or ethnic origin.

A first set of cases concentrates on discrimination on the ground of disablement or illness. A prohibitory injunction was for example granted in a judgment of 4 November 2009 of the court of first instance of Dendermonde (in interim proceedings).[82] In this

[80] Verslag namens de commissie voor justitie over het Wetsontwerp houdende wijziging van de wet van 30 juli 1981 tot bestraffing van bepaalde door racisme of xenofobie ingegeven daden, no. 1294/3 93/94, p 2.

[81] See e.g. in general about discriminatory refusal to contract: A De Boeck, 'Doorwerking van het gelijkheidsbeginsel in het contractenrecht. De contractsvrijheid in het nauw gedreven?' in *Vrijheid en gelijkheid. De horizontale werking van het gelijkheidsbeginsel en de nieuwe antidiscriminatiewet*, Maklu, Antwerp 2003, pp 424–428.

[82] Court of first instance of Dendermonde 4 November 2009, AR no. 08/3009/A, not published (www.unia.be). Based on different Articles of the general antidiscrimination law. Comp. Court of first instance of Ghent 24 June 2014, AR no. GE 56.LA.41677/13-SW4, not published (www.unia.be) (a shop owner refused access to an assistance dog and its boss because of an allergy (which he could prove with a medical certificate); no discrimination based on the general antidiscrimination law but a breach of Article 3 of the Decree of 20 March 2009 '*houdende de toegankelijkheid van publieke plaatsen voor personen met een assisentiehond*' (free translation: 'concerning the accessibility of public spaces for persons with an assistance dog'); the fine of the shop owner was delayed).

case access to a restaurant was denied to an assistance dog of a physically disabled person. The restaurant owner was of the opinion that the prohibition was justified by the aim to operate a small and cosy restaurant, displaying directly the meat that is be grilled. The judge decided that this refusal had to be considered a direct discrimination and imposed a prohibitory injunction subject to the payment of a lump sum. The judge also grants the victim damages and orders to make the judgment public in a local newspaper. This judgment was confirmed upon appeal except that the court of appeal decided that it was an indirect discrimination and that the publication in a local newspaper was not necessary.[83] Another case is closely linked to the next set of cases, related to discrimination of the ground of religion by wearing the headscarf (see *infra*). This case did not concern a religious headscarf but a headwear to cover one's baldness because of a cancer treatment. A cancer patient wanted to eat out in a bowling restaurant with her family and was told by one of the servants that a headscarf was prohibited. At the time she was wearing a headscarf to cover her baldness due to cancer treatment. The court of first instance of Huy granted in a judgment of 26 May 2010 an injunction and a lump sum to execute the order in order to stop this indirect discrimination on the ground of the state of health.[84] This judgment has been appealed by the bowling owner and the appeal has been granted in favour of the bowling owner, five years later, by the court of appeal of Mons in a judgment of 29 September 2015.[85]

We also observe discrimination on the ground of religion in the catering sector, often related to headscarves. In a nuanced case two sisters were denied access to a cocktail bar because they wore a headscarf. The court of appeal of Ghent made clear in a judgment of 8 October 2015[86] that in this case, the bar owner had not directly discriminated the two sisters because he based his refusal on internal rules displayed at the entrance door. These rules prohibited any kind of headgear and were applicable to

83 Ghent 6 December 2012, AR no. 2010/AR/264, not published (www.unia.be).

84 Court of first instance of Huy 26 May 2010, AR no. 09/928/B, not published (www.unia.be). Based on Articles 3, 4, 5, 20 of the general antidiscrimination law.

85 Mons 29 September 2015, not published (www.unia.be) (no indirect discrimination because the current case was the fruit of a miscommunication of a servant who did not know that there was an exception in the internal rules for female headwear (except for caps)). See also, but in the fitness sector: Brussels 8 September 2015, AR 2014/AR/2354, not published (www.unia.be) (no (direct or) indirect discrimination found because of the fact that the indirect differentiation by prohibiting headwear in a fitness centre was legitimized by the security reasons; the measures taken were proportionate, apt and necessary to achieve the legitimate aim; headwear for medicinal reasons was inserted as an exception in the internal rules of the fitness company, after negotiations with the Centre; confirmation of the decision of the Court of first instance of Brussels 2 June 2014, not published (www.unia.be)).

86 Ghent 8 October 2015, not published, (www.unia.be). Mainly based on Articles 4, 8°, 9, and 14 of the general antidiscrimination law (Ghent 8 October 2015 is the appeal to the judgement of the Court of first instance of Veurne 2 July 2014, AR no. 14:043/C, not published, (www.unia.be) (in this case was decided that there was no (in)direct discrimination on one of the protected grounds)). Compare: Court of first instance of Brussels 22 December 2009, no. R.G. 2009/12.031/A, not published (www.unia.be) (based on Articles 5 and 14 general antidiscrimination law. The owner of a drinking premise refused to serve a lady because of her headscarf. The court established a direct and at least an indirect discrimination and orders a prohibitory injunction and the publication of the judgement during three months in the said drinking premises).

everyone. Nevertheless, the court was of the opinion that these rules, applicable to everyone, amounted to an indirect discrimination of the two sisters. Moreover, the indirect differentiation could not be legitimized by a necessary and justified aim. The bar owner intended to improve the social/nightlife climate with his internal rules; but the judge was of the opinion that the rules were not necessary to obtain the intended aim. The court finally decided that the internal rules of the bar should provide for an exception in case of religious headwear.

Discriminating refusal to contract in the catering sector happens very often on the ground of race.[87] A judgment of the criminal court of Mechelen of 5 January 2011 found discrimination in a case where a person was denied access to a drinking-house based on racist motives.[88] The court condemned the owner to a community service. By a judgment of the court of appeal of Brussels of 2 May 2002 the Interfederal Centre for Equality of Chances (*'Interfederaal Gelijkekansencentrum'*; formerly: 'Centre for Equality of Chances and for the Fight Against Racism'; hereafter 'the Centre') has been attributed damages in a case where someone was discriminatorily denied access to a dancing by the owner and the porter.[89] The porter of a dancing denied a potential customer access because of his ethnic background. The Court decides that this is a case of direct discrimination based on race, skin colour, origin, or national or ethnic descend.

18. In the *fitness sector* the discriminatory refusal to access has also been invoked because of headwear and 'women-only' policies.[90] In a case decided by the court of appeal of Brussels of 8 September 2015[91], the judge found no (direct or) indirect discrimination on religious grounds or health state because of the fact that the indirect

[87] See also extensively D De Prins, S Sottiaux and J Vrielink, *Handboek Discriminatierecht*, Kluwer, Mechelen 2005, pp 353 *et seq.*

[88] Corr. Mechelen 5 January 2011, AR no. ME56.11.12931-10, not published (www.unia.be).

[89] Brussels 2 May 2012, 13th Chamber, *not published* (*www.unia.be*) (based on Article 5, 1° and 8° and Article 7 of the antiracism law)). See similarly: Antwerp 4 December 2008, 13th chamber, AR no. 811 P 2007, not published (www.unia.be) (discriminatory refusal of an immigrant to access a dancing. The owner of the café is found guilty and has to pay the victim damages); Corr. Ghent 13 October 2009, 21st chamber, AR no. GE 56.L5.5102/08, unpublished (www.unia.be) (discriminatory refusal of an immigrant to access a dancing. The owner of the café is punished by a delayed jail sentence and a fine and its porter with a fine. The victim and the Centre receive jointly damages; confirmed by an appeal brought by the owner of the café: Ghent 28 June 2011, AR no. GE/56.L5.5102/08, unpublished (www.unia.be) (except for the criminal conviction which is not anymore delayed but suspended)); Brussels 2 May 2012, unpublished (www.unia.be) ((direct) discriminatory refusal of a Belgian with an immigrant background to access a dancing based on race, skin colour, origin, or national or ethnic descend (anti-racism law). The victim was awarded moral damages). See for a similar case, but there is insufficient proof to establish a discrimination: Corr. Hasselt 13 October 2009, AR no. rep. 1958, unpublished (www.unia.be).

[90] Comp. also: Court of first instance of Antwerp 25 March 2011, AR no. AN56.99.77-06, unpublished (www.unia.be) (no discrimination on the ground of race, skin colour, origin, descend or nationality, because people (whether or not they had an immigrant background) were only refused if they acted violently and disturbed the peace in the fitness club).

[91] Brussels 8 September 2015, AR 2014/AR/2354, not published (www.unia.be) (no (direct or) indirect discrimination found because of the fact that the indirect differentiation by prohibiting headwear in a fitness centre was legitimized by the security reasons; the measures taken were proportionate, apt and necessary to achieve the legitimate aim; headwear for medicinal reasons was inserted as an exception

differentiation by prohibiting headwear in a fitness centre was justified by the security reasons; the measures taken were proportionate, apt and necessary to achieve the legitimate aim. The fitness centre even inserted in its internal rules an exception for headwear for medical reasons (in exceptional circumstances), after negotiations with the Centre. In another fitness case, the court of first instance of Liège found a discrimination based on gender due to a 'women-only' policy and ordered an injunction as an interim measure.[92] The defendants could not justify their refusal to accept men by difficult economic circumstances. The economic difficulties were not considered an objective justification and the measures taken (the women-only policy) did not necessarily or appropriately lead to the economic revival of the fitness centre.

19. Discriminatory refusal to contract also happens in the *real estate industry*.[93] In a case of 23 April 2008 before the criminal court of Brussels, a real estate agent refused in a discriminatory way to contract, hiding behind the request of an owner to not rent to 'black' people.[94] The Centre received damages. A judgment of 23 June 2010 of the criminal court of Antwerp also finds direct discrimination on the ground of ethnical origin in a case of renting a residence by a real estate agent.[95] The court stresses that the facts are serious and that a professional real estate agent has to be a role model and may not, under any circumstance, make a direct differentiation based on ethnical origin. The defendant was found guilty and is sentenced to a community service. Moreover, the victim and the Centre received damages. Direct discrimination on the ground of ethnical origin was also found in a judgment of the court of first instance of Antwerp of 26 June 2014 in which a real-estate agent discriminated against a couple of foreign origin that

in the internal rules of the fitness company, after negotiations with the Centre; confirmation of the decision of the Court of first instance of Brussels 2 June 2014, not published (www.unia.be)).

92 Court of first instance Liège 23 January 2014, AR no. 13:4948/A, not published (www.unia.be). Based on the gender law. The court correctly points out that the gender law does not only have an influence in contractual relations (because also the sport complex company, besides the fitness company (with which the victim has a contractual relation) was sued).

93 See also: N Bernard, 'Les lois anti-discrimination et le secteur du logement (privé et social)' in C Bayart, S Sottiaux and S Van Drooghenbroeck (eds), *De nieuwe federale antidiscriminatiewetten*, die Keure, Bruges 2008, pp 801–826; C Cauffman, 'Discriminatie bij bijzondere overeenkomsten', (2006–07) *RW* 287, 303–304; M Dambre, 'De wet bestrijding discriminatie en het huurrecht' in M De Vos and E Brems (eds), *De Wet bestrijding discriminatie*, Intersentia, Antwerp 2004, pp 321–347; D De Prins, S Sottiaux and J Vrielink, *Handboek Discriminatierecht*, Mechelen, Kluwer 2005, p 359; J Kusters, 'Discriminatie ten opzichte van allochtonen op de private huurmarkt' in *Vrijheid en gelijkheid. De horizontale werking van het gelijkheidsbeginsel en de nieuwe antidiscriminatiewet*, Maklu, Antwerp 2003, pp 541–571; N Van Leuven, 'De Antidiscriminatiewet en de huurovereenkomst' in S Stijns and P Wéry (eds), *Antidiscriminatiewet en contracten*, Bruges, die Keure 2006, pp 111–141. Comp.: no discrimination found by the Court of first instance of Dendermonde of 14 February 2011, AR no. DE.56./4.13277/09/7, unpublished (www.unia.be) (no discrimination by a real estate agent in the pre-contractual phase by refusing a veiled woman to view a property that she wanted to rent because of lack of evidence).

94 Corr. Brussels 23 April 2008, 58th chamber, unpublished (www.unia.be) (based on Article 2 of the old Law of 30 July 1981, *BS* 8 August 1981. Currently the anti-racism law).

95 Corr. Antwerp 23 June 2010, chamber 1C, AR no. AN56.99.570–08, unpublished (www.unia.be) (based on the Articles 5, 61, 1° and 24 anti-racism law).

wanted to rent an apartment.[96] The victim and the Centre both received damages and the landlord was convicted to a (delayed) fine.

We must point out that in case of the intervention of a real estate agent the question arises who should be charged with discrimination: the real estate agent and/or the landlord. Case law is not decisive.[97] Bernard proposes that this must depend on the degree of intensity of the power of representation given by the landlord to the real estate agent. If the mandate is very specific, the real estate agent has little room to manoeuvre and will be hold less easily accountable, and the other way around. We are convinced, with regard to the civil aspects, that the rules of representation have to be applied strictly. If the landlord has ordered the real estate agent to act in a discriminatory way and stipulated this in their contract, this part of the contract between the landlord and the real estate agent will be null and void because it is contrary to public order to stipulate such a thing in a contract.[98] There will be no valid representation of the landlord by the real estate agent with regard to this aspect. This means that the real estate agent will not act in the name of the landlord but in its own name, with regard to the discriminatory refusal to contract. Consequently, the real estate agent must be hold accountable and responsible for any discriminatory act towards prospective tenants, such as a discriminatory refusal to contract. The landlord can also be held accountable, not the least because he incited / ordered the discriminatory refusal to contract by the real estate agent.[99] If the landlord has nothing to do with a discriminatory refusal to contract by a(n) (real estate) agent, Van Leuven argues correctly that the real estate agent must be held accountable, because an agent who acts in his own name, will be held obliged personally.[100] In this situation, it seems far reaching to also hold accountable the landlord (principal). Nevertheless, a judgment of the Court of Cassation of 16 February

96 Court of first instance of Antwerp of 26 June 2014, AR no. AN56.LB.48751-12, not published (www.unia.be). Based on, among others, Articles 5, 24 and 27 anti-racism law.

97 See for an extensive description of the case law: N Bernard, 'Les lois anti-discrimination et le secteur du logement (privé et social)' in C Bayart, S Sottiaux and S Van Drooghenbroeck (eds), *De nieuwe federale antidiscriminatiewetten*, die Keure, Bruges 2008, pp 823 *et seq*.

98 Moreover, the antidiscrimination laws of 2007 state that discriminating terms in contracts are void and null (see *supra*, no. 14). Dambre seems to infer from this that the nullity is restricted to discriminatory terms in tenancy contracts (see with regard to the former antidiscrimination law: M Dambre, 'De wet bestrijding discriminatie en het huurrecht' in M De Vos and E Brems (eds), *De Wet bestrijding discriminatie*, Intersentia, Antwerp 2004, p 341); nevertheless, we are convinced that also an agency-contract that orders or incites to discriminate is null and void with regard to this aspect.

99 See also C Cauffman, 'Discriminatie bij bijzondere overeenkomsten', (2006-07) *RW* 287, 307; J Kusters, 'Discriminatie ten opzichte van allochtonen op de private huurmarkt' in *Vrijheid en gelijkheid. De horizontale werking van het gelijkheidsbeginsel en de nieuwe antidiscriminatiewet*, Maklu, Antwerp 2003, pp 554-555.

100 N Van Leuven, 'De Antidiscriminatiewet en de huurovereenkomst' in S Stijns and P Wéry (eds), *Antidiscriminatiewet en contracten*, die Keure, Bruges 2006, p 133. See also: N Bernard, 'Les lois anti-discrimination et le secteur du logement (privé et social)' in C Bayart, S Sottiaux and S Van Drooghenbroeck (eds), *De nieuwe federale antidiscriminatiewetten*, die Keure, Bruges 2008, p 825.

2001 seems to make this possibility acceptable.[101] With regard to the criminal law aspects, the required intent to commit the crime must be fulfilled for each actor in order to criminalize their behaviour.[102]

Not only real estate agents, but also individual landlords can behave in a discriminatory way. In a case of 18 March 2016 before the Court of first instance of Antwerp a landlord and a couple of foreign origin were negotiating a tenancy contract.[103] The landlord broke off the negotiations in a discriminatory way because she motivated it by referring to the fact that they were dressed like Muslims, that the man had a big beard, and that the neighbours would not agree with them moving into the block. This motivation was sent by a text message from the landlord's mobile phone to the mobile phone of the tentative tenants. The court decided that the charges were proven and the landlord was sentenced to one month of imprisonment and a fine of 200 EUR.[104] Moreover, the victims got a moral compensation of 1 EUR. In another case a landlord and his mandatory discriminated on the ground of skin colour and nationality in refusing to rent the property of the landlord to black people and non-Belgians. The court of first instance of Liège granted in a judgment of 6 May 2014 an injunction to stop the discriminatory behaviour of the two defendants.[105]

The following case has even risen the interest of the national newspapers.[106] In a judgment of 5 May 2015 of the court of first instance of Namur has been decided that a landlord directly discriminated on the ground of wealth (fortune) and handicap by requiring of its prospective tenants an employment contract of an indeterminate time and a minimum wage before they were eligible to rent his apartments.[107] He has explicitly mentioned these requirements in ads promoting the apartments he wanted to rent out. The court granted the Centre an injunction prohibiting the landlord to continue this discriminatory behaviour under the threat of a lump sum. It was the first

101 Cass. 16 February 2001, *Arr.Cass.* 2001, 303, *Huur* 2002, 107, *Pas.* 2001, 301, *JDSC* 2002, 116, note P. Kileste, *Res Jur.Imm.* 2001, 123, *Rev.prat.soc.* 2001, 348, *RW* 2002–03, 340 and *TBH* 2002, 698, note C.N. Geys. See also C Cauffman, 'Discriminatie bij bijzondere overeenkomsten', (2006–07) *RW* 287, 307; N Van Leuven, 'De Antidiscriminatiewet en de huurovereenkomst' in S Stijns and P Wéry (eds), *Antidiscriminatiewet en contracten*, die Keure, Bruges 2006, p 134.

102 J Kusters, 'Discriminatie ten opzichte van allochtonen op de private huurmarkt' in *Vrijheid en gelijkheid. De horizontale werking van het gelijkheidsbeginsel en de nieuwe antidiscriminatiewet*, Maklu, Antwerp 2003, p 555.

103 Court of first instance of Antwerp 18 March 2016, AN56.LB.99609-I4, not published (www.unia.be). Based on, among others, Articles 5, 19 and 24 anti-racism law.

104 Which is delayed due to the fact that she has never been convicted to an imprisonment of more than 12 months or an equivalent criminal sanction.

105 Court of first instance Liège 6 May 2014, not published (www.unia.be). Based on, among others, Article 7 of the anti-racism law (no discrimination found on the ground of fortune prohibited in the general antidiscrimination law).

106 See e.g.: www.standaard.be/cnt/dmf20150511_01674465.

107 Court of first instance Namur 5 May 2015, not published (www.unia.be). Based on, among others, Article 20 of the general antidiscrimination law.

time that discrimination *on the ground of wealth*[108] was recognised in the real estate sector.[109]

20. The *travel business* is another domain where discriminatory refusal to contract occurs. A judgment of 20 January 2011 of the court of appeal of Ghent decided in a case about the participation of a deaf man in a group tour to the Kingdom of Jordan. He could not participate, unless he would be accompanied – at own expenses – by an accompanying person to optimize communication.[110] The appellate judges confirmed the first instance judgment and decided it amounted to a discriminatory refusal to contract on the ground of a handicap. The refusal could not be justified objectively. The judgment also confirmed the first instance judgment by granting a prohibitory injunction subject to the payment of a lump sum, but decided to grant the victim higher damages, claimed by way of an appeal on the same occasion.

21. The refusal *to publish* an *advertisement in a journal* of a politician of a controversial political party was also judged to be discriminatory on the ground of political conviction. The court of appeal of Brussels made this very clear in a judgment of 26 January 2016.[111] The politician received a compensation because of the discriminatory treatment.

2.1.2.2.2. Discriminatory cancellation of the contract

22. It is also possible that one of the parties decides unilaterally to cancel the contract in a discriminatory way. Think for example that a bank would cancel in a discriminatory way the bank accounts of an Islamic organisation. The court of first instance of Brussels decided in a judgment of 13 July 2015 such a case.[112] The bank closed the bank accounts of an Islamic organisation due to the fact that large amounts of deposits were done without proper identification of the donator. An internal procedure to prevent money

108 See with regard to the former antidiscrimination law: M Dambre, 'De wet bestrijding discriminatie en het huurrecht' in M De Vos and E Brems (eds), *De Wet bestrijding discriminatie*, Intersentia, Antwerp 2004, pp 333 *et seq.*; N Van Leuven, 'De Antidiscriminatiewet en de huurovereenkomst' in S Stijns and P Wéry (eds), *Antidiscriminatiewet en contracten*, die Keure, Bruges 2006, p 128.

109 Www.unia.be/nl/artikels/erkenning-van-discriminatie-op-basis-van-vermogen-in-de-huisvestingssector-uitspraak-vormt-precedent-in-belgie. Comp. Court of first instance Liège 6 May 2014, not published (www.unia.be) (no discrimination found on the ground of fortune, prohibited in the general antidiscrimination law); Court of appeal of Mons 16 May 2013, not published (www.unia.be) no discrimination on the ground of fortune (general antidiscrimination law): a real estate agent (acting upon the wishes of the landlord) refused a prospective tenant based on its mission to select solvent tenants whose profile fits the nature and situation of the property (*'Attendu qu'il est parfaitement légitime pour un professionnel de l'immobilier de se soucier de la solvabilité des candidats locataires et de la correspondance de leurs profils respectifs à la nature et à la situation du bien'*).

110 Ghent 20 January 2011, AR no. 2010/AR/2943, not published (www.unia.be); confirmation of Kh. (commercial court) Ghent 29 September 2010, AR no. WK A/10/02142, not published (www.unia.be). Based on Articles 5 and 14 general antidiscrimination law.

111 Brussels 26 January 2016, 3rd Dutch speaking chamber, not published (www.unia.be). Based on Articles 3, 5, 14, 18, and 20 general antidiscrimination law.

112 Court of first instance Brussels 13 July 2015, not published (www.unia.be).

laundry had been activated, explaining the sudden cancellation of the bank accounts. The court found no (in)direct discrimination on the ground of religion because the rule was applicable to all its clients and was not particularly harming for Islamic organisations. Even if there would be an indirect discrimination it would have been necessarily justified by a legitimate aim, namely to be in conformity with the obligations of the law of 11 January 1993 preventing money laundry. Another example is the cancellation of a fitness contract due to the fact that a woman does not want to remove her headscarf (because of health reasons). The court of appeal of Brussels decided in a judgment of 8 September 2015 that there was no discrimination anymore because of a negotiated change of the internal regulations of the fitness company, allowing a headscarf for health reasons and the fact that she has been received a free offer to fitness in one of the other accommodations of the company (one in which she has not been fighting with the staff).[113]

2.1.2.2.3. Discriminatory content of contractual terms

23. Discriminating behaviour in contractual relations can also be reflected by introducing discriminatory contractual terms.[114] The court of appeal of Antwerp has decided for example that one is using discriminating contractual terms on the ground of age if the terms offer discounts according to the age of the buyer (e.g. 32 years, 32% discount).[115]

2.2. *Horizontal effect of Articles 10 and 11 of the Constitution in the law of obligations*

24. Whether or not the public law prohibition to discriminate (Articles 10 and 11 of the Constitution[116]) – which is primarily aimed at prohibiting discrimination of citizens by the government – also limits the (pre-)contractual freedom, other contractual relations

113 Brussels 8 September 2015, no. 2014/AR/2354, not published (www.unia.be) (no (direct or) indirect discrimination found because of the fact that the indirect differentiation by prohibiting headwear in a fitness centre was legitimized by the security reasons; the measures taken were proportionate, apt and necessary to achieve the legitimate aim; headwear for medicinal reasons was inserted as an exception in the internal rules of the fitness company, after negotiations with the Centre; confirmation of the decision of the Court of first instance of Brussels 2 June 2014, not published (www.unia.be)).

114 See also about discriminatory contractual terms: A De Boeck, 'Doorwerking van het gelijkheidsbeginsel in het contractenrecht. De contractsvrijheid in het nauw gedreven?' in *Vrijheid en gelijkheid. De horizontale werking van het gelijkheidsbeginsel en de nieuwe antidiscriminatiewet*, Maklu, Antwerp 2003, pp 428–430.

115 Antwerp, 26 April 2007, AR no. 2004/AR/1793, *Jaarboek Handelspraktijken & Mededinging* 2007, 469, note J Stuyck, *RABG* 2007, 1351 (www.unia.be) (the Court decided that the discounts did not respect the (old) antidiscrimination law of 25 February 2003 and also had to be qualified as breaching the prohibition of unfair commercial practices).

116 We must point out that these Articles of the Constitution have to be read in conjunction with Article 14 ECHR and Article 26 of the International Covenant on Civil and Political Rights. See e.g. Constitutional Court 12 February 2009, no. 17/2009, B.14.2 and B.14.4.

and tort relations between individuals, remains the subject of a sharp debate. Different stances have been developed with respect to this 'horizontal effect' of the constitutional principle of equality.[117]

25. The first stance defends that the principle of equality, like other fundamental rights in the Constitution, regulates in the first place the relation between the government and her citizens and does not regulate the relations between individual persons. A second stance defends that fundamental rights, such as the principle of equality, are directly applicable between individuals (*direct horizontal effect*). A third opinion makes an appeal to indirect means to apply the principle of equality between individuals (*indirect horizontal effect*). The prohibition to discriminate will indirectly influence the law of obligations by means of existing concepts such as the requirement to act in good faith, the general duty of care (*bonus pater familias* criterion) in Article 1382 CC, the prohibition to abuse your rights, and the incompatibility with public order and public decency...[118] Consequently, the principle of equality can influence the relations between individuals by means of 'open norms' in private law. Most of the authors only accept this form of *indirect horizontal effect* of fundamental rights.[119] According to us, the Constitutional Court has also defended this point of view in a judgment of 12 February 2009 by stating: 'Even if it concerns relations between private persons, the legislator cannot deviate from the general principle that prohibits discriminations and that is expressly protected by the constitutional and treaty provisions mentioned in (...)' and 'Any discrimination in the relations between citizens, for which no justification can be given, amounts to

117 See extensively S Jansen, 'De invloed van het Europese antidiscriminatierecht op privaatrechtelijke verhoudingen' in I Samoy, V Sagaert and E Terryn (eds), *Invloed van het Europese recht op het Belgische privaatrecht*, Intersentia, Antwerp 2012, no. 37–39. See e.g. also F De Ly, 'Het gelijkheidsbeginsel in het contractenrecht', (1991–92) *RW* 1141, 1143 *et seq*; E Dirix, 'Grondrechten en overeenkomsten' in K Rimanque (ed), *De toepasselijkheid van grondrechten in private verhoudingen*, Kluwer, Antwerp 1982, pp 40–43; I Samoy, 'Recente wetgeving en Europese richtlijnen: invloed op het verbintenissenrecht' in *Verbintenissenrecht*, die Keure, Bruges 2004, no. 33.

118 See also implictly K Vanderschot, 'De bestrijding van discriminatie in het gemeen contractenrecht', in S Stijns and P Wéry (eds), *Antidiscriminatiewet en contracten*, die Keure, Bruges 2006, pp 50–68. See also with regard to discrimination with regard to foreigners on the private tenancy market (and discriminatory refusal to contract): J Kusters, 'Discriminatie ten opzichte van allochtonen op de private huurmarkt' in *Vrijheid en gelijkheid. De horizontale werking van het gelijkheidsbeginsel en de nieuwe antidiscriminatiewet*, Maklu, Antwerp 2003, pp 567 *et seq*.

119 See e.g. A De Boeck, 'Doorwerking van het gelijkheidsbeginsel in het contractenrecht. De contractsvrijheid in het nauw gedreven?' in *Vrijheid en gelijkheid. De horizontale werking van het gelijkheidsbeginsel en de nieuwe antidiscriminatiewet*, Antwerp, Maklu 2003, pp 423–424. See similarly: S Jansen, 'De invloed van het Europese antidiscriminatierecht op privaatrechtelijke verhoudingen' in I Samoy, V Sagaert and E Terryn (eds), *Invloed van het Europese recht op het Belgische privaatrecht*, Intersentia, Antwerp 2012, no. 39; K Rimanque and P Peeters, 'De toepasselijkheid van grondrechten in de betrekkingen tussen private personen. Algemene probleemstelling' in K Rimanque (ed), *De toepasselijkheid van de grondrechten in private verhoudingen*, Kluwer, Antwerp 1982, pp 19–21; S Somers, 'De Drittwirkung van grondrechten', (2011) *NJLP* 44, 44–62; J Velaers, 'De horizontale werking van het discriminatieverbod in de antidiscriminatiewet, enkele constitutionele beschouwingen' in *Vrijheid en gelijkheid: de horizontale werking van het gelijkheidsbeginsel en de nieuwe antidiscriminatiewet*, Maklu, Antwerp 2003, p 294.

discrimination and has therefore to be considered faulty behaviour that may result in a civil sanction, in particular damages. In addition, the court can declare discriminatory contractual provisions void under the Articles 6, 1131, and 1133 of the Civil Code because it is contrary to public policy'.[120]

26. Special attention has been devoted to the horizontal effect of human rights in contract law by Van Leuven in her dissertation.[121] She defends a nuanced approach towards the effect of the (constitutional) human rights between individuals: somewhere between direct and indirect horizontal effect. Van Leuven calls it 'enhanced indirect effect'. In the dissertation of Somers the horizontal effect of human rights has been explored with regard to tort law.[122] He argues that the Belgian legal order in principle only accepts an indirect horizontal effect but that the application of international and constitutional illegality has a result that comes near to a direct horizontal effect of human rights. He nevertheless favours an indirect approach because this is more in line with the requirements of legal certainty and the design of our constitutional order and because it can be used as a tactic to avoid state liability for the violation of a positive obligation to protect human rights in horizontal relations.

27. The Court of Cassation has, however, decided in a judgment of 29 March 2010 clearly that the Articles 10 and 11 of the Constitution only regulate the regulation between citizens and the government as a body of public law.[123] The Court decides that these Articles do not imply any direct duties among citizens and that they are not applicable in a labour relationship between a public institution and its employees. This judgment raises many questions. What is the relationship of this judgment with the case law of the Constitutional Court which points at the direction that Articles 10 and 11 of the Constitution have indirect horizontal effect in private law by means of open norms? We are of the opinion that the vision of the Constitutional Court has to be followed.[124] Next to this, the judgment of the Court of Cassation of 29 March 2010 seems to be extremely broad, so that one can wonder whether it is the role of the Court of Cassation,

120 Free translation: '*Zelfs wanneer het gaat om verhoudingen tussen privépersonen, zou de wetgever niet kunnen afwijken van het algemene discriminatieverbod dat uitdrukkelijk is gewaarborgd bij de in B.14.2 vermelde grondwets- en verdragsbepalingen.*' and '*Elke ongelijke behandeling in de verhoudingen tussen burgers waarvoor geen verantwoording kan worden gegeven, maakt immers een discriminatie uit en derhalve een foutief gedrag, dat tot een burgerrechtelijke sanctie, met name een schadevergoeding, aanleiding kan geven. Bovendien kan de rechter een discriminerend contractueel beding op grond van de artikelen 6, 1131 en 1133 van het Burgerlijk Wetboek nietig verklaren omdat het indruist tegen de openbare orde*'. Constitutional Court 12 February 2009, no. 17/2009, B.14.4.

121 See about the so-called 'enhanced' indirect effect: N Van Leuven, *Contracten en mensenrechten. Een mensenrechtelijke lezing van het contractenrecht*, Intersentia, Antwerp 2009, pp 291–292.

122 S Somers, *Het buitencontractueel aansprakelijkheidsrecht en de rechten van de mens: kruisbestuiving in een meergelaagde rechtsorde*, Antwerp, Intersentia 2016, pp 50–62 and 180–184.

123 Cass. 29 March 2010, *Soc. Kron.* 2011, 44, note J JACQMAIN.

124 Moreover, this vision fits with the harmonious interpretation of the treaty of e.g. Article 14 ECHR which obliges member states positively to enforce the principle of equality between individuals by way of legislation and case law.

after the inclusion of Article 26, §4 in the Special law of 6 January 1989 regarding the Constitutional Court, to decide upon a matter of fundamental rights.[125]

28. For the sake of completeness, we have to point out that the principle of equality, such as regulated in the antidiscrimination legislation, has evidently acquired horizontal effect by means of this legislation.[126] In the domain of our concern (the law of obligations) this legislation has undoubtedly horizontal effect: e.g. the freedom to contract or not, with which person you want to contract and the freedom to determine freely the terms of your contract are affected by the principle of equality (*supra*, no. 5 *et seq.*).

29. In a judgment of 7 October 2011 the Court of Cassation has accepted that the refusal to contract can imply an abuse of rights.[127] Although this was not explicitly treated or mentioned in the judgment, this case could also be analysed in light of the prohibition to discriminate. In this case a certain doctor was refused to get the title of '*médecin intégré*'. This means that he was treated differently in comparison to his colleagues of the same department that received this title. Because no specific (discrimination) ground or protected criterion of the antidiscrimination laws could be invoked (see *supra*, no. 11), this legislation will not be applicable.[128] The question arises whether this unequal treatment is prohibited by the horizontal effect (between the hospital and the doctor) of Articles 10 and 11 of the Constitution. If we apply the theory of the judgment of 12 February 2009 of the Constitutional Court, the principle of equality can govern horizontal relationships between individuals by open norms in the law of obligations. By means of the theory of 'unlawful refusal to contract' the refusal to contract is under some circumstances in breach with the general duty of care contained in Article 1382 CC. The duty of care (as an open norm) can be read in the light of the constitutional principle of equality. But even if the doctor can prove that the hospital treats him differently, the hospital will try to justify this differentiation in treatment by a proportionate and legitimate aim. Also, it has to be pointed out that the Court of Cassation refuses any influence of the constitutional principle of equality in relations between individuals. We must conclude that the outcome of this reasoning would be highly uncertain.

125 Special law of 12 July 2009 'tot wijziging van artikel 26 van de bijzondere wet van 6 januari 1989', *BS* 31 July 2009.

126 See for the same remark with regard to the relationship between tenants and landlords: M Dambre, 'De wet bestrijding discriminatie en het huurrecht' in M De Vos and E Brems (eds), *De Wet bestrijding discriminatie*, Intersentia, Antwerp 2004, pp 324–325.

127 Cass. 7 October 2011, *Juristenkrant* 2011, 1, *Pas.* 2011, 2148, concl. Henkes, *RCJB* 2013, 537, note T Leonard, *RW* 2012–13, 1181, note S Jansen and S Stijns, *TBBR* 2012, 489, note A De Boeck.

128 This case would fall within the material scope of application of the antidiscrimination laws: namely labour relations.

3. Principle of equality and vertical relationships (government to citizen): the jurisprudence of the Belgian Constitutional Court

30. In the previous part (2) we have seen that the principle of equality can be used in horizontal relations as an instrument to limit the freedom to refuse to contract, to cancel a contract and to freely decide upon the content of a contract. It is clear from these observations that the principle of equality and non-discrimination has an important impact on people's freedom of contract. The principle of equality and non-discrimination does, however, not only address private persons, but also the government. Just as the principle forbids citizens to discriminate one against another, it forbids the three branches of government to discriminate citizens against one another. In this contribution, only the legislative and judicial branches of government will be discussed, since the application of the principle of equality on the executive branch is more relevant for the field of administrative law than for the law of obligations. Accordingly, the question that this part addresses, is whether parties can invoke the principle of equality when rules treat tort victims or contracting parties, who are in a similar situation, in a discriminatory way. In order to answer this question, we will discuss the relevant jurisprudence of the Constitutional Court.

31. Before we will deal with the jurisprudence of the Constitutional Court in detail, it is important to discuss the so-called "*lente-arrest*".[129] This judgment was the first one in which the Constitutional Court found a violation in the field of the law of obligations. The facts of this case were simple. On 27 October 1983, a car accident occurred causing injury to one of the involved parties. The injured party only sued the alleged tortfeasor for the court of first instance many years later, on 30 August 1989. Consequently, the defendant argued that the claim was time-barred. He noticed that the alleged wrongful act had to be qualified as a crime. In such a case, Article 26 of the preliminary title of the code of criminal procedure stipulated that the civil claim must be subjected to the prescription periods of the criminal claim,[130] which in this case was five years.[131] The injured party contested this line of reasoning and argued that the claim was based on tort law and thus that the general prescription period of Article 2262 of the Civil Code had to be applied according to which (at that time) a claim was only time-barred after thirty years. The court of first instance qualified the alleged wrongful act as a crime, following the reasoning of the defendant and judged that the claim in principle was time-barred. However, the court noticed that this strangely made the situation of the plaintiff

[129] Constitutional Court 15 May 1996, no. 32/96.

[130] Including the application of interruption and suspension grounds: Memorie van toelichting, *Parl. St.* Kamer 1996–97, no. 49K1087/001, 7–8; I Claeys, 'De nieuwe verjaringswet: een inleidende verkenning', (1998–99) *RW* 277, 383; A Jacobs, 'La loi du 10 juin 1998 modifiant certaines dispositions en matière de prescription', (1999) *TBBR* 10, 18; A Van Oevelen, 'Recente ontwikkelingen inzake de bevrijdende verjaring in het burgerlijk recht', (2000–01) *RW* 1433, 1436; T Vansweevelt, 'De verjaring van de buitencontractuele vordering (art. 2262*bis* BW)' in H Vuye and Y Lemense (eds), *Springlevend aansprakelijkheidsrecht*, Intersentia, Antwerp 2011, p 295.

[131] Article 21 of the preliminary title of the code of criminal procedure.

worse than it would have been if the defendant committed a wrongful act that was not qualified as a crime. Accordingly, the court of first instance addressed to the Constitutional Court the question whether or not this application of the prescription rules, in the given context, violated the principle of equality.

32. The Constitutional Court observed that the situations of claimants in tort law who are confronted with time limitations are comparable, whether or not the wrongful act of the defendant can be qualified as a crime. Moreover, the Court found that the different treatment of both categories of victims is based on a legitimate aim and an objective criterion of differentiation. Nevertheless, the Court ruled that the different treatment of both categories of persons is in violation with the principle of equality. It found that the limitation of the rights of victims of a wrongful act which is also considered a crime was unreasonable, since it was not outweighed by the objectives of the legislature, namely the promotion of legal certainty and the aim of preventing old conflicts to disturb the social peace after years by starting to inquire into criminal acts in a civil context after the criminal claim was already expired. In this regard, the Court stressed that a wrongful act that cannot be qualified as a crime, is less serious than one that is criminalised by the legislature. The Court implicitly ruled that a more serious wrongful act (such as one that can be qualified as a crime) cannot be time-barred by the lapse of a shorter period of time than a similar, less wrongful act. By doing so, the Court actually rejected the main idea of the legislator. The legislator enacted this legislation for two reasons. First, the legislator was of the opinion that a private law claim only concerns individual legal relationships and does not interfere with public order (as is the case with criminal law). Secondly, the legislator was of the opinion that with regard to prescription, there should be 'solidarity' between the different actions (civil and criminal) that can rise from the same facts. It is clear that the Constitutional Court neglected these main reasons of the legislator, especially the notion that a civil claim might only be barred after the lapse of a long time because it does not interfere with public order.

33. With this judgment, the Constitutional Court upset all existing rules of liberative prescription at that time and caused a lot of legal uncertainty as to its consequences in legal practice.[132] This case illustrates that the principle of equality can have far reaching consequences in the law of obligations. Indeed, when the Constitutional Court in a procedure on a prejudicial question rules that legislation violates the constitutional principle of equality, the Court dealing with the case will have to judge in a manner as if the particular legislation does not exist.[133] Moreover, if a violation of the principle of equality has been caused due to the lack of a regulation in a specific

[132] H Bocken, 'Gelijkheid in aansprakelijkheid – De rechtspraak van het Arbitragehof en de ontwikkeling van het aansprakelijkheidsrecht' in *De herziening van de bevrijdende verjaring door de wet van 10 juni 1998; De gelijkheid hersteld?*, Kluwer, Antwerp 1999, p 5; P Traest, 'De verjaring van de burgerlijke vordering voortspruitend uit een misdrijf: de geschiedenis en de onzekere toekomst', (1994–95) *RW* 1324, 1325.

[133] P Popelier, 'De doorwerking van prejudiciële arresten van het Grondwettelijk Hof in de rechtspraak', (2010) *CDPK* 392, 393.

situation that is very similar to a situation where legislation does exist, courts will have to expand the field of application of the existing legislation via analogy.[134] Consequently, the finding of a violation of the constitutional principle of equality by the legislator can indirectly influence the law that judges have to apply in conflicts between private persons with regard to the law of obligations.[135] With regard to the "*Lente-arrest*", the legislator was pushed[136] to enact new prescription rules for the law of obligations.[137] However, this judgment was only the first important judgment in which the Constitutional Court found violations of the principle of equality in the field of the law of obligations. Other judgments followed. In order to discuss the impact of this jurisprudence on the law of obligations, we will discuss this jurisprudence in the following paragraphs. This will not be done in a chronological way. The following titles will be structured on the basis of the test that the Constitutional Court applies when it interprets the principle of equality as enshrined in the Belgian Constitution.[138] The assessment of the Court is structured on the comparability of the situations, the legitimate aim, the presence and relevance of an objective criterion for differentiation and the proportionality test.[139]

134 Constitutional Court 31 July 2008, no. 111/2008; Cass. 2 September 2008, no. P.08.1317.N; Cass. 29 September 2011, no. C.09.0570.N. This, however, is only possible if the expansion of an existing regime does not impact other legal provisions or requires a new balancing of societal interests. If this would be the case, it is up to the lawmaker to solve the violation of the Constitution: Cass 3 November 2008, no. S.07.0013.N. Thus, in principle, a violation of the constitution that exists because there is a gap in the legislation must be solved by the legislator: Constitutional Court 15 May 1996, no. 31/96, B.5.; Constitutional Court 13 March 2002, no. 54/2002, B.5. For a more elaborated discussion of this topic see P Popelier, 'De rechtspraak van het Arbitragehof inzake lacunes in de wetgeving' in A Alen (ed), *20 jaar Arbitragehof*, Kluwer, Mechelen 2005, pp 76 *et seq.*; J De Jaegere, 'Actieve rechtsvorming door het Grondwettelijk Hof. Waar ligt de grens?', (2014) *TBP* 22, 22–32; M Melchior and C Courtoy, 'Het verzuim van de wetgever of de lacune in de grondwettelijk rechtspraak', (2008) *TBP* 587, 599 *et seq.*

135 It is argued that the other party in such cases might be able to sue the government on the basis of state liability: S Somers, 'De horizontale werking van mensenrechten en het verticaal aansprakelijkheidsrecht', (2014) *TBP* 353, 365–368.

136 Verslag over het wetsontwerp tot wijziging van sommige bepalingen betreffende de verjaring, *Parl. St.* Kamer 1997–98, no. 49K1087/015, 4.

137 Law of 10 June 1998 'tot wijziging van sommige bepalingen betreffende de verjaring', *BS* 17 July 1998, 23.544.

138 One must keep in mind that the Constitutional Court oversees compliance by the legislative authorities in Belgium of the Constitution by way of actions for annulment and preliminary issues. The Constitutional Court can thus not apply the principle of equality directly in conflicts between private citizens; it can, however, answer on prejudicial questions of courts that are competent to deal with private litigation. For a general overview of the procedures and competences of the Belgian Constitutional Court in English, Dutch, French or German see the website: <www.const-court.be/en/common/home.html>.

139 See extensively D De Prins, S Sottiaux and J Vrielink, *Handboek discriminatierecht*, Kluwer, Mechelen 2005, pp 250–266; J Theunis, 'Het gelijkheidsbeginsel. Juridisch interpretatiekader, met bijzondere aandacht voor 'corrigerende ongelijkheden' en doorwerking in private rechtsverhoudingen', in *Publiekrecht. De doorwerking van het publiekrecht in het privaatrecht, Postuniversitaire cyclus Willy Delva 1996/199*, Mys and Breesch, Ghent 1997, pp 135 *et seq.*; J Vande Lanotte, G Goedertier and T De Pelsmaeker, *Handboek Belgisch Publiekrecht*, die Keure, Brugge 2013, pp 334–345.

3.1. The assessment scheme

3.1.1. Comparability of the situation

34. When the Constitutional Court has to assess a potential violation of the principle of equality, it will first assess whether the situations under which people seem to be discriminated, are comparable. If this is not the case, people are treated differently in different situations and no violation of the principle of equality can be found. In this context it is important to notice that the comparability must be perceived in a practical, and not a formal way. The Court will assess whether people in actual situations are in a comparable position whether or not their situation, from a formal legal perspective, is qualified differently. With regard to the law of obligations this can be illustrated by the jurisprudence concerning the liability scheme for motorized vehicles. To protect vulnerable road users, the Belgian lawmaker enacted a faultless liability scheme so that victims of traffic accidents do not have to prove the fault of the motorized vehicles that cause physical harm to them.[140] This law was applicable for motorized vehicles that made use of the public space with the exception of trams and trains. As a consequence, the question was posed to the Court whether victims of road accidents caused by trams or trains in places accessible to the public[141] were not discriminated against in comparison to victims of road accidents caused by cars, trucks or buses. The victims of road accidents caused by motorized vehicles of the first category had to rely on the general liability rules as enshrined in Article 1382 Civil Code (CC)[142] and thus had to prove the fault of the tram- or train conductor whereas the victims in the second category did not have to demonstrate this. The Constitutional Court found that victims of a road accident caused by a tram were in a comparable situation to the victims of accidents caused by cars, trucks or buses because all these vehicles participate in traffic on streets that are accessible to the public and the drivers of all these vehicles have to take into account the traffic regulations.[143]

35. If an accident is, however, caused by a motorized vehicle on an area that is not accessible to the public, for instance a closed railway, there is no comparable situation since the risk for accidents on inaccessible areas is considerably lower.[144] The same holds

140 Law of 21 November 1989 'betreffende de verplichte aansprakelijkheidsverzekering inzake motorrijtuigen', *BS* 8 December 1989, 20122.

141 It must, however, be noted that the Court in one case even found that the principle of equality is violated if the special liability regime for accidents with motorized vehicles is not expanded to victims of train accidents on places that are not open to the public but in which the victim was authorized to be present: Constitutional Court 28 May 2015, no. 74/2015.

142 Article 1382 of the Civil Code provides compensation for damage that is wrongfully caused by a third person. In addition, Article 1383 states that people can be held liable not only for positive acts but also for omissions.

143 Constitutional Court 15 July 1998, no. 92/98; Constitutional Court 10 December 2003, no. 158/2003; Constitutional Court 7 June 2006, no. 93/2006.

144 Constitutional Court 6 November 2002, no. 158/2002; Constitutional Court 8 March 2012, no. 35/2012, B.6.3.

true for boats because traffic on water is much less intense than traffic on the road. The Constitutional Court thus found that victims of boat accidents are not in a situation similar to victims of a car accident.[145] Thus, the exclusion of boat accidents and accidents in places that are not open to the public from the faultless liability scheme of motorized vehicles does not conflict with the principle of equality.

36. Other interesting cases can be found in the jurisprudence of the Court with regard to employees-liability. According to Article 18 of the law on employment contracts, employees can only be held liable for intentional, heavy or repeated light errors that they make in the context of their employment.[146] Thus, if an employee commits a normal error, he cannot be held liable. In that case his employer will be held liable. In the past, this regulation only applied to employees that were hired on a contractual basis. Employees in the public sector that were hired via a statutory regime could still be held liable via general tort law when they committed a normal error in the context of their work. In a case of 18 December 1996, the Constitutional Court had to rule whether this difference in treatment violates the principle of equality and non-discrimination.[147] In its judgment the Court observed that the legislator differentiates between, on the one hand, employees hired on a contractual basis and, on the other hand, those hired on a statutory basis. However, it did rule that the principle of equality was violated because both groups of employees, when making an error, were in a very similar situation since both of them act under authority and to the benefit of their employer.[148] As a result of this jurisprudence, judges had to apply Article 18 of the law on employment by analogy on statutory hired governmental employees.[149] The Court on the contrary decided that the exclusion of the members of the board of directors from this liability scheme did not violate the principle of equality since they do not act under the authority of their employer.[150] The lack of subordination makes the situations of normal employees and members of the board of directors incomparable and thus not discriminatory. The same

145 Constitutional Court 21 December 2005, no. 193/2005.

146 Article 18 of the Law of 3 July 1978 concerning labour agreements, *BS* 22 August 1978, 9277.

147 Constitutional Court 18 December 1996, no. 77/96. See also: B Elias, 'Naar een gelijkschakeling werknemers-ambtenaren inzake burgerlijke aansprakelijkheid tegenover derden', (1996–97) *AJT* 553, 555; L Deridder, "noot onder Arbitragehof 77/96", (1997) *T.Gem.* 302, 302–305.

148 Constitutional Court 18 December 1996, no. 77/96, B.3; Constitutional Court 9 February 2000, no. 19/2000. This led to a law reform: Article 2 of the Law of 10 February 2003 'betreffende de aansprakelijkheid van en voor personeelslieden in dienst van openbare rechtspersonen', *BS* 27 February 2003. See on this topic: B Dubuisson, 'La loi du 10 février 2003 relative à la responsabilité civile des personnes publiques et de leurs agents', (2003) *JT* 507, 509; H Vandenberghe, 'Aansprakelijkheid van de uitvoerende macht', in H Vandenberghe (ed), *Overheidsaansprakelijkheid*, die Keure, Bruges 2005, pp 78–99; T Vansweevelt and B Weyts, *Handboek buitencontractueel aansprakelijkheidsrecht*, Intersentia, Antwerp, 2009, pp 443–450.

149 I Boone and I Geers, 'Het Arbitragehof en het aansprakelijkheidsrecht' in *Gandaius Actueel III*, Kluwer, Antwerp 1998, p. 39; P Popelier, 'De beoordeling door het Arbitragehof van het ontbreken van een wettelijke regeling', (1996–97) *RW* 1249, 1249–1250.

150 Constitutional Court 4 March 2008, no. 36/2008.

holds true for industrial accidents[151] and accidents on the way to work.[152] Because of the different nature of these accidents, both situations cannot be compared. Consequently, a different liability regulation can apply. This, however, is not the case when the regulation concerning the protection of employees for industrial accidents also covers some accidents of employees on the way to work, but not all of them.[153] In such a situation, the principle of equality can be violated.

3.1.2. Legitimate aim

37. If the Constitutional Court finds that people are treated differently in comparable situations, it will in a second step verify whether the different treatment of both situations serves a legitimate aim. Although in principle this is a second criterion that must be differentiated from the comparability of the situations, both criteria can also be viewed as one: the comparability of the situation is often perceived from the viewpoint of the legitimate aim, as can be derived from the previous cases wherein the Constitutional Court found that some situations were not comparable because one of them could not serve the aim that was pursued by a special regulation. Nonetheless, even if one could investigate the comparability without looking at the aim of a regulation, one still has to inquire whether the aim is legitimate.

38. In most cases this requirement does not cause many problems. A legitimate aim for a special regime can be found in the specific risks regulated by the scheme[154] or the special position of one of the involved parties. This is for example the case with regard to the position of the close relatives of a leaseholder to whom the leaseholder wants to transfer the lease of a farm. Their family tie constitutes a legitimate aim to grant them some prerogatives.[155] Also the fact that long-term lease contracts are subjected to special notification- and registration rules is legitimate since the risk that troubles arise between a landlord and a tenant is much higher in long-term compared to short-term leases.[156] In the same way, the different treatment of distance-selling of immovable and movable goods is based on the higher occurrence, and thus higher risk, of the selling over distance of movable goods.[157]

39. Some problems with regard to the criterion of the legitimate aim appear for the reason that the Constitutional Court assesses the legitimacy of the pursued aim from a present-day perspective and not from the viewpoint at the time the lawmaker enacted a

151 A faultless liability scheme that only grants partial compensation.

152 Liability based on fault but with the possibility to receive full compensation.

153 Constitutional Court 16 January 1997, no. 3/97; Constitutional Court 9 June 2004, no. 102/2004.

154 E. Karner, *Der Ersatz ideeller Schäden bei Körperverletzung bei Körperverletzung*, Springer, Vienna 1999, p 18.

155 Constitutional Court 9 January 2002, no. 4/2002.

156 Constitutional Court 29 April 2010, no. 50/2010.

157 Constitutional Court 17 September 2015, no. 120/2015.

law.[158] This is important since the Court looks at the legitimate aim from a practical and not from a formalistic perspective. Thus, when the societal context on which rules apply changes over time, an aim that used to be legitimate may no longer be so. This can be illustrated by a case of 21 January 1997.[159] The law under scrutiny in this case dated from the nineteenth century.[160] This law enacted a faultless liability scheme of the holders of the right to hunt for exceptional damages created by rabbits on the harvest of farmers in the area of their license. On top of that the law provided for punitive damages in the sense that the person to whom the damage occurred could receive three times the value of the damages. A holder of the right to hunt who was held liable argued that he was discriminated against because there was no valid reason why in this specific case alone the law provided for punitive damages. The Constitutional Court remarked that the lawmaker at the time pursued a legitimate aim: protecting farmers from a rabbit-plague. But since this risk had ceased to exist, the Court found that foresters were indeed discriminated against because of the higher compensation they were required to pay.[161]

3.1.3. The presence and relevance of an objective criterion of differentiation

40. In this step of the assessment scheme, the Constitutional Court will look whether or not the different treatment is based on an objective criterion of differentiation and whether this criterion is relevant for the pursued legitimate aim.[162] The application of these principles in the field of the law of obligations can best be illustrated by a judgment of 1 December 2011.[163] This case relates to the specific rule according to which a tenant exceptionally does not have to take into account a notification period and does not have to pay a compensation for the cancellation of his tenancy-contract, in case this contract is not registered.[164] The question raised whether or not the principle of equality was

158 E Karner, *Der Ersatz ideeller Schäden bei Körperverletzung bei Körperverletzung*, Springer, Vienna 1999, p 15.

159 Constitutional Court 21 January 1998, no. 5/98. In another case in the field of social security law the Court found that the different treatment by a compensation scheme for disability of people who work fulltime in one job, on the one hand, and people who work two jobs, on the other hand, was discriminatory. The law only took into account the situation where people held only one job. The Court found that this might have been legitimate at the time of the enactment of the law because at that time most people indeed only had one job but that this was no longer the case in present times: Constitutional Court 28 March 2013, no. 51/2013.

160 Law of 28 February 1882 'jachtwet', *BS* 3 March 1882, 841.

161 In a later case, however, the Court found that the mere fact that the liability of the holders of a hunting right for the exceptional damage that wild animals caused to the harvest of farmers was faultless did not breach the principle of equality. This legitimate aim was still valid: Constitutional Court 11 June 2003, no. 80/2003.

162 Constitutional Court 26 October 2005, no. 159/2005. In this case, the Court ruled that the principle of equality would be violated if the law on commercial practices was interpreted in such a way so that the governmental railway company would be excluded from the rules with regard to the judicial control on penalty clauses that protect consumers.

163 Constitutional Court 1 December 2011, no. 182/2011.

164 Article 3, §5, third section of book III, title VIII, chapter II, division 2 of the Civil Code (also called 'woninghuurwet').

violated if this exception was interpreted in such a way so that it only applied to written tenancy contracts and not to oral agreements. The Court in this case found that the exceptional possibility – in case of non-registration of the tenancy contract – of a tenant to cancel a contract without having to respect a notification period or to pay a compensation, served a legitimate aim. This exception is introduced as a sanction against landlords who do not fulfil their obligation to register their tenancy contracts. This registration is an important instrument to protect tenants when the property they rent is sold. Moreover, the Court found that the limitation of this rule to written tenancy contracts constituted an objective criterion of differentiation. Nevertheless, it ruled that this criterion was not relevant for the legitimate aim of the exception. Indeed, whether or not a tenancy contract is written for a tenant, in either situation it is important that his landlord is forced to register the contract so that the tenant will be protected in case of a sale. Consequently, the Court ruled that a reading of the law, according to which the exception only applies to written tenancy contract, violates the principle of equality.

41. The Constitutional Court sometimes does not explicitly mention that the criterion of differentiation is irrelevant for the pursued aim of the different treatment, but only does so implicitly (often when applying the proportionality-test). Take for example its jurisprudence concerning the exclusion of trams and buses from the application of the faultless liability scheme for motorized vehicles (see also *supra*, no. 34 *et seq.*).[165] The Court in these cases found a legitimate aim in these cases and applied the proportionality test, but the aim that the Court referred to was the protection of vulnerable road users and the difficulty they encounter in proving the fault of a driver causing a road accident. Since this is the aim of the faultless liability scheme in general, and not of the different treatment that was caused by the exclusion of trams and busses from this scheme, it seems obvious that the Court would find that the different treatment of victims of road accidents caused by these particular type of vehicles was disproportionate with the aim of the different treatment that, in fact, did not exist. The same holds true for a case of 7 March 2013.[166] This case related to the exclusions of some types of vehicles owned by the state from the liability regime for motorized vehicles. Because of the exclusion of this type of vehicles from the liability regime for motorized vehicles, in the event that an accident was caused by a vehicle of this type, the victim could not invoke the faultless liability scheme. The Court however judged that, since a vulnerable road user has no choice regarding whether they are hit by a vehicle that requires insurance or not, and since those vehicles excluded from the insurance obligation were very few in number, their exclusion from the faultless liability scheme was not proportionate. By developing these arguments, it seems that the Court essentially found that there was no legitimate reason to apply different liability rules for accidents caused by state owned vehicles.

165 Constitutional Court 15 July 1998, no. 92/98; Constitutional Court 10 December 2003, no. 158/2003; Constitutional Court 7 June 2006, no. 93/2006.

166 Constitutional Court 7 March 2013, no. 31/2013.

42. A similar line of reasoning can be found in a judgment of 26 November 2009.[167] The case related to the duty *of landlords* to motivate the cancellation of the tenancy contract with regard to a dwelling. The question raised whether this duty is also applicable to a situation where a tenant cancels the contract and the landlord counter-cancels the contract. It was claimed that the principle of equality is violated if this would not be the case. The Court followed this line of reasoning. It did so by referring to the legitimate aim of the rules on the duty to motivate a cancellation of a tenancy contract and stated that the right to housing of the tenant had to be protected, whether or not the tenant aimed to cancel the contract himself. Thus, it seems that the criterion of differentiation in this case was not relevant for the pursued aim.

3.1.4. Proportionality

43. If the Constitutional Court finds a legitimate aim and a relevant differentiation criterion, it generally accepts that the different treatment by the two regimes is not discriminatory. The Court, for example, accepts that liability for traffic accidents that cause physical injuries is faultless because of the large risk and because of the difficulty of victims in proving the faultiness of the action of the driver.[168] The Court also accepts that a faultless liability scheme for industrial accidents provides only partial compensation. It rules that the reduction of the compensation is a concession for the faultless nature of liability and to protect social peace.[169] In another case, the Court ruled that the principle of equality was not violated if a victim in a similar situation but in a different regime has to start a second legal procedure in order to receive compensation, as long as it is possible to receive a compensation in the long-run.[170] Moreover, also the fact that different rules apply on similar regimes cannot be considered a violation of the principle of equality if people are free to choose which regulation scheme they apply.[171] In the context of tenancy law, the Court easily ruled that landlords that conclude a written rent agreement are treated better than those that only make an oral rent agreement (by awarding them the right to index the rent), because the lawmaker legitimately aimed to encourage landlords to make written rent agreements in order to promote legal certainty.[172] Also in the context of tenancy law, the Court was unwilling to find a violation of the principle of equality for the reason that the notification periods of the parties differ,[173] for the reason

[167] Constitutional Court 26 November 2009, no. 189/2009.

[168] Constitutional Court 15 July 1998, no. 92/98; Constitutional Court 6 November 2002, no. 158/2002; Constitutional Court 10 December 2003, no. 158/2003; Constitutional Court 7 June 2006, no. 93/2006; Constitutional Court 8 March 2012, no. 35/2012.

[169] Constitutional Court 1 March 2001, no. 31/2001.

[170] Constitutional Court 16 July 2009, no. 118/2009, B.8.

[171] Thus, the fact that employers can be sued for an industrial tort by temporary workers they attract via employment agencies whereas they cannot be sued in a similar situation by normal workers, does not violate the principle of equality for the reason that employers are not obliged to use temporary workers: Constitutional Court 11 May 2005, no. 88/2005.

[172] Constitutional Court 26 April 2007, no. 65/2007. See also: Constitutional Court 26 June 2008, no. 93/2008.

[173] Constitutional Court 10 May 2007, no. 76/2007.

that members with a special family tie are protected in one way or another[174] and it accepts that differences exist between the rules that apply on the lease of a house, a business or a farm.[175]

44. All these cases illustrate that the Court does not apply the proportionality test very strictly. It often argues that it is reasonable that a regulation diverges from a general rule in one way or another if the enactment of a special regime in general has a legitimate aim.[176] Moreover, the Court also takes into account financial consequences of regulations, for example by taking into account the consequences of a small discrimination on the costs of insurances,[177] or by taking into account the financial situation of the involved parties (for example when contractors and subcontractors or legal persons and natural persons are treated differently).[178] Take for example a judgment of 28 June 2006.[179] In this case, the Constitutional Court had to assess whether the principle of equality was violated for the reason that subcontractors, under the conditions of Article 1798 of the Civil Code, have a direct right of action against building owners, whereas building owners have no such right against the subcontractors. The Court observed that the direct right of action of subcontractors was motivated by the will to protect subcontractors, who are often very dependent on the main contractor, in the same way as the employees of the main contractor are. The Court ruled that this was a legitimate and reasonable aim that is not relevant for the position of the building owner. In this context, a violation only seems to occur when a differentiation is made that is not relevant for the pursued aim. So, when the direct right of action is limited to the first subcontractors and not to the subcontractors in the second or third degree (subcontractors of subcontractors), the principle of equality is violated for the reason that the unequal treatment of subcontractors on the basis of their degree is not relevant from the perspective of the legitimate aim to protect subcontractors, because of their dependence and weaker economic situation.[180]

45. By doing so, the Court grants the lawmaker a certain margin of appreciation for the reason that the topics in the context of the law of obligations generally concern socio-

174 Constitutional Court 20 November 2008, no. 164/2008; Constitutional Court 27 March 2014, no. 53/2014; Constitutional Court 3 December 2008, no. 177/2008.

175 Constitutional Court 22 May 2014, no. 84/2014.

176 Constitutional Court 1 March 2001, no. 31/2001; Constitutional Court 1 April 2001, no. 52/2001; Constitutional Court 13 March 2002, no. 47/2002; Constitutional Court 26 June 2002, no. 115/2002. In most judgments the Court does not state so explicitly, but does not elaborate into the proportionality after it found that there is a legitimate aim for the different treatment, e.g.: Constitutional Court 24 September 1998, no. 98/98; Constitutional Court 9 July 2009, no. 109/2009.

177 Constitutional Court 23 January 2002, no. 23/2002, B.4.3 *in fine*.

178 Constitutional Court 28 January 2003, no. 17/2003; Constitutional Court 20 June 2006, no. 111/2006; Constitutional Court 28 October 2010, no. 121/2010, B.6.2 *in fine*; Constitutional Court 18 May 2011, no. 86/2011; Constitutional Court 2 February 2012, no. 12/2012.

179 Constitutional Court 20 June 2006, no. 111/2006.

180 Constitutional Court 2 February 2012, no. 12/2012.

economic policy.[181] But this does not mean that there is no judicial control at all. It is not so that because a certain level of deviation is accepted, the lawmaker can do anything he wishes. The Court still applies the proportionality test in all these cases. When doing so, two elements seem to be crucial for finding a violation in context of the law of obligations: the presence of a grave or intentional error and the impossibility to receive a compensation.

3.1.4.1. The presence of a grave or intentional error

46. The first principle that seems to be determinative in deciding whether a different treatment is proportionate or not is the presence of a grave or intentional fault. This element dates back to the "*lente-arrest*", as already discussed before (*supra,* no. 31).[182] Indeed, we have seen that the Constitutional Court ruled it was contradictory that if someone commits a crime, or even a serious crime, he can only be summoned to court within a shorter period of time than someone who is sued in tort for a minor wrong. From this reasoning, the rule derives that the lawmaker has to provide prescription periods that are proportionate to the gravity of the fault. This reasoning was also confirmed in two later judgments where the Court ruled that the principle of equality was not violated in case a longer prescription period applies to torts that are also criminal offences as opposed to those that are not.[183]

47. The Constitutional Court also applied the notion of a 'grave or intentional fault', although not explicitly, in the framework of a liability scheme for industrial accidents. As a starting point, the Court argued that a faultless liability-scheme of employers that provides only for partial compensation for industrial accidents of employees and excludes grave and intentional faults or omissions of the employer, is not discriminatory.[184] The scheme for industrial accidents aims to protect social harmony within companies by precluding legal cases between employees and employers. It does so by a faultless liability scheme in terms of which employees automatically receive compensation from the employer (who is expected to take out insurance). As a concession towards the employers, this compensation is limited in the sense that moral damages are not included. Thus, the exclusion of grave or intentional faults from this scheme has as a result that an employee can receive full damages when his employer gravely or intentionally causes an industrial accident. The gravity or the intentionality of the fault is thus the reason why the different treatment is not disproportionate.[185] Similarly, the Court found that the inability of a tortfeasor who committed a crime to be granted remission of liability was not disproportionate.[186]

181 Constitutional Court 22 May 2014, no. 84/2014.

182 Constitutional Court 21 March 1995, no. 25/95.

183 Constitutional Court 18 March 1997, no. 13/97; Constitutional Court 19 December 2002, no. 190/2002.

184 Constitutional Court 1 March 2001, no. 31/2001.

185 In the same sense as the possibility of tortfeasors to be granted remission of liability in cases where they did not commit a crime: Constitutional Court 20 December 2012, no. 162/2012.

186 Constitutional Court 1 March 2001, no. 31/2001; Constitutional Court 20 December 2012, no. 162/2012.

3.1.4.2. The impossibility to receive compensation

48. Secondly, the Court takes into account the impossibility to receive compensation for all damages or for a specific type of damages when applying the proportionality test. This means, that the Court will, in principle, find a breach of the principle of proportionality, and hence a violation of the principle of equality, if in two comparable situations, it establishes the impossibility to receive compensation at all in one of the situations. In the opposite way, the Court seldomly finds a violation when the law provides a limited compensation or a standard fee if the specific regulation is motivated by a legitimate aim.[187] A standard fee might even be intended to have a deterrent effect, as is the case with the damages a landlord receives for his losses that are caused by a transfer of a right of pre-emption by a leaseholder of a farm.[188]

49. As with the principle of the presence of grave or intentional fault, this principle first arose in cases where the rules of prescription were under scrutiny. The core problem regards a specific regulation according to which a claim in tort against the government was time-barred after five years, starting from the first of January of the budget year in which the damage-occurring event took place. The discrepancy between this short limitation period and the longer period that applies to claims against private persons led to different complaints before the Constitutional Court.[189] The Court found that the shorter prescription period was in principle legitimate because the government, in serving the public interest, must make up its budget within a reasonable time.[190] This is not only important for budgetary reasons, but also to guarantee parliamentary control of the state budget. Because the victims of faults caused by the state still had a reasonable time to sue the government, the Court found that the difference in treatment of these victims was, in principle, proportionate with the legitimate aim.[191] However, the Court further argued that the principle of equality is violated when the *damages* occur only *after* this period (*i.e.* in case of latent damages) and the victim is unable to sue the government within this 'reasonable time'; whereas the victim would be able to lodge a claim and possibly receive restitution if the tortfeasor were a private person.[192] This is clear expression of the principle we pointed at before: indeed, the Court has found a breach of the principle of proportionality if it establishes the impossibility to receive compensation at all in one of two comparable situations. In the same line, the Court found a breach of the principle of equality in a case concerning the special liability

187 E.g.: Constitutional Court 1 March 2001, no. 31/2001, Constitutional Court 14 June 2006, no. 95/2006; Constitutional Court 16 July 2009, no. 118/2009.
188 Constitutional Court 17 September 2003, no. 114/2003.
189 Constitutional Court 15 May 1996, no. 32/96; Constitutional Court 18 October 2006, no. 153/2006; Constitutional Court 20 June 2007, no. 90/2007.
190 Constitutional Court 15 May 1996, no. 32/96, B.12; Constitutional Court 20 June 2007, no. 90/2007, B.3.
191 Constitutional Court 20 June 2007, no. 90/2007, B.4. Also: Constitutional Court 18 October 2006, no. 153/2006, B.6.
192 Constitutional Court 15 May 1996, no. 32/96, B.18; Constitutional Court 14 January 2004, no. 1/2004, B.5.

scheme for industrial accidents.[193] In this case the surviving relatives were *unable* to receive moral damages for the death of a relative that was caused during work hours by a third person.

50. An explicit affirmation of this principle was given in a judgment of 6 November 2014.[194] This case relates to clauses in favour of third parties. When a husband and his wife divorced, they signed a contract in which the husband offered half of the family house to his wife and promised to grant the other half within a month after the signing of the contract to their son and daughter. The husband did however not respect this promise. Many years later, the husband wanted to sell his part of the house. His children then filed a claim before the court on the basis of the clause in which their father promised to give them his share in the family house. However, their claim was time-barred because of the lapse of the ten years prescription period of Article 2262*bis*, §1, section one CC. The children argued that the application of the ten-year prescription period in this particular case violated the constitutional principle of equality and non-discrimination. They noticed that a similar claim in tort law would not have been prescribed due to the application of Article 2262*bis*, §1, second and third section CC. This, of course, raised the question of whether claims in contract law and tort law can be compared. The Constitutional Court found that this was the case. It ruled that both victims of a tort and a contractual fault are confronted with errors (either contractual or non-contractual) that are committed by another person. Thus, the situation of both persons was comparable. The different treatment is however based on an objective criterion and serves a legitimate interest. Thus, the lawmaker in principle has a margin of appreciation in order to enact different regulations in prescription law for contract and tort law. The Court nevertheless ruled that in this particular case, the principle of equality can be violated if it would seem that the children who are third parties to the contract could only have had knowledge of the stipulation after their claim was already time-barred.

51. This last case illustrates two things. Firstly, the case illustrates that the Constitutional Court easily finds a violation of the principle of equality in the context of the law of obligations if in two comparable situations, it is made impossible to file a claim in only one of the situations.[195] Secondly, the case illustrates that the Court easily accepts the comparability of situations. By doing so, the Court makes it possible to apply the principles of equality even on the points of differentiation between contract and tort law. Nevertheless, the impact of these conclusions can easily be exaggerated. Indeed, it is hard to imagine situations where the Court will find a violation of the principle of equality due to a different treatment by tort and contract law. The Court takes into account a margin of appreciation and it will normally find a legitimate aim for the differentiation on the

[193] Constitutional Court 7 July 2004, no. 124/2004. Also: Constitutional Court 1 March 2001, no. 31/2001; Constitutional Court 1 April 2001, no. 52/2001; Constitutional Court 13 March 2002, no. 47/2002; Constitutional Court 26 June 2002, no. 115/2002; Constitutional Court 29 January 2004, no. 16/2004.

[194] Constitutional Court 6 November 2014, no. 163/2014.

[195] See more extensively: S Somers, 'De objectieve kenbaarheid als criterium voor de grondwettelijke toets van verjaringsregels bevestigd', (2015) *TBBR* 448, 448–459.

basis of the existence of a contract. For example with regard to prescription periods, it must be noticed that one can expect from a contract party to be aware of the emergence of damages in the execution of the contract, also when these damages are not visible at first sight. In tort law, one cannot be expected to investigate on a regular basis whether latent damages arise due to the acts of third parties. In the context of contract law, only the position of benefactors of a clause in favour of a third party can be compared with the position of victims in tort law because they might not have been aware of the existence of the contract on the basis of which they can make a claim.

3.2. *The limits of constitutional review*

52. The foregoing paragraphs illustrate that the constitutional principle of equality and non-discrimination can potentially influence large areas of the law of obligations. This raises the question of how far the constitutional review of the law of obligations via the principle of equality can reach. In what follows, we will examine whether the field of application of the principle of equality can be limited by the presence of other constitutional rights or by the necessity to have different rules that apply in similar situations. Finally, we will discuss the possibility to use the principle of equality as an interpretative instrument for judicial interpretation of general rules of the law of obligations.

3.2.1. The presence of other constitutional rights

53. Another element that seems to be decisive in the application of the proportionality test, is the presence of other constitutional rights. It seems that regulations in the law of obligations that are based on other constitutional rights or principles of constitutional value have a considerable influence on the balancing exercise that the Constitutional Court must do. This is reasonable, one might argue that constitutional rights can be considered a *lex specialis* that have priority over the principle of equality that must be qualified as a *lex generalis*.[196]

54. The importance of this notion was clearly illustrated in a judgment of 22 March 2006.[197] At the origin of the judgment was a defamation case in which two journalists of the newspaper "*Le Soir*" had been held liable. The journalists however found that they were discriminated because they could not appeal to the rules of employee liability, according to which employees can only be held liable for intentional, heavy or repeated light errors that they make in the context of their employment and not for normal errors (for which their employer can be hold accountable).[198] In its judgment, the Constitutional Court recognised that journalists are treated differently from other employees, but ruled that this did not

[196] One might also say that the enjoyment of certain human right constitutes an exception on the substantive scope of application of the principle of equality: S Sottiaux, 'Het gelijkheidsbeginsel: langs oude paden en nieuwe wegen', (2008–09) *RW* 690, 691.

[197] Constitutional Court 22 March 2006, no. 47/2006.

[198] Article 18 of the Law of 3 July 1978 concerning labour agreements, *BS* 22 August 1978, 9277.

cause a violation of the principle of equality because of the necessity to protect the right to free speech as enshrined in Article 25 of the Constitution. The Court indicated that the drafters of the Constitution, when drafting this provision, explicitly intended to prevent private censorship and that the application of the rules of employee liability on journalists would cause the risk that employers would censor their journalists employees in order not to be held accountable for their errors.[199] Accordingly, it ruled that the different treatment of journalists in the context of professional liability is caused by the Constitution itself and that it has no authority to assess the choices of the constituent power.

55. The judgment of 22 March 2006 is very interesting because the Constitutional Court explicitly stated that it had no authority to judge the choices of the constituent power. There are however other judgments where the Court did not go that far, but where it attached heavy weight to constitutional rights when assessing the proportionality of an infringement of the principle of equality and non-discrimination. With regard to the payment of attorney's fees via tort law, this led to some interesting cases. For example, in a case of 16 April 2006 the Court found a violation of the principle of equality and the right to a fair trial for the reason that the claimant could receive compensation for his attorney's fees but a defendant could not.[200] As a consequence of this judgment, the lawmaker introduced a new regulation according to which general tort law did not apply anymore to the compensation of attorney's fees.[201] Instead, a scheme of standard fees was introduced. As a result, it was argued that this scheme was discriminatory for the reason that it made a full compensation of attorney's fees impossible. The Constitutional Court observed that there was indeed a different treatment of the compensation of attorney's fees and other types of damages, but found that this difference in treatment did not violate the requirement of proportionality for the reason that, on the one hand, a compensation was still awarded, and, on the other hand, the scheme that the legislator had provided aimed to protect the equality of arms between claimants and defendants.[202]

199 Constitutional Court 22 March 2006, no. 47/2006, B.5.

200 Constitutional Court 19 April 2006, no. 57/2006.

201 Law of 21 April 2007 'betreffende de verhaalbaarheid van de erelonen en de kosten verbonden aan de bijstand van een advocaat', *BS* 31 May 2007, 29541.

202 Constitutional Court 18 December 2008, no. 182/2008, B.9.1-9.5; Constitutional Court 5 February 2009, no. 15/2009. B.10.2; Constitutional Court 8 December 2011, no. 186/2011, B.28.2. The fact that the government could not receive a compensation for attorney's fees in procedures before the Council of State did however not violate the principle of equality for the reason that the government, according to the Constitutional Court, could not be compared with other defendants because it has specific tasks and more means to defend itself: Constitutional Court 19 July 2012, no. 96/2012, B.10 and B.11. For a similar reason, the Court ruled that the impossibility of labour unions to receive compensation for the pleadings of their delegates did not violate the principle of equality: Constitutional Court 14 October 1999, no. 113/99, B.8; Constitutional Court 5 May 2009, no. 73/2009, B.4.3-4.4; Constitutional Court 30 September 2009, no. 149/2009, B.2.3). The same holds true for the costs made by provisional administrators (Constitutional Court 13 March 2014, no. 43/2010, B.5) and of curators (Constitutional Court 11 March 2009, no. 46/2009, B.5.5). Similarly, the Court found no violation of the principle of equality with regard to the special system for legal assistance for poor people in the form of the *pro Deo* system: Constitutional Court 5 May 2009, no. 73/2009, B.2.3; Constitutional Court 30 September 2009, no. 149/2009, B.2.3; Constitutional Court 3 February 2011, no. 19/2011, B.7.1 *et seq*.

3.2.2. The need to find a different regulation that applies in a similar situation

56. The field of application of the constitutional review via the principle of equality is also limited by the requirement to find a different regulation that applies in a similar situation. Indeed, in order to find a violation of the principle of equality and non-discrimination, it is first required that different rules apply in a similar situation. If a claimant wants to appeal to the principle of equality, he must find a regulation that is applicable in a similar situation to his and that would be beneficial to him if it would apply on his situation. If no such regulation can be found, it will not be useful for a claimant to invoke the principle of equality. Take for example the law of prescription. Invoking the principle of equality in this context will only be useful for a claimant that is confronted with a time-bar if he finds a prescription period that applies in a similar situation and that would not yet have been time-barred. The Constitutional Court is however easily inclined to accept that different situations are comparable. Indeed, we have seen that the Court does not take into account formal legal qualifications (*supra*, no. 34) and that it recently accepted that the situation of a defendant in tort law is comparable to the situation of a defendant in contract law since both are confronted with the error of another person (*supra*, no. 50–51). Consequently, it seems almost impossible not to find a comparable situation where different rules apply, thus making constitutional review on the basis of the principle of equality possible in almost any case.

57. The ease with which the Constitutional Court applies the principle of equality in the field of the law of obligations, can be illustrated by a judgment of 5 July 1990.[203] The applicants in this particular case were shipping companies who challenged a law that retroactively excluded the liability of the state for faults of pilots of ships at sea (in Belgium these pilots are employees of the state). Since the pilots of the ships themselves were only liable for grave and intentional faults,[204] it became impossible for ship owners who were the victims of normal faults of pilots, to receive a compensation. Accordingly, shipping companies contended that the law contradicted the requirements of the principle of equality. The victims of damages caused by other public servants could indeed claim damages from the state. On top of this, the applicants argued that the principle of governmental liability, as developed by the Belgian Court of Cassation prior to the existence of the Constitutional Court, was actually grounded on a refinement of the constitutional principle of equality of citizens towards the public burden. Indeed, if a governmental action causes damages to some citizens, it seems that these citizens have to bear a larger portion of the public burden and, as a consequence, are discriminated against. If one accepts this reasoning, the principle of equality constitutionalises governmental liability in such a way that it is no longer necessary to refer to a similar situation in order to circumvent the impossibility of receiving compensation for damages caused by the government. The Constitutional Court did not, however, explicitly accept this line of reasoning. Nor, however, did it expressly reject it. On the contrary, the Court

203 Constitutional Court 5 July 1990, no. 25/90.

204 Law of 3 November 1967 'betreffende het loodsen van zeevaartuigen', *BS* 5 January 1968, 101.

applied the principle of equality and non-discrimination to the case. In doing so it did not find a violations of the principle of equality[205] but, rather, that the captain of a ship, apart from the pilot, has an important responsibility and that this kind of liability would pose a heavy burden on the state budget. By applying the proportionality-test, the Court implicitly seems to accept the argument of the applicants and, thus, that the principle of equality in the field of governmental liability can be applied without reference to a similar situation. Also, even if this argument does not suffice, one cannot but admit that the Constitutional Court applied the comparability of different situations in this case in a very flexible way. It is, for example, far from obvious that all persons who are the victim of damages caused by public services are in a similar situation. Those involved in delivering public services engage in different activities that cause very different risks and damages. Thus, this case at least illustrates that one can broaden the scope of application of the principle of equality by using very abstract points of comparison to the extent that it seems that a point of comparison is, in fact, no longer necessary.

3.2.3. The principle of equality as an interpretative instrument

58. In some cases, the constitutional principle of equality is applied in situations where there is no different legislation that applies on similar situations at hand. In those cases, the Constitutional Court is required to control the reconcilability of *judicial interpretation* of legislation or general legal principles with the principle of equality. The principle of equality in these cases becomes an instrument to interpret general rules of the law of obligations. As such, this is an interesting illustration of the *indirect horizontal effect* of the principle of equality.

59. Take for example the case of 17 July 2014.[206] At the origin of this case was an accident between a car and a motorbike that caused the death of the driver of the motorbike. In the procedures that followed, the judges found that the driver of the car had to be held liable, but that the victim made a contributory fault. Consequently, the lower Courts ruled that both parties had to bear half of all the damages. The accident did however not only cause direct damages to the involved parties, but also caused reflected damages to the relatives of the deceased person. With regard to these damages, the lower courts ruled that the driver of the car (and his insurer and employer) had to pay all the damages. By doing so, the lower courts neglected the established case law of the Court of Cassation according to which the contributory fault of the direct victim has to be taken into account when estimating the compensation of indirect damages.[207] Consequently, the Court of Cassation

205 In later proceedings the ECtHR found, however, that the retroactivity of the law was contrary to the requirements of the right to property: ECtHR *Pressos Compania Naviera S.A. v Belgium*, 20 November 1995, no. 17849/91.

206 Constitutional Court 17 July 2014, no. 111/2014.

207 Cass. 19 December 1962, *RW* 1962–63, 1235, concl. Adv. Gen. F. Dumon; Cass. 17 June 1963, *Pas.* 1963, I, 1096 and *RCJB* 1964, 446, note J. Kirkpatrick; Cass. 15 April 1980, *Arr.Cass.* 1979–80, 1010; Cass. 14 April 1981, *Arr.Cass.* 1980–81, 942, *Bull.* 1981, 915, *Pas.* 1981, I, 915 and *RW* 1981–82, 1491, note; Cass. 1 February 1994, AR P.93.0037.N, *Arr.Cass.* 1994, 129, *Bull.* 1994, 133, *Pas.* 1994, I, 133, *RGAR*

quashed the judgment of the lower courts and referred the case to another one.[208] The relatives of the deceased person however found that they were discriminated by this jurisprudence for the reason that they could only receive a part of their damages whereas relatives that would also be direct victims of the accident would have been able to receive a full compensation of their damages. The Constitutional Court did not follow this line of reasoning. It ruled that the Court of Cassation had found a reasonable balance between the interests of the liable persons on the one hand and the relatives of deceased persons on the other. The Court also indicated that the situation wherein a relative is also a direct victim differs from the situation where a relative only suffers indirect losses because the direct losses of a second victim are not determined by the affective bond between the relatives (as is the case with indirect losses). Accordingly, the Court made clear that indirect damages and direct damages of second relatives have to be treated in a different way in case a contributory fault is at hand.[209] Thus, although the Court in this case did not find a violation of the principle of equality, it is a relevant case because it illustrates that the Constitutional Court can indicate whether or not jurisprudential developments, even when indicated by the Court of Cassation, can be reconciled with the principle of equality. By doing so, the Court can act as the highest Court in the Belgian legal order, also when it comes to the interpretation of general rules in the law of obligations.

60. It must be noticed that this is not the only case in which the Constitutional Court applied the principle of equality on a legal interpretation of a rule. Other cases can be discussed in order to affirm this observation, some of which have been discussed before (e.g. *supra*, no. 42). Moreover, in a recent case of 21 January 2016 the Constitutional Court made an important judgment with regard to the interpretation of a judge of Article 1382 CC with regard to the estimation of moral damages and the possibility of non-governmental organisations to claim damages for the degradation of public goods.[210] Similarly, the Constitutional Court made changes to the jurisprudential criteria that have to be used in order to assess a case of state liability for errors committed by the judiciary.[211] In another case, the Court also acted as jurisprudential controller by

1995, no. 12.444, *RW* 1995–96 (shortened), 338, note and *Verkeersrecht* 1994, 147; Cass. 2 March 1995, AR C.94.209.F, *Arr.Cass.* 1995, 255, *Bull.* 1995, 264, *T.Verz.* 1995, 572, *JLMB* 1996, 339, note A Pirard, *JT* 1995, 542, *Pas.* 1995, I, 264, *RGAR* 1995, no. 12.513, *RRD* 1996, 605, note J Fagnart and *RW* 1995–96 (shortened), 338; Cass. 28 June 2006, AR P.05.1141.F, *Arr.Cass.* 2006, 1508 and *Pas.* 2006, 1534; Cass. 16 February 2011, AR P.10.1232.F, *Arr.Cass.* 2011, 524, *Pas.* 2011, 529, concl. D Vandermeersch and *RGAR* 2012, no. 14814; Cass. 23 January 2012, AR C.09.0228.F, *Arr.Cass.* 2012, 202, *Pas.* 2012, 180, *RGAR* 2012, no. 14930 and *RW* 2013–14 (summary), 1099; Cass. 30 May 2013, AR C.12.0344.F, *Arr.Cass.* 2013, 1342, *Pas.* 2013, 1214, *RGAR* 2014, no. 15.051, note, *T.Verz.* 2013, 439, note and *VAV* 2013, 33, note J Muyldermands.

208 Cass. 28 April 2011, AR C.09.0097.F, unpublished.

209 See: S Somers, 'Enkele beschouwingen inzake de schadeloosstelling van benadeelden die schade bij weerkaatsing lijden in geval van een eigen fout van de rechtstreekse benadeelde' (2015) *RW* 1256, 1260.

210 Constitutional Court 21 January 2016, no. 7/2016.

211 Constitutional Court 30 June 2014, no. 99/2014, B.8.3. It seemed that the Constitutional Court in this case was inspired by the criteria that the European Court of Justice uses in similar cases: M Storme, *Ontwikkelingen verbintenissenrecht 2000–2014*, https://www.law.kuleuven.be/personal/mstorme/recyclageverbintenissenrecht.pdf, 40.

describing the field of application of consumer contract law in such a way so that it does not violate the principle of equality.[212]

Conclusion

61. This contribution showed that the principle of equality and non-discrimination influences the Belgian law of obligation in different ways. First of all, the emergence of the antidiscrimination laws and the horizontal effect of the constitutional principle of equality had as a result that the freedom to contract in (pre-)contractual relations has been restricted. This restriction affects all aspects of the freedom to contract: the freedom to choose whether to contract or not; one's ability to freely choose with whom to contract, and the freedom to determine the content of the contract.

In this contribution we have seen that the antidiscrimination laws have influence on the freedom to contract in the nightlife businesses, the entertainment sector, the catering industry, the fitness sector, the real estate industry, the travel business and the publishers industry… The influence of the principle of non-discrimination generally relates to the freedom to refuse to contract. The case law in which the principle of equality limits the freedom to cancel a contract or to determine the content of contractual terms is more limited. However, this does not necessarily mean that the principle of equality is not relevant for these elements of contract law. It might be that these kind of cases until present do not lead to legal procedures. Indeed, as we have seen, there is an ever growing number of cases that can be found about non-discrimination in the law of obligations.

62. Secondly, we have seen that the principle of equality has been used by the Constitutional Court as an instrument to control the coherence of legislation and jurisprudence. At first sight, it seems that the Court not easily finds a violation of the principle of equality in this context. It easily accepts a legitimate aim of a different treatment in the form of a special risk, or in the special position of one of the involved parties. When the Court finds such a legitimate aim, it grants the legislator a wide margin of appreciation and accepts that people under the different regimes are treated differently in one way or another. It can thus be concluded that the Constitutional Court generally is cautious to find a violation of the principle of equality. The cases where the Court finds a violation of the principle of equality seem to relate to situations where an unequal treatment is based on an objective criterion that is *not relevant* for the pursued aim, where a regime connects lighter consequences to grave or intentional errors as to normal errors or where a regime makes it impossible to receive a compensation.

Although the Court is cautious when it applies the principle of equality, we have seen that the possibility to apply the principle of equality in the law of obligations seems to be boundless. The only hard boundary that seems to exist can be found in the protection of other constitutional rights that are to be considered *lex specialis* with regard to the principle of equality. If a special regime in the law of obligations is based on a constitutional provision other than the principle of equality, it seems that this regime is free from

212 Constitutional Court 26 October 2005, no. 159/2005.

constitutional review. Apart from this, no hard limitations of the field of application seem to exist. It is of course required to find a point of comparison in order to find an unequal treatment, but the Court easily accepts that two situations are comparable and the principle of equality can also be used as an instrument to interpret general rules in the law of obligations. This has as a result that the Constitutional Court acts more and more as an 'interpreter' of the law of obligations.

63. All of this illustrates that there are general mechanisms by which the principle of equality and non-discrimination has influenced the law of obligations. Indeed, his principle is used as an instrument to control the quality of the decision making by the lawmaker, judges and private persons in the law of obligations. It forces them to examine their motives in the light of their actual impact and relevance. Accordingly, the principles that were described in this contribution can be used to assess new initiatives in the law of obligations as a reaction to future societal evolutions.

Stefaan Voet*

'WHERE THE WILD THINGS ARE' REFLECTIONS ON THE STATE AND FUTURE OF EUROPEAN COLLECTIVE REDRESS

> *"And when he came to the place where the wild things are they roared their terrible roars and gnashed their terrible teeth and rolled their terrible eyes and showed their terrible claws till Max said "BE STILL" and tamed them with the magic trick of staring into all their yellow eyes without blinking once and they were frightened and called him the most wild thing of all".*
> (M Sendak, *Where the Wild Things Are,*
> HarperCollins Children's Books, New York 1963)

1. Introduction

Almost a decade ago, I started to dig into the topic of complex litigation and collective redress. My supervisor, who had written a PhD about *res iudicata* and had touched on the issue of the binding effect of a judicial decision on third parties, recommended me to talk with an American scholar, since the class action mechanism was seen as 'the hallmark feature of the American legal system'.[1] Over the course of the years, this (now) colleague, provided me with a wealth of information about American class actions. However, the very first book (s)he gave me was a children's book. It was Maurice Sendak's epic book 'Where The Wild Things Are'.[2] Since then, I have looked with boundless curiosity and inquisitiveness at the 'wild things'. Over the years, and as in the book, they have looked tantalizing and enticing. Other times, I perceived them as unfriendly and

* Associate Professor KU Leuven, Host Professor UHasselt, 2016–2017 TPR Chair University of Utrecht. Stefaan.Voet@kuleuven.be. With the exception of the table in subchapter 4.1, the law is stated as at 1 January 2017. I thank Prof Peter Cashman (University of Sydney), Prof Deborah Hensler (Stanford Law School), Prof Christopher Hodges (Oxford University), Prof Jasminka Kalajdzic (University of Windsor), Prof Hans-Wolfgang Micklitz (European University Institute), Prof Linda Mullenix (University of Texas), Prof Catherine Piché (Université de Montréal); Michael Spyres (one of the best tenors of our time) and Eline Verhage (PhD fellow Leiden University) for their insightful comments.

1 CH Miller, 'The Adaptive American Judiciary: From Classical Adjudication to Class Action Litigation' (2009) 72 *Albany Law Review* 117, 130.

2 M Sendak, *Where the Wild Things Are*, HarperCollins Children's Books, New York 1963.

menacing. Because in some places they are being ousted, the 'wild things' decided to move to other places, where they encountered other species. The fact that almost a decade later there is still much ado about the 'wild things' stands out like a sore thumb.

In this chapter, I want to reflect about the state and future of European collective redress. The goal is to look at the broader perspective. Various (complex) litigation tools exist, which all aim at achieving collective redress. I see the latter as the goal or outcome of dispute resolution processes. The objective is not to sketch a comprehensive overview of what is going on in the (currently) 28 Member States, but to share some general observations that, according to me, should and could steer the sometimes highly controversial debate.

2. Common law class actions[3]

The class action mechanism is generally known as a common law device that originated in medieval group litigation in England.[4] In the 20th century, it became well developed in the U.S. and it later spread to other common law jurisdictions. The current state of class actions in these jurisdictions is ambivalent.

The most prominent and well-known class action regime is the American Rule 23 of the Federal Rules of Civil Procedure, which was substantially amended in 1966.[5] American class actions start as class complaints. After a pretrial discovery phase, that is vigorously supervised and accompanied by monetary sanctions against lawyers and parties in case rules are violated, defendants usually bring summary judgment motions. In case these are granted, which happens frequently, the case ends. If, at this point, the merits of the case look bad for the defendants, the parties usually enter into settlements negotiations. Very few cases (about 10%) get to the point of class certification. Most cases settle at this stage. American class actions are brought under a 'speculative fee regime'. Class counsel, who is appointed by the court (that acts as a fiduciary for the class), funds and finances the procedure. If the class loses, their notional cost of the litigation falls on the plaintiff's lawyer. There is no loser pays rule. If the class wins, the plaintiff's lawyer usually receives a percentage of the total sum paid to the class. Occasionally, courts reduce class counsel's fees. American class actions are opt-out class actions. Opt-out rates are generally low, particularly in class action settlements where the class member is not in a position to pursue his claim individually. Sometimes opt-out occurs when there

3 The following brief overview is based on the notes that Prof Jasminka Kalajdzic and I drafted at the occasion of an Expert Seminar 'Principles for Collective Actions: When EU and Nation-State Principles Collide', which was organized at the KU Leuven in Leuven on 16 September 2016. I am grateful to Prof Kalajdzic (University of Windsor) (for the notes and the Canadian overview), Prof Deborah Hensler (Stanford Law School) (for the U.S. overview) and Prof Peter Cashman (University of Sydney) (for the Australian overview). These notes are on file with the author. Any error is my own responsibility.

4 See SC Yeazell, *From Medieval Group Litigation to the Modern Class Action*, Yale University Press, New Haven 1987, p 306. See also R Mulheron, *The Class Action in Common Law Legal Systems. A Comparative Perspective*, Hart Publishing, Oxford 2004, p 536.

5 For a historical overview see RG Bone, 'Walking the Class Action Maze: Towards a More Functional Rule 23' (2013) 46 *University of Michigan Journal of Law Reform* 1097.

is a controversy about whether the settlement is fair and/or adequate. On occasion, this is triggered by objectors who oppose a settlement.

In the U.S., class actions seem to have a hard time, at least when looking at the titles of recent class action scholarship: 'The Decline of Class Actions',[6] 'The End of Class Actions?',[7] 'Ending Class Actions As We Know Them',[8] 'Is the Class Action Really Dead?'[9] What is for sure is the fact that the U.S. Supreme Court has been slowly closing the class action doors[10] and that there is a shift to other (non-class action) mechanisms, such as MDL.[11] Although this has probably tempered the rate of federal class actions, there does not seem to be solid (empirical) data showing that the overall number of class actions is declining. The conclusion seems to be that 'the class action rule is not a bad thing; it is just not working, or it is working poorly'.[12] The current debate focuses on amending or modifying the existing rule framework. Some propose a mild reform,[13] others advocate a more radical revision.[14] Some have even suggested newfangled conceptual models, such as a better coordination between public and private enforcement, in the form of an alliance under which a 'gatekeeper' (ie, a public enforcement agency) retains a 'private attorney general' (ie, a law firm) on a contingent fee basis.[15] It remains to be seen whether these proposals will go anywhere, especially under the new (conservative) administration.

American style class actions were adopted in almost all Canadian provinces.[16] Canadian class actions seem to thrive well. There is no solid empirical evidence that the

6 RH Klonoff, 'The Decline of Class Actions' (2013) 90 *The Washington University Law Review* 729.

7 BT Fitzpatrick, 'The End of Class Actions?' (2015) 57 *Arizona Law Review* 161.

8 LS Mullenix, 'Ending Class Actions As We Know Them: Rethinking the American Class Action' (2014) 64 *Emory Law Journal* 399.

9 GM Vairo, 'Is the Class Action Really Dead? Is that Good or Bad for Class Members?' (2014) 64 *Emory Law Journal* 477.

10 See eg, *Morrison v Nat'l Austl. Bank Ltd.* 130 S. Ct. 2869 (2010); *Wal-Mart Stores, Inc. v Dukes* 131 S. Ct. 2541 (2011); *AT&T Mobility LLC v Concepcion* 131 S. Ct. 1740 (2011); *Comcast Corp. v Behrend* 133 S. Ct. 1426 (2013) and *Am. Express Co. v Italian Colors Rest.* 133 S. Ct. 2304 (2013).

11 Multidistrict litigation (28 U.S.C.A. §1407) that permits civil lawsuits with at least one common (and often intricate) question of fact that have been pending in different federal district courts to be transferred and consolidated for pretrial proceedings before one judge.

12 LS Mullenix, above n 8, p 448.

13 Eg, R Klonoff, above n 6, p 823–30 (arguing that courts should return to the basic principles of the class action rule, not losing sight of the fact that the class action can be a useful and efficient device, and not allowing an abstract concern about blackmail settlements or the possibility of abuse by class counsel to raise the overall bar for certification.) and BT Fitzpatrick, above n 7, p 193–98 (suggesting ia to amend the Federal Arbitration Act and abrogating *Concepcion* and *American Express*).

14 LS Mullenix, above n 8, p 436–47 (suggesting ia the introduction of one class action regime and eliminating the existing class categories; abolishing damages class action and limiting them to injunctive relief, introducing an opt-in system and a preliminary merits review, etc).

15 JC Coffee, jr., *Entrepreneurial Litigation. Its Rise, Fall and Future*, Harvard University Press, Cambridge 2015, pp 225–28.

16 The three provinces with the oldest class action procedures are Québec (Book IX of the Code of Civil Procedure), Ontario (Class Proceedings Act, 1992, S.O. 1992, c. 6) and British Columbia (Class Proceedings Act [RSBC 1996] Chapter 50). See WK Winkler, PM Perell, J Kalajdzic and AM Warner, *The Law of Class Actions in Canada*, Canada Law Book, 2014, p 420. In Quebec, Prof Catherine Piché (University of Montreal) recently created a 'Class Actions Lab' (<www.classactionslab.ca/>).

system is abusive. About 20% of all initiated cases do not get certified or are dismissed on summary judgment. Once certified, most class actions are settled. However, the rate of cases going to trial is on the increase, and plaintiffs lose roughly 50% of the cases that go to trial. There are no bad experiences with (excessive) punitive damages, since plaintiffs who abuse the system face large cost orders. Pretrial discovery, which is permitted in all jurisdictions but Quebec, is strictly limited to issues of class action certification. Fishing expeditions on the merits of the case are not allowed. Almost all Canadian class actions are brought by an individual class member, who needs to have a cause of action against one of the defendants. The prerequisite that there must be an aligned interest between the class representative and the rest of the class is regarded as beneficial. All class actions are funded by a third party: usually lawyers (on a contingency fee basis; as in the U.S., courts regularly reduce fees), private third party funders or not-for-profit funding entities.[17] The latter entities, that only pay the expenses (not the lawyers) and provide a security for indemnity cost orders, receive a 10% levy if the case is won. There is no evidence of frivolous litigation. Canada also is an opt-out jurisdiction. Opt-out rates are very low which is considered as a positive factor since it offers finality to the defendant.

Finally, class actions also spread to Australia.[18] Each of the three statutory regimes (the Federal Court of Australia, the Supreme Court of Victoria and the Supreme Court of NSW) has adopted an opt-out regime. The legislation in each jurisdiction provides that a class action proceeding may be brought on behalf of 'some or all' of those with potential claims. Moreover, there are a number of statutory mechanisms for government regulators to bring class action proceedings to recover damages on behalf of persons who have suffered loss as a result of contravention of specified federal laws (either as separate actions or as an adjunct to regulatory proceedings, eg for civil penalties). However, each of these regulatory regimes provide that the regulator can only bring claims on behalf of persons who consent. Thus, these are opt-in regimes. Accordingly, they are rarely used. The most interesting feature of Australian class actions is how they are financed. Most class actions are funded by third party litigation funders. Up until recently, litigation funders have taken the view that to secure their legal entitlement to a share of the damages (which they are permitted to do, unlike lawyers who are not allowed to charge a percentage of the amount recovered) they should sign up persons with claims and limit (most) funded class actions to those who have entered into litigation funding agreements. The Australian Full Federal Court has validated this practice.[19] However, more recently, the Full Federal Court has endorsed the notion of a 'common fund'.[20] In other words: permitting the

17 Eg, the Ontario Class Proceedings Fund (<www.lawfoundation.on.ca/class-proceedings-fund/>) or the Fonds d'aide aux actions collectives in Quebec (<www.faac.justice.gouv.qc.ca/>).

18 Three class action regimes currently operate in Australia: Part IVA of the Federal Court of Australia Act 1976 (federal), Part 4A of the Supreme Court Act 1986 (Victoria) and Part 10 of the Civil Procedure Act 2005 (New South Wales). The latter two are based on the first federal regime. See D Grave, K Adams and J Betts, *Class Actions in Australia 2nd Edition*, Thomson Reuters, Pyrmont 2012, p 1212.

19 *Multiplex Funds Management Ltd v P Dawson Nominees Pty Ltd* 164 FCR 275 (2007). See also J Kalajdzic, P Cashman and A Longmoore, 'Justice for Profit: A Comparative Analysis of Australian, Canadian and U.S. Third Party Litigation Funding' (2013) 61 *The American Journal of Comparative Law* 93, 102–03.

20 *Money Max Int Pty Ltd v QBE Insurance Group Limited* FCAFC 148 (2016).

funder to receive a commission from the whole of (an opt-out) class, but subject to the Court deciding whether this is fair and reasonable and subject to the Court (rather than the funder) determining the appropriate percentage. This has one downside from the funder's perspective: the Full Court said that normally a determination of what is a reasonable percentage should be made at the end of the case, when all relevant information is available (whereas funders have previously contracted for a specified percentage from individual prospective group members before the proceedings are commenced).

3. European guarded interest

3.1. Three leagues

3.1.1. European frontrunners

In Europe, things evolve at a different pace. Previously, I have discerned three categories.[21] First, there are the European frontrunners: jurisdictions that have had relatively long-standing class action procedures. The most notable examples are Portugal (1995)[22] and the Scandinavian countries (Sweden (2003),[23] Finland (2007),[24] Norway (2008)[25] and Denmark (2008)[26]). These regimes are essentially based on an opt-in system. A remarkable feature of some of the Scandinavian class actions is the fact that standing is given to regulatory bodies. This is for example the case in Finland and Denmark where the Consumer Ombudsman, who is an enforcer and not an ombudsman in the traditional sense,[27] can bring a class action. In Denmark, the Consumer Ombudsman is the only entity that can bring an opt-out class action representing consumers.

21 S Voet, 'Cultural Dimensions of Group Litigation: The Belgian Case' (2013) 41 *Georgia Journal of International and Comparative Law* 433, 435–40.

22 Law No 83/95 of 31.08.1995. See C Gonçalves Borges and M Serra Baptista, 'Portugal' in PG Karlsgodt (ed), *World Class Actions. A Guide to Group and Representative Actions around the Globe*, Oxford University Press, New York 2012, pp 312–22.

23 Section 4 Swedish Group Proceedings Act of 2002. See G Sparrman and L Göransson, 'Sweden' in PG Karlsgodt (ed), *World Class Actions. A Guide to Group and Representative Actions around the Globe*, Oxford University Press, New York 2012, pp 198–213 and L Ervo, 'Group Actions in Sweden – A Moderate Start' in V Harsági and CH van Rhee (eds), *Multi-Party Redress Mechanisms in Europe: Squeaking Mice?*, Intersentia, Cambridge 2014, pp 243–57.

24 Section 4 Finnish Act on Class Actions No 444/2007. See P Kiurunen, 'Finland' in PG Karlsgodt (ed), *World Class Actions. A Guide to Group and Representative Actions around the Globe*, Oxford University Press, New York 2012, pp 214–28.

25 Section 35–3(1)(a) Norwegian Dispute Act of 2005. See P Kiurunen and N Lindström, 'Norway' in PG Karlsgodt (ed), *World Class Actions. A Guide to Group and Representative Actions around the Globe*, Oxford University Press, New York 2012, pp 229–40.

26 Section 254(c) Danish Administration of Justice Act of 1995. See P Kiurunen, N Lindström and M Bylov Rath, 'Denmark' in PG Karlsgodt (ed), *World Class Actions. A Guide to Group and Representative Actions around the Globe*, Oxford University Press, New York 2012, pp 186–97.

27 Ie, a governmental or private entity that receives, investigates and attempts to resolve complaints and problems.

3.1.2. Jurisdictions with recent class action procedures

Second, there are European countries that have adopted class action procedures more recently. Most of these regimes are limited to a specific sector, and are not of a universal or transsubstantive nature. In Belgium,[28] the most important class action prerequisite is that the cause of action must be a possible infraction by the defendant of his contractual obligations or one of the 33 European or Belgian consumer regulations or acts that are enumerated in the Class Action Act.[29] The procedure is limited to C2B (consumer-to-business) disputes. Standing is given to authorised consumer associations and non-profit organisations whose statutory aim corresponds with the collective harm. The Consumer Ombudsman, who is a traditional ombudsman,[30] only has standing to initiate a class action and to negotiate a collective settlement. If the class action is certified, the court can freely choose between an opt-in or opt-out system.

In France, the new 2014 Consumer Code provides for a consumer and competition class action.[31] Only accredited associations have standing. With respect to consumer class actions, the court will decide on liability on the basis of individual test cases brought by the association. Where liability is established, the court will determine the scope of the class action. In a second phase, the claimants who meet the class criteria, can join the class via an opt-in system. In other words, class members opting in know that, in theory, they will receive compensation. French law also allows for a competition class action, but only as a 'follow-on' action. Such an action can only be brought when the decision of the national or European competition authorities has become final. The procedure will be limited to the causation and damages issues. Since November 2016 class actions for health-related cases (which can be brought against pharmaceutical companies, public or private hospitals, organisations producing medical devices, cosmetic products, etc) are also possible.[32] The procedural framework resembles the one for consumer and competition class actions. However, in health-related class actions, compensation to class members will always be assessed on an individual basis. Moreover, in November 2016 the class action mechanism was expanded to privacy and data protection,[33] environmental[34] and discrimination cases (including discriminatory practices at the

[28] Arts XVII.35–69 Belgian Code of Economic Law. See S Voet, 'Consumer Collective Redress in Belgium: Class Actions to the Rescue?' (2015) 16 *European Business Organization Law Review* 121.

[29] These regulations and acts relate to some provisions regarding competition law and banking, market practices, consumer protection, payment and credit services, product safety, intellectual property, privacy, electronic signature, prices, insurance and professional liability, travels, energy and transport of passengers.

[30] See above n 27.

[31] Arts L.623–1 et seq and R.623–1 French Consumer Code. See A Biard, 'Class Action Developments in France (August 2016)' <http://globalclassactions.stanford.edu/content/class-action-developments-france> accessed 29.12.2016.

[32] Arts L.1143–1 et seq and R.1143–1 et seq French Code of Public Health.

[33] Art 43*ter* French Data Protection Act of 06.01.1978.

[34] Art 142–3–1 French Environmental Code.

workplace).[35] Additionally, a general framework providing for horizontal rules for class actions filed before civil and commercial courts was introduced.[36]

In the UK, the 2015 Consumer Rights Act introduced a competition class action.[37] The Competition Appeal Tribunal (CAT), the UK's specialist competition law tribunal, has exclusive jurisdiction. The procedure can be used by any person who has suffered harm as a result of anticompetitive behaviour. The CAT has always been able to hear collective opt-in actions, but only one case was brought.[38] Since 2015 and under a new procedural framework, the CAT can hear follow-on or stand-alone actions, and it (not the parties) will decide if the procedure is to be opt-in or opt-out. The CAT has broad discretion to certify the procedure that can be brought by a person or a (consumer or trade) association. The class action will be certified if it is just and reasonable for the proposed representative to act as representative of the claimants and all the claims raise the same, similar or related issues of fact or law.

Other European countries are in the phase of creating class actions procedures. This is for example the case in Hungary[39] and Slovenia. I will discuss below the well-known Dutch Collective Settlement Act. This framework allows a collective settlement to be approved by the Amsterdam Court of Appeal. However, there needs to be an out-of-court collective settlement. In the absence thereof, the procedure cannot be used. In November 2016, the Dutch Minister of Justice proposed a fully-fledged opt-out damages class action procedure,[40] which would serve as a 'big stick'. According to the proposal the corporate governance criteria for representative associations are tightened. Where more than one association wants to be the class representative, the court appoints a 'lead representative organization', while the other associations remain a party to the proceedings. The decision appointing a 'lead representative organization' is published, after which class members may opt out. The Amsterdam courts have exclusive jurisdiction. Moreover, the lead representative organization would need to demonstrate

35 Art 10 Act No 2008–496 of 27.05.2008 and Art L.1134–6 et seq French Labour Code.

36 Art 60 et seq French Act on the modernization of justice and art L.77–10–1 French Administrative Justice Code.

37 Section 47B of the Competition Act of 1998. See A Higgins, 'Driving with the Handbrake On: Competition Class Actions under the Consumer Rights Act 2015' (2016) 79 *Modern Law Review* 442 and BJ Rodger, 'The Consumer Rights Act 2015 and collective redress for competition law infringements in the UK: a class act?' (2015) 3 *Journal of Antitrust Enforcement* 258.

38 *1078/7/9/07 The Consumers Association v JJB Sports PLC* (see <www.catribunal.org.uk/239-640/1078-7-9-07-The-Consumers-Association.html> accessed 27.01.2017).

39 See V Harsági, 'The Need for Further Development of Collective Redress in Hungary' in V Harsági and CH van Rhee (eds), *Multi-Party Redress Mechanisms in Europe: Squeaking Mice?*, Intersentia, Cambridge 2014, pp 171–83.

40 <https://www.rijksoverheid.nl/ministeries/ministerie-van-veiligheid-en-justitie/nieuws/2016/11/16/wetsvoorstel-collectieve-schadevergoedingsactie-naar-tweede-kamer> accessed 30.12.2016. For a brief summary in English see I Tzankova, 'New Dutch bill on collective damages action' <http://conflictoflaws.net/2016/new-dutch-bill-on-collective-damages-action/> accessed 29.12.2016. For a first critical analysis see E Bauw and S Voet, 'Van stok achter de deur tot keurslijf? Een eerste verkenning van het wetsvoorstel tot invoering van een collectieve schadevergoedingsactie' (2017) 4 *Nederlands Juristenblad*, 240–47.

a sufficient link with the Netherlands. It still remains to be seen whether the proposal will be approved and enacted.

3.1.3. Jurisdictions with complex litigation tools

Third and finally, one can distinguish countries that do not have class actions, in the sense of representative collective or group actions, but that have created instruments to deal with 'mass cases'. The two most notable examples are Germany and the Netherlands. The 2005 German Act on Model Case Proceedings in the Capital Markets (KapMuG) established a model, or test case procedure, of which the core is to detect common issues of law in a multitude of individual cases, have them decided by a higher court, and resolve the previously suspended individual cases taking into account the outcome of the test cases.[41] The procedure only applies to claims for damages caused by false, misleading or omitted public capital market information of a company, or for damage caused by false or misleading investment consulting based on such information. Investors have to sue the defendant individually. When at least 10 of them agree, the model case procedure will be initiated and the court will appoint a test case plaintiff. In 2012, the KapMuG was extended to 2020 and the possibility was introduced for the court to approve a settlement between the model claimant and the defendant that becomes binding on all parties, unless they opt out.[42] Any settlement has to be accepted by 70% of the investors who have started individual proceedings.

The 2005 Dutch Collective Settlement Act provides for settlement-only class actions.[43] An association or special purpose foundation, representing the victims of a mass harm, tries to reach an all-embracing settlement with the defendant. This settlement is then approved by the Amsterdam Court of Appeal, which has exclusive jurisdiction. Class members who disapprove of the settlement can opt out. If not, they are bound by the court decision approving the settlement. One decision of the Amsterdam Court of Appeal has attracted great attention.[44] In the 2010 *Converium* case the court ruled that it had international jurisdiction to approve the settlement for non-U.S. class members, even

41 Capital Markets Model Case Act of 02.10.2011. See M Bakowitz, 'The German Experience with Group Actions – The *Verbandsklage* and the Capital Markets Model Case Act (KAPMUG)' in V Harsági and CH van Rhee (eds), *Multi-Party Redress Mechanisms in Europe: Squeaking Mice?*, Intersentia, Cambridge 2014, pp 153–65 and L Röckrath, 'Germany' in PG Karlsgodt (ed), *World Class Actions. A Guide to Group and Representative Actions around the Globe*, Oxford University Press, New York 2012, pp 246–49. See also E Steinberger, *Die Gruppenklage im Kapitalmarktrecht. Vorschläge zur Weiterentwicklung des Kapitalanleger-Musterverfahrensgesetzes (KapMuG)*, Nomos, Baden-Baden 2016, p 321.

42 Capital Markets Model Case Act Amendment of 25.10.2012. See A Stadler, 'Developments in Collective Redress: What's New in the 'New German KapMuG'?' (2013) 24 *European Business Law Review* 731.

43 Arts 7:900-:910 Dutch Civil Code and arts 1013–18 Dutch Judicial Code. See J Fleming and JJ Kuster, 'The Netherlands' in PG Karlsgodt (ed), *World Class Actions. A Guide to Group and Representative Actions around the Globe*, Oxford University Press, New York 2012, pp 286–300 and CH van Rhee and I Tzankova, 'Collective Redress in the Netherlands' in V Harsági and CH van Rhee (eds), *Multi-Party Redress Mechanisms in Europe: Squeaking Mice?*, Intersentia, Cambridge 2014, pp 209–24.

44 S Voet, above n 21, p 438–39.

though the class mainly consisted of non-Dutch class members.[45] In its final decision of January 2012, the court declared the settlement binding on all class members. Moreover, the court had no problem with the contingency fee arrangement for the American lawyers, which involved up to 20% of the amount of the settlement.[46] After the U.S. Supreme Court's decision in *Morrison* invalidated class actions brought in the U.S. on behalf of foreign class members,[47] Amsterdam has the ambition of becoming the settlement hub for claims involving non-U.S. class members in mass cases.[48] In other words, the Dutch Collective Settlement Act could be a possible avenue for the current Volkswagen case.[49]

3.2. *European policy*

3.2.1. Piecemeal legislation

For a long time, Europe struggled with taking a clear position on consumer collective redress and establishing a coherent legal framework. Over the years, the European legislator enacted piecemeal legislation, of which the effectiveness is limited. The 2004 Regulation on Cooperation between Member States for Consumer Protection (CPC Regulation) established a network of national authorities, each having national investigation and enforcement powers for monitoring the application of legislation concerning consumer protection.[50] The Regulation establishes a framework for mutual assistance which covers the exchange of information, requests for enforcement measures and coordination of market surveillance and enforcement activities. In May 2016, the Commission proposed to reform the CPC Regulation.[51] Besides expanding the toolbox of national enforcement authorities so they can work faster and more efficiently,[52] the

45 Court of Appeal Amsterdam 12 November 2010, ECLI:NL:GHAMS:2010:BO3908.

46 Court of Appeal Amsterdam 17 January 2012, ECLI:NL:GHAMS:2012:BV1026.

47 *Morrison v Nat'l Austl. Bank Ltd.* 130 S. Ct. 2869 (2010).

48 XE Kramer, 'Securities Collective Action and Private International Law Issues in Dutch WCAM Settlements: Global Aspirations and Regional Boundaries' (2014) 27 *Pacific McGeorge Global Business & Development Law Journal* 235 and B Krans, 'The Dutch Class Action (Financial Settlement) Act in an International Context: The Shell Case and the Converium Case' (2012) 31 *Civil Justice Quarterly* 141.

49 In early 2016 a Dutch (special purpose) foundation, Volkswagen Investor Settlement Foundation, was established to represent 'the interests of investors in Volkswagen securities worldwide, including common or preferred shares, and public or private debt, during the period from 23 April 2008 through 4 January 2016'. See <http://volkswageninvestorsettlement.com/> accessed 31.12.2016.

50 Regulation 2006/2004/EC of the European Parliament and of the Council of 27 October 2004 on consumer protection cooperation [2004] OJ L 634/1.

51 Proposal for a Regulation of the European Parliament and of the Council on cooperation between national authorities responsible for the enforcement of consumer protection laws COM(2016) 283 final 25.5.2016. See <http://ec.europa.eu/consumers/enforcement/cross-border_enforcement_cooperation/index_en.htm> accessed 01.01.2017.

52 'Authorities will be able to request information from domain registrars and banks to detect the identity of the responsible trader, carry out mystery shopping to check geographical discrimination or after-sales conditions, and to order the immediate take-down of websites hosting scams. The harmful practices covered will also include advertisement campaigns of short duration that may have a lasting impact, by trapping consumers in unwanted subscriptions'. (ibid).

Commission wants to coordinate common actions to address Union-wide problematic practices (eg, by adopting a one-stop-shop approach to consumer law where enforcement authorities will notify the businesses concerned of the issues, asking them to change their practices and, if necessary, to compensate the affected consumers). In order to detect market problems more easily, consumer organizations will be able to signal bad cross-borders practices to enforcers and to the European Commission. Finally, the Commission wants to expand the scope of application of the CPC Regulation (eg, to transport and retail financial services).

On the other hand, collective actions for injunctive relief have been possible for a while. The key and oldest Directive in this regard is the Injunctions Directive, which ensures the defense of collective interests of consumers in the internal market.[53] It aims at terminating or prohibiting infringements (regarding consumer credit, package travel, unfair terms in contract concluded with consumers, distance contracts and unfair commercial practices) which are contrary to the collective interests of consumers. Only qualified authorities having a legitimate interest in ensuring that the collective interests of consumers are complied with (eg, independent public bodies or consumer protection organizations), may bring an action. The Injunctions Directive was evaluated in 2012.[54] The Commission concluded that injunctive actions constitute a useful tool for the protection of the collective interests of consumers and that qualified entities are gradually becoming aware of the possibilities offered to them by the Directive and gaining experience with its use. However, the Commission noted that important disparities exist among Member States in its level of use and effectiveness. In Member States where injunctions are used, their potential is not fully exploited, inter alia, because of the high costs linked to the proceedings, the length of the proceedings, the complexity of the procedures, the relatively limited effects of the rulings on injunctions and the difficulty of enforcing them.

Yet, regarding these effects reference must be made to the case law of the Court of Justice of the European Union (CJEU) under the Unfair Contract Terms Directive.[55] In the *Invitel* case the CJEU held that where the unfair nature of a term included in the general conditions of consumer contracts has been recognised in an action for an injunction, the national courts of the Member States are required, *of their own motion, and also as regards the future*, to draw all the consequences provided for by national law in order to ensure that consumers who have concluded a contract to which those general conditions apply will not be bound by that term.[56] However, the CJEU also held that a

53 Directive 2009/22/EC of the European Parliament and of the Council of 23 April 2009 on injunctions for the protection of consumers' interests [2009] OJ L 110/30. This Directive repealed Directive 98/27/EC of the European Parliament and of the Council of 19 May 1998 on injunctions for the protection of consumer interests [1998] OJ L 166/51.

54 Report from the Commission to the European Parliament and the Council concerning the application of Directive 2009/22/EC of the European Parliament and of the Council on injunctions for the protection of consumers' interest COM(2012) 635 final 06.11.2012.

55 Art 7 Council Directive 93/13/EEC of 5 April 1993 on unfair terms in consumer contracts [1993] OJ L 95/29.

56 Case C-472/10 *Nemzeti Fogyasztóvédelmi Hatóság v Invitel Távközlési Zrt*, ECLI:EU:C:2012:242. Emphasis added. See also case C-191/15 *Verein für Konsumenteninformation v Amazon EU Sàrl*, ECLI:EU:C:2016:612.

collective action procedure against a trader, under the Unfair Contracts Terms Directive, may not have the result that as long as that procedure is pending, individual procedures are suspended as this would have as a result that the consumer could no longer have all circumstances of the case taken into account, such as the negotiations that may have taken part between the parties, and could not waive the non-application of the unfair term. A national rule requiring a court to suspend an individual action brought before it by a consumer until a final judgment in a parallel collective action brought by an association is reached, does not constitute an adequate or effective means of bringing to an end the continued use of unfair clauses.[57]

3.2.2. EC Recommendation on common principles for injunctive and compensatory collective redress mechanisms[58]

3.2.2.1. Ratio legis

In June 2013, and after a series of studies and preparatory policy documents,[59] the European Commission published a Recommendation on common principles for injunctive and compensatory collective redress mechanisms in the Member States concerning violations of rights granted under Union Law.[60] The Commission recommends that all Member States should have collective redress mechanisms in those areas where Union law grants rights to citizens and companies: consumer protection, competition, environment protection, protection of personal data, financial services legislation and investor protection. The principles set out in the Recommendation should be applied horizontally and equally in those areas but also in any other areas where collective claims for injunctions or damages in respect of violations of the rights granted under Union law would be relevant.

57 Joined Cases C-381/14 and 385/14 *Jorge Sales Sinués v Caixabank SA*, ECLI:EU:C:2016:252. In the Fernández Oliva case the court ruled that Art. 7(1) of the Unfair Contract Terms Directive must be interpreted as precluding a provision of national law which does not permit a court seized of an individual action brought by a consumer seeking a declaration that a term of a contract binding him to a seller or supplier is unfair to adopt interim relief of its own motion, for as long as it considers appropriate, pending a final judgment in an ongoing collective action, the outcome of which may be applied to the individual action, when such relief is necessary in order to ensure the full effectiveness of the judgment to be given on the existence of the rights claimed by the consumer under the Unfair Contract Terms Directive (Joined Cases C-568/14 to 570/14 *Ismael Fernández Oliva v Caixabank SA*, ECLI:EU:C:2016:828).

58 This subchapter is largely based on S Voet, 'European Collective Redress: A Status Quaestionis' (2014) 4 *International Journal of Procedural Law* 97.

59 For an overview see ibid, p 102–06.

60 Recommendation 2013/396/EU of the European Commission of 11 June 2013 on common principles for injunctive and compensatory collective redress mechanisms in the Member States concerning violations of rights granted under Union Law [2013] OJ L 206/60. See also Communication from the Commission to the European Parliament, the Council, the European Economic and Social Committee and the Committee of the Regions. Towards a European Horizontal Framework for Collective Redress COM(2013) 401/2 11.06.2013.

The goal is not to harmonize the national systems, but to list some common, non-binding, principles relating both to judicial (compensatory and injunctive) and out-of-court collective redress that Member States should take into account when crafting such mechanisms. The Commission wants to facilitate access to justice, stop illegal practices and enable victims of mass cases to obtain compensation, and at the same time to provide appropriate procedural safeguards to avoid abusive litigation.[61]

Although the Recommendation is of a non-binding, declaratory nature, it seeks to oblige the Member States to implement the principles set out in it in national collective redress systems by 26 July 2015 at the latest.[62] The Commission will assess the implementation of the Recommendation on the basis of practical experience. It will evaluate its impact on access to justice, on the right to obtain compensation, on the need to prevent abusive litigation and on the functioning of the single market, on SMEs, the competitiveness of the economy of the European Union and consumer trust. The Commission will also assess whether further measures to consolidate and strengthen the horizontal approach reflected in the Recommendation should be proposed.[63]

As an aside, it should be noted that legislative initiatives were taken in other fields too. However, these fall outside the scope of this chapter. At the same time as the Recommendation, the Commission proposed a Directive on certain rules governing actions for damages under national law for infringements of competition law.[64] The proposal became a Directive in 2014.[65] It aims to remove the practical obstacles victims of infringements of the EU antitrust rules currently face when trying to get full compensation, whether or not an infringement decision was issued by a competition authority. The new General Data Protection Regulation includes statutory rights for individuals who have suffered damages to seek compensation from organizations, and for public interest organizations to bring (a sort of) class action on behalf of such individuals.[66]

[61] Art 1 Recommendation and recitals (10) and (13) Recommendation.

[62] Art 38 Recommendation.

[63] Art 41 Recommendation.

[64] Proposal for a Directive of the European Parliament and of the Council on certain rules governing actions for damages under national law for infringements of the competition law provisions of the Member States and of the European Union, COM(2013) 404 final 11.06.2013. See S Voet, above n 58, p 114–17.

[65] Directive 2014/104/EU of the European Parliament and of the Council of 26 November 2014 on certain rules governing actions for damages under national law for infringements of the competition law provisions of the Member States and of the European Union [2014] OJ L 349/1. See M Bergström, M Iacovides and M Strand (eds), *Harmonising EU Competition Litigation. The New Directive and Beyond*, Hart Publishing, Oxford 2016, p 343 and F Wijckmans, M Visser, S Jaques and E Noël, *The EU Private Damages Directive Practical Insights. Minutes of the Closed Workshop 2015*, Intersentia, Cambridge 2016, p 110. Based on the Directive, national courts can order companies to disclose evidence when victims claim compensation, a final decision of a National Competition Authority (NCA) finding an infringement will automatically constitute proof of that infringement before national courts, victims will have at least one year to claim damages once an infringement decision by a NCA has become final and consensual settlements between victims and infringing companies will be made easier by clarifying their interplay with court actions.

[66] Chapter VIII of Regulation 2016/679/EU of the European Parliament and of the Council of 27 April 2016 on the protection of natural persons with regard to the processing of personal data and on the free movement of such data, and repealing Directive 95/46/EC [2016] OJ L 119/1.

3.2.2.2. (Procedural) principles

Although these concepts are not defined, the Recommendation states that national collective redress procedures should be fair, equitable, timely and not prohibitively expensive.[67] The Recommendation applies to injunctive and compensatory collective redress.[68] The former is 'a legal mechanism that ensures a possibility to claim cessation of illegal behaviour collectively by two or more natural or legal persons or by an entity entitled to bring a representative action'. The latter is 'a legal mechanism that ensures a possibility to claim compensation collectively by two or more natural or legal persons claiming to have been harmed in a mass harm situation or by an entity entitled to bring a representative action'. A representative action is described as 'an action which is brought by a representative entity, an ad hoc certified entity or a public authority on behalf and in the name of two or more natural or legal persons who claim to be exposed to the risk of suffering harm or to have been harmed in a mass harm situation whereas those persons are not parties to the proceedings'.[69]

A threefold distinction is made between principles common to injunctive and compensatory redress, principles relating to injunctive collective redress, and principles relating to compensatory collective redress.[70] Some principles apply to both types. Only associational or organizational plaintiffs can bring a representative action. Besides public authorities,[71] officially designated representative entities and entities certified on an ad hoc basis by a national authority or court for a particular representative action have standing to bring a representative action.[72] These entities must have a non-profit making character and must have sufficient capacity in terms of financial resources, human resources and legal expertise.

The class representative should be able to disseminate information about a claimed violation of rights granted under Union law and his or her intention to seek an injunction to stop it as well as about a mass harm situation and his or her intention to pursue an action for damages in the form of collective redress. The same possibilities for the representative entity, ad hoc certified entity, a public authority or for the group of claimants should be ensured as regards the information on the ongoing compensatory actions.[73] The dissemination methods should take into account the particular circumstances of the mass harm situation concerned, the freedom of expression, the right to information, and the right to protection of the reputation or the company value of a defendant before its responsibility for the alleged violation or harm is established by the final judgment of the court.[74]

67 Art 2 Recommendation.
68 Art 3 (a) Recommendation.
69 Art 3 (d) Recommendation.
70 Some of the principles are discussed below in the other (more relevant) subchapters.
71 Art 7 Recommendation.
72 Arts 4 and 6 Recommendation.
73 Art 10 Recommendation.
74 Art 11 Recommendation.

Some principles only relate to injunctive collective redress. On the one hand, courts and competent public authorities should treat claims for injunctive orders requiring cessation of or prohibiting a violation of rights granted under Union law with all due expediency, where appropriate by way of summary proceedings, in order to prevent any or further harm causing damage because of such violation.[75] On the other hand, the Member States should establish appropriate sanctions against the losing defendant with a view to ensuring the effective compliance with the injunctive order, including the payments of a fixed amount for each day's delay or any other amount provided for in national legislation.[76]

Finally, there are specific principles relating to compensatory collective redress. The Recommendation puts forward the opt-in principle as the default position. The claimant group should be formed on the basis of express consent of the natural persons claiming to have been harmed.[77] Nevertheless, opt out is possible as exception, by law or by court order, as long as this is duly justified by reasons of sound administration of justice (whatever this may mean).[78]

A member of the claimant group should be free to leave the claimant group at any time before the final judgment is given or the case is otherwise validly settled, subject to the same conditions that apply to withdrawal in individual actions, without being deprived of the possibility to pursue its claims in another form, if this does not undermine the sound administration of justice.[79] Natural or legal persons claiming to have been harmed in the same mass harm situation should be able to join the claimant party at any time before the judgment is given or the case is otherwise validly settled, if this does not undermine the sound administration of justice.[80]

The Commission prohibits contingency fees and punitive damages. The Member States should ensure that the lawyers' remuneration, and the method by which it is calculated, do not create any incentive to litigation that is unnecessary from the point of view of the interest of any of the parties.[81] Contingency fees risk creating such an incentive. When contingency fees are exceptionally allowed in collective redress cases, appropriate national regulation should be provided, taking into account in particular the right to full compensation of the members of the claimant party.[82]

The compensation awarded to natural or legal persons harmed in a mass harm situation should not exceed the compensation that would have been awarded, if the claim had been pursued by means of individual actions. In particular, punitive damages, leading to overcompensation in favour of the claimant party of the damage suffered, should be prohibited.[83]

75 Art 19 Recommendation.
76 Art 20 Recommendation.
77 Art 21 Recommendation.
78 Ibid.
79 Art 22 Recommendation.
80 Art 23 Recommendation.
81 Art 29 Recommendation.
82 Art 30 Recommendation.
83 Art 31 Recommendation.

3.2.2.3. Reception

Despite the fact that the Recommendation is of a non-binding nature, it purports to oblige the Member States to implement the principles set out in it in national collective redress systems.[84] When one analyzes the recent legislative initiatives and proposals with respect to damages class actions – as discussed above in subchapter 3.1. –, one cannot but conclude that the Recommendation does not have a major impact. Most Member States adhere to their own views on how to deal with mass harms, and follow only few of the proposed principles. Most of the recent initiatives and acts are of a sectoral nature, in the sense that the class action procedure only applies to a specific field of substantive law (eg, consumer law). This is the case, for example, in Belgium, France and the UK. Nevertheless, the Recommendation proposes collective redress mechanisms in *all* areas where Union law grants rights to citizens and companies (consumer protection, competition, environment protection, protection of personal data, financial services legislation and investor protection). While the Recommendation favours the opt-in principle, which is followed in some Member States (eg, the Scandinavian countries and France), other jurisdictions adhere to the opt-out principle (eg, Portugal and the Netherlands) or allow the court to choose between opt-in or opt-out (eg, Belgium and the UK). The proposed principles relating to the dissemination of information on a collective redress action and the ones regarding injunctive collective redress are not to be found in the legislative framework of most Member States. As discussed below, the Recommendation provides for specific principles relating to the funding and financing of collective redress mechanisms and the establishment of a registry of collective redress actions. With some exceptions, most Member States disregard these issues.

All but indirectly, other principles are applied by the Member States, the most notable one being the standing principle. Almost all Member States prefer (non-profit) organizations, associations or foundations as class representatives. In some Member States special purpose foundations are allowed (eg, in the Netherlands), while others give standing to public authorities (eg, Belgium, Denmark and Finland). The traditional continental rules on the prohibition of contingency fees and punitive damages are embedded in most legal regimes.[85] France and the UK provide for collective follow-on actions as proposed by the Recommendation. Finally, and as discussed below, most jurisdictions focus on the out-of-court resolution of mass harm situations, which resembles the Commission's policy.

The Recommendation was received with mixed skepticism by most scholars. Some pointed out that the principles regarding injunctive collective redress are no more than a reiteration or confirmation of the model as laid down in the Injunctions Directive, despite the call of the European Parliament to 'strengthen and increase the effectiveness of existing instruments such as [the Injunctions Directive and the CPC Regulation] in

84 Art 38 Recommendation.

85 However, there are some exceptions. For example under the Lithuanian class action regime, contingency fees are allowed (Z Juška, 'Country Report. Class Actions in Lithuania' <http://globalclassactions.stanford.edu/sites/default/files/documents/LITHUANIA.pdf> accessed 02.01.2017).

order to ensure appropriate public enforcement of consumers' rights in the EU'.[86] With respect to the proposed compensatory collective redress mechanism some observed that 'the approach seems to be defendant oriented and, therefore, too reluctant in promoting effective collective redress mechanisms'.[87] Others have pointed out that the Recommendation is unlikely to achieve the aim of producing procedural coherence and consistency in respect of collective redress actions.[88] Besides the non-binding nature of the Recommendation and the fact that it does not mandate action on the part of any of the Member States, ample room is left for the Member States to deviate from the proposed principles (for example with respect to the opt-in vs opt-out system and the allowance of contingency fees), which is likely to leave the 'patchwork' of national procedures as it is right now.[89] Looking at the most recent initiatives and proposals in the various Member States post-2013, one cannot but conclude that this 'patchwork', in the sense of uncoordinated or inconsistent sectoral approaches, is becoming a reality. Moreover, most of these reforms seem to stem from Member States' legal traditions or from the necessity to have a 'quick' tool to manage sometimes high-profile mass cases,[90] rather than from the terms of the Recommendation.[91] In that sense, the Recommendation is not considered as a normative guide to increase harmonization and coherence, but rather as a 'damp sqibb',[92] or 'squeaking mouse'.[93] Hodges rightfully points out the 'porousness' of the proposed safeguards,[94] including the absence of appropriate funding and financing rules, the importance of national contexts and the existing empirical evidence. These issues deserve some further consideration.

4. Limited success

4.1. (Limited) data

The basic empirical question underlying the debate, is how many class action procedures are being brought in the Member States. It should be noted that almost no jurisdiction

86 E Silvestri, 'Group Actions *À La Mode Européenne*: A Kinder, Gentler Class Action for Europe?' in CB Picker and GI Seidman (eds), *The Dynamism of Civil Procedure – Global Trends and Developments*, Springer, 2016, pp 210–11 (referring to European Parliament resolution of 2 February 2012 on 'Towards a Coherent European Approach to Collective Redress' (2011/2089(INI), paras 11–14)).

87 B Hess, 'European Perspectives on Collective Litigation' in V Harsági and CH van Rhee (eds), *Multi-Party Redress Mechanisms in Europe: Squeaking Mice?*, Intersentia, Cambridge 2014, p 7.

88 J Sorabji, 'Reflections on the Commission Communication on Collective Redress' (2014) 17 *Irish Journal of European Law* 62, 66–70.

89 E Silvestri, above n 86, p 214.

90 I once spoke of a trigger-effect (S Voet, above n 21, p 448).

91 J Sorabji, above n 88, p 67–69.

92 C Hodges, 'Collective Redress: A Breakthrough or a *Damp Sqibb*?'(2014) 37 *Journal of Consumer Policy* 67.

93 V Harsági and CH van Rhee (eds), *Multi-Party Redress Mechanisms in Europe: Squeaking Mice?*, Intersentia, Cambridge 2014, p 264.

94 Hodges, above n 92, p 78–79. Hodges also refers to the subsidiarity principle as laid down in Art 67(1) TFEU. 'That constraint gives rise to both the safeguards and also the exemptions' (ibid, p 78).

has reliable (public or private) sources on the number of cases. And this is despite the fact that the Recommendation wants the Member States 'to establish a national registry of collective redress actions, which should be available free of charge to any interested person through electronic means and otherwise. Websites publishing the registries should provide access to comprehensive and objective information on the available methods of obtaining compensation, including out of court methods'.[95] Moreover, the same Recommendation states that once the Member States have implemented collective redress mechanisms, they should collect reliable annual statistics on the number of out-of-court and judicial collective redress procedures and information about the parties, the subject matter and outcome of the cases.[96] To date, this seems to be an idle statement.

The information collected in the table below is based on personal contacts with scholars from the relevant jurisdictions. Exceptionally, there are public (eg, in Poland) or private (eg, in Italy) sources. The possible forthcoming Dutch class action act establishes a public registry.[97]

Jurisdiction	Year of Introduction	Act	Number of Cases
Portugal	1995	Law 83/95 of 31 August 1995 on the right to take part in administrative proceedings and the right of popular action	179 filed[98] (2007–2015) 29 pending in 2015
Lithuania	2002	2015 Amendments to the Code of Civil Procedure (introduction group legal actions)	5[99] (January 2015 - August 2017) - 2 pending - 3 dismissed
Sweden	2003	2003 Group Proceedings Act	17[100] (2003–2014)
the Netherlands	2005	2005 Dutch Collective Settlement Act	9[101] (2005 - October 2016)
Finland	2007	2007 Class Action Act	0[102]
Denmark	2008	Chapter 23a (§254a-254k) Administration of Justice Act	2[103] (2008–2012)

95 Articles 35–36 Recommendation.

96 Art 39 Recommendation.

97 See above n 40.

98 Correspondence with Henrique Sousa Antunes, Católica Global School of Law, November 2016 (on file with author).

99 Correspondence with Renata Juzikiene, director of the Supreme Court of Lithuania, August 2017 (on file with author).

100 L Ervo, above n 23, p 255.

101 <https://www.rechtspraak.nl/>.

102 Correspondence with Lauro Ervo, Örebro University, November 2016 (on file with author).

103 P Kiurunen, N Lindström and M Bylov Rath, above n 26, p 197.

Jurisdiction	Year of Introduction	Act	Number of Cases
Italy	2010[104]	2009 Law no. 99 – Article 140*bis* Italian Consumer Code	58[105] (January 2010 – November 2016)
Poland	2010	Class Actions Act of 17 December 2009	210[106] (2010–2016)
Belgium	2014	2014 Act Introducing a Consumer Collective Redress Action in the Code of Economic Law	5 (September 2014 – August 2017) – 2 certified (1 finished and 1 pending) – 2 pending – 1 withdrawn
France	2014	Articles L.623-1 *et seq.* and R.623-1 *et seq.* of the French Consumer Code (Code de la Consommation) and the similar procedures in health, discrimination, environment, privacy and data protection law	11[107] (October 2014 – August 2017) – 1 settled (consumer) – 1 dismissed (consumer) – 9 pending (7 consumer, 1 health and 1 discrimination)
England & Wales	2015	2015 Consumer Rights Act (Competition Class Action)	2[108] (2015 – August 2017) – 1 dismissed – 1 withdrawn

4.2. *Scope and standing*

This is not the place extensively to analyse why the overall number of class action cases is low. This requires a more in-depth quantitative and qualitative analysis. Some will argue that the data is too scant right now to draw general conclusions and that the ideal would be to obtain data about the outcomes of all the actions filed (eg, settlement, distributions, judgments, case dismissed, abandoned, etc.). Although this is true, I think some issues can be identified that *might* explain the *prima facie* low rates. Some of them

104 This is the new 2009 version (Law no. 99) of Article 140*bis* Italian Consumer Code.

105 <www.osservatorioantitrust.eu/it/azioni-di-classe-incardinate-nei-tribunali-italiani/> (Osservatorio permanente sulle regole della concorrenza accessed 03.01.2017). The website contains a disclaimer, specifying that the data reported are not official, but come from the press and the websites of the major consumer associations. 18 cases have been declared inadmissible. 40 cases are still pending at various stages of the procedure.

106 Correspondence with Magdalena Tulibacka, December 2016 (on file with author). See <https://isws.ms.gov.pl/pl/baza-statystyczna/opracowania-wieloletnie/> accessed 03.01.2017. 203 cases were civil cases brought before district courts (first instance). 7 cases were commercial cases also brought before district courts (first instance).

107 Correspondence with Alexandre Biard, August 2017 (on file with author).

108 <www.catribunal.org.uk/237-9391/1266-7-7-16--Walter-Hugh-Merricks-CBE-.html> and <www.catribunal.org.uk/237-9255/1257-7-7-16-Dorothy-Gibson.html> accessed 03.01.2017.

have to do with the procedural design and features of European-style class actions. These will be analysed below in subchapters 4.2., 4.3. and 4.4. Others relate to more fundamental policy choices and will be analysed in subchapters 5 and 6.

The procedural design of many class action regimes is characterized by a panoply of safeguards. The aim is to avoid abusive or frivolous litigation: 'collective redress mechanisms should preserve procedural safeguards and guarantees of parties to civil actions. In order to avoid the development of an abusive litigation culture in mass harm situations, the national collective redress mechanisms should contain the fundamental safeguards identified in this Recommendation'.[109] However, creating too many safeguards can result in a catch-22 situation: 'weak or superfluous safeguards will not prevent abusive litigation; overly restrictive safeguards will create insurmountable barriers to justice'.[110] Striking the right balance between collective access to justice and avoiding abusive litigation is a tricky exercise.

As mentioned above, the Recommendation stipulates that all Member States should have collective redress mechanisms in *all* areas where Union law grants rights to citizens and companies. The proposed principles should be applied horizontally and equally.[111] Conversely, most European class actions are of a sectoral nature, in the sense that their scope is limited to for example consumer or competition law. At first sight this is at odds with the access to justice goal of the Recommendation.[112] For some disputes collective access to justice is provided, while for other disputes, falling outside the scope of the law, there is only individualized access to justice. In Belgium, where the class action regime is limited to consumer law cases, the Belgian Constitutional Court held that the act's limited scope of application did not render it unconstitutional.[113] The Court stated that most mass cases are consumer cases and that the list of European and Belgian consumer regulations and Acts (limiting the scope of the Belgian class action procedure) was sufficiently comprehensive. Moreover, the Court found that because it concerns a novel and complicated procedure, the Belgian legislature was right to limit, in the first instance,[114] its scope to consumer cases. This reasoning is not convincing. The fact that most mass cases are consumer cases (which is not substantiated by empirical evidence) on the one hand, and the complexity (whatever that means) of the class action procedure on the other hand, are not reasonable (and in my opinion even fallacious) grounds to exclude other kinds of cases from the procedure. Nevertheless, and as discussed below, there might be another plausible and more acceptable reason why Member States limit

109 Recital (16) Recommendation.

110 R. Money-Kyrle and C. Hodges, 'European Collective Action: Towards Coherence?' (2012) 19 *Maastricht Journal of European and Comparative Law* 477, 479.

111 See subchapter 3.2.2.1.

112 Recitals (9) and (10) Recommendation.

113 Belgian Constitutional Court 17 March 2006, case 41–2016, available at <www.const-court.be/en/common/home.html>. In France, the constitutional council also seemed to validate the limited scope of application of the consumer and competition class action procedure as laid down in the new Consumer Code (Conseil Constitutionnel, decision n° 2014–690 DC of 13.03.2014; see <www.conseil-constitutionnel.fr/conseil-constitutionnel/francais/les-decisions/acces-par-date/decisions-depuis-1959/2014/2014–690-dc/decision-n-2014–690-dc-du-13-mars-2014.140273.html> accessed 04.01.2017).

114 The procedure will be evaluated in 2017, after which its scope could be expanded.

their class action procedures to specific sectors, namely the existence of other (more efficient) means of resolving (mass) disputes in other sectors.[115]

The overall policy of the Member States is to give standing to organizational, associational or public entities, which coincides with the Recommendation. While this is a laudable choice,[116] there is a danger of market monopolization, which can be detrimental to the interests of potential class members. There is also a risk of ineffectiveness, if the wrong intermediary – generically, a consumer association – is selected. The fact that in some jurisdictions, such as Belgium and France, only authorized or accredited associations or organizations have standing can be criticized because this could mean too much government dependency. The possibility to initiate a class action would de facto depend on governmental authorization.[117] In Belgium, there is a real monopolization of the class action market. To date, all (five) class action procedures have been brought by Belgium's biggest consumer association, Test-Aankoop/Test-Achats. In France on the other hand, there seems to be more diversity in standing.[118] Under the Dutch Collective Settlement Act, established associations defending the interests of consumers, tenants, minority shareholders etc, as well as special-purpose foundations or ad hoc entities established at the occasion of a specific mass harm situation can conclude a collective settlement. These entities will also have standing under the possible new class action regime. However, as mentioned above, the Dutch legislator wants to tighten the admissibility criteria for these class representatives if they want to bring a class action. As in Belgium, this could lead to a restricted litigation market. These examples make clear that limiting, or even constraining, standing to a limited number of players can lead to a possible lack of enforcement. Bringing a class action will depend on the financial willingness of these, usually non-profit, entities. The question arises how big this willingness is under a loser-pays system and in the absence of external funding sources.

4.3. *Procedural design flaws*

Many class action regimes are characterized by procedural complexity, making them sometimes unmanageable and therefore difficult to bring. Three random examples make this clear. In some jurisdictions, it is possible to appeal the class action certification decision, for example in Belgium.[119] At first instance, the Brussels Court of First Instance or the Brussels Commercial Court has exclusive jurisdiction to hear class action cases. Their class action certification decision can be appealed. According to Belgian law,[120]

115 C Hodges, above n 92, p 85. See also B Hess, above n 87, p 8–9.

116 S Voet, above n 21, p 457–64. It has to be underlined that some of these associations are successful in collecting claims and have established a reputation over the years. A leading example is the VKI (Verein für Konsumenteninformation) in Austria (see <www.konsument.at>).

117 S Voet, above n 28, p 127.

118 Cases have been brought by UFC Que Choisir (a consumer association), Confédération Syndicale des Familles (CSF); Consommation, Logement et Cadre de Vie (CLCV); Confédération Nationale du Logement (CNL) and Familles Rurales. See A Biard, above n 31.

119 S Voet, above n 28, p 140.

120 Art 1068 Belgian Judicial Code.

when a decision is appealed, all the (factual and legal) issues that were not decided by the first court are transferred to the appellate court that will decide them. There is no referral back to the court of first instance in case the appellate court affirms the decision. In other words, there is a full re-trial of the case. There are some exceptions to this rule. For example, when the appellate court affirms, on the same grounds, an investigative measure ordered by the first court, it will refer the case back to the first court. The exception does not apply when the Brussels Court of Appeals affirms a class action certification decision. In that case, the Court of Appeals has jurisdiction to deal with the rest of the procedure. Because the stakes in class action procedures are usually high, the certification decision will almost always be appealed (especially, of course, if no collective settlement is reached). This means that the procedure at first instance will be de facto limited to the certification issue. It will be the Brussels Court of Appeal that will approve a collective settlement reached after certification or that will render a decision on the merits of the case. Because of the backlog in this court it currently takes sometimes four or five years to have an individual lawsuit decided. In other words, class members will have to wait for years to get compensated.

Another example deals with the opt-out regime in some jurisdictions. In the Belgian class action act and in the proposed Dutch class action procedure there is only one opt-out 'round'. In Belgium, class members can opt out (or opt in, if the court has imposed an opt-in regime) after the certification decision has been notified. In the Netherlands, class members could opt out after the decision appointing a 'lead plaintiff' has been notified. In both instances, the choice is irrevocable. If a class member has not opted out, and afterwards disagrees with a collective settlement or the decision on the merits of the case, he will be bound by the *res iudicata* effect of that settlement or decision. Such a setting allows determination of the definite size of the group at an early stage of the proceedings, which can facilitate and encourage a collective settlement. However, this could also have the adverse effect that class members will simply opt out because their choice will be final and they do not know what the outcome of the procedure will be. If that happens, this could be detrimental to the interests of the defendants who want finality (ie, the lowest possible opt-out rate) when they enter into a collective settlement.

Finally, a lot of class action regimes struggle with devising a coherent and clear (back-end) framework for the distribution of damages after a collective settlement or decision. Problems of individual quantification of loss can present huge difficulties. Usually specific tailor-made techniques are missing.[121] Most jurisdictions (eg, the Netherlands) start from the naïve premise that the traditional tort rules can simply be applied. In other jurisdictions (eg, Belgium and France) complicated sub-procedures exist where one of the parties or a claims settler has to distribute the funds among the class members. In Poland, all class members have to claim the same amount, which forces people arbitrarily to form subgroups around specific but arbitrary amounts of money.[122]

121 In Belgium, Falla recently proposed a Quebecian-inspired toolbox to deal with the distribution of damages under the Belgian class action regime (E Falla, *Les dommages de masse. Propositions pour renforcer l'efficacité de l'action en réparation collective. Thèse visant à l'obtention du titre de docteur en sciences juridiques*, p 740, unpublished (on file with author); see <http://difusion.ulb.ac.be/vufind/Record/ULB-DIPOT:oai:dipot.ulb.ac.be:2013/239308/Details> accessed 04.01.2017).

122 See M Tulibacka, 'Class Actions in Poland – 2015 Update' <http://globalclassactions.stanford.edu/content/update-polish-class-actions> accessed 27.01.2017.

4.4. *Lack of appropriate funding and financing rules*[123]

The biggest obstacle to the effectiveness of many European class action regimes is the funding and financing controversy, which goes to the heart of any class action system. At the outset, it should be noted that most jurisdictions assume that class action procedures can and will be financed in the same way as individual procedures. This is simply not the case. Funding and financing class actions is a complex issue. It is challenging to embed this kind of procedure in the existing one-on-one litigation funding rules. In individual litigation, the costs and lawyer fees are (pre)financed by the identifiable plaintiff pursuing his individual claim, or a third party (eg, a lawyer, a legal-expenses insurer, a legal-aid scheme or a third-party litigation fund) directly connected with that plaintiff. In class action litigation, and at least at the outset of the procedure, the plaintiff acts on behalf of a group of unquantifiable and unidentified class members. Rational apathy and free-rider problems minimize the incentive for those members to invest in the litigation, leaving the funding to be paid for or organized by their agent (ie, the class representative) who will in most cases be confronted with wealthy and sophisticated repeat players as counterparties in the litigation. This results in an investment asymmetry.[124]

The fees and costs in question are also substantial. Collective redress procedures not only entail court costs and lawyer fees, but also specific class action related costs connected to: an intensive preparation stage, a complicated certification phase, multiple individual or non-individual notifications to class members, reaching a settlement, court ordered investigations, a possible elaborate trial on the merits of the case, internal administration and communication processes, potential distribution procedures etc. All these costs and fees need to be pre-financed, irrespective of the outcome of the case.

Due to the loser pays rule, which is well entrenched in the European legal tradition,[125] the final outcome of the case will ultimately determine who will have to bear some or all of these costs and fees. That the loser pays rule also should apply in collective redress procedures is suggested as the preferred policy option by the Commission in its Recommendation.[126] The rule is viewed as a safeguard against abusive litigation.

In a one-on-one setting, there are two principal actors on the initiator side: the plaintiff pursuing his individual claim and his (representing) counsel. Collective redress procedures are, from the plaintiff's side, characterized by a triangular structure. In addition to the class representative and the class lawyer, there are a number of unquantifiable and unidentified class members. Although they are not formal parties to

123 This subchapter is largely based on S Voet, 'The Crux of the Matter: Funding and Financing Collective Redress Mechanisms' in B Hess, M Bergström and E Storskrubb (eds), *EU Civil Justice. Current Issues and Future Outlook*, Hart Publishing, Oxford 2016, pp 201–22.

124 I Tzankova, 'Funding of Mass Disputes: Lessons from the Netherlands' (2012) 8 *Journal of Law, Economics & Policy* 549, 554. However, it should be noted that the financing issue is codependent on the scope of the litigation in terms of the amounts at stake. In Canada for example there is a lot less financing of class actions because Canadian cases are much less important in financial terms than American cases.

125 See C Hodges, S Vogenauer and M Tulibacka, *The Costs and Funding of Civil Litigation. A Comparative Perspective*, Hart Publishing, Oxford 2010, p 562.

126 Art 13 Recommendation.

the procedure, it is their rights that are being adjudicated in a decisive manner, in the sense that they are directly bound by the *res iudicata* effect of the decision, unless they have not opted in or have opted out. Therefore, the funding issue should be approached from this triangular structure: funding by the class representative (an individual class member, a governmental body or an association/foundation), funding by the class counsel, and funding by a third party (public funding, legal aid, legal-expenses insurance and third-party litigation funding). I have analysed this elsewhere.[127] My conclusion was that there is no clear-cut answer to the question of how collective redress actions should best be financed. The most sustainable solution seems to be a mixture of options: direct funding by a governmental body or organizational plaintiff, a governmental fund, tailor-made designed legal aid and legal-expenses insurance, regulated third-party litigation funding, and one-way cost shifting.

One funding method that is at the centre of attention is third-party litigation funding (TPLF).[128] The Recommendation supports TPLF, but recommends 'soft' regulation.[129] For example, the funder may not seek to influence procedural decisions of the plaintiff and may not charge excessive interest on the funds provided. Courts should be able to stay the proceedings where there is a conflict of interest between the funder and the plaintiff, or if the funder has insufficient resources. It is unclear whether some of the cases mentioned in the table in subchapter 4.1. were funded through TPLF. On the other hand, some TPLFs openly disclose on their websites the cases that they are currently funding.[130] In some jurisdictions, there is case law that could (negatively) impact future cases. In *Excalibur Ventures v Texas Keystone and others* the English Court of Appeal held that a private funder is required to pay the defendants' costs on an indemnity basis even if the funder is no party to the misconduct that led to the award of indemnity costs. The Court emphasised that third-party funders seek to derive financial benefit from claims just as much as funded claimants and that the 'derivative nature of a commercial funder's involvement should ordinarily lead to his being required to contribute to the costs' on the same basis as the funded claimant.[131]

127 See above n 123.

128 See J Kalajdzic, P Cashman and A Longmoore, above n 19; R Mulheron and P Cashman, 'Third Party Funding: A Changing Landscape' (2008) 27 *Civil Justice Quarterly* 312 and WH van Boom, 'Financing Civil Litigation by the European Insurance Industry' in M Tuil and L Visscher (eds), *New Trends in Financing Civil Litigation in Europe: A Legal Empirical and Economic Analysis*, Edward Elgar, Cheltenham 2010, pp 99–104. See also WH van Boom (ed), *Litigation, Costs, Funding and Behaviour. Implications for the Law*, Routledge, Abingdon 2017, p 246.

129 Arts 15–16 Recommendation.

130 Bentham Europe currently is funding the European Truck Cartel Claim, the Volkswagen AG Shareholder Action and the Tesco Shareholder Action (see <www.benthameurope.com/en/> accessed 04.01.2017). Claims Funding Europe is funding the European Truck Cartel Litigation, the European Air Cargo Cartel and an Action on behalf of investors against Volkswagen AG ('VW') (see <http://claimsfundingeurope.eu/projects/> accessed 04.01.2017).

131 *Excalibur Ventures v Texas Keystone and others* [2016] EWCA Civ 1144. See R Wheal, P Brumpton, A Hart and T Wingfield, 'Excalibur Litigation: Court of Appeal Confirms that Funders Will Be Put to the Sword' (November 2016)), <www.whitecase.com/sites/whitecase/files/files/download/publications/excalibur-litigation.pdf> accessed 04.01.2017.

5. Context

5.1. Public vs private enforcement

Another reason that could explain the limited success of European class actions, besides the sometimes problematic procedural design, has to do with the broader context in which these procedures are embedded. This first of all relates to the traditional dichotomy between public and private enforcement. I describe here the European policy in this regard. How this should be assessed, will be discussed in subchapter 7.

In common law jurisdictions, and most notably in the U.S., private class actions are viewed not just as vehicles for mass compensation, but also as regulatory enforcement mechanisms, intended to supplement the (by some arguable) failures of public enforcement. This relates to the 'private attorney general' role of class actions.[132] In Europe, the division between public and private enforcement has been much stronger, mainly because of historical reasons (the Napoleonic commitment to a strong central state and the Bismarckian support for an equally strong bureaucracy emphasizing technical expertise).[133] Public enforcement, through its reliance on state power, benefits from more effective investigative and sanctioning powers, by comparison to private enforcement. Moreover, public enforcement has the advantage of allowing better control in setting the optimal amount of the sanction.[134] Private actions for damages are driven by the private interests of the parties concerned, which may diverge from the general interest.[135] Private actions for damages are regarded as superior to public enforcement only with regard to the pursuit of corrective justice through compensation.[136]

This approach is echoed in the policy on collective redress. The Recommendation points out that the collective redress mechanisms it envisages are not of a regulatory nature. It is a core task of public enforcement to prevent and punish the violations of rights granted under Union law. The possibility for private persons to pursue claims based on violations of such rights only supplements public enforcement.[137] The Commission adheres to the principle that the compensation awarded to natural or legal persons harmed in a mass harm situation should not exceed the compensation that would have been awarded if the claim had been pursued by means of individual actions.

[132] See eg, JC Coffee, jr., 'Rescuing the Private Attorney General: Why the Model of the Lawyer as Bounty Hunter is not Working' (1983) 42 *Maryland Law Review* 215; B Garth, IH Nagel and S Jay Plager, 'The Institution of the Private Attorney General: Perspectives from an Empirical Study of Class Action Litigation' (1987–88) 61 *Southern California Law Review* 353 and W Rubenstein, 'On What a 'Private Attorney General' Is – and Why It Matters' (2004) 57 *Vanderbilt Law Review* 2129.

[133] See eg, WH van Boom and M Loos (eds), *Collective Enforcement of Consumer Law. Securing Compliance in Europe through Private Group Action and Public Authority Intervention*, Europe Law Publishing, Groningen 2007, p 258.

[134] WPJ Wils, 'The Relationship between Public Antitrust Enforcement and Private Actions for Damages' (2009) 32 *World Competition* 3, 10–11.

[135] Ibid, p 11–12.

[136] Ibid, p 15.

[137] Recital (6) Recommendation.

Punitive damages, which might lead to overcompensation of the claimant for the purpose of deterrence, should therefore be banned.[138]

On the other hand, the Commission recognises that in fields where public enforcement plays a key role (eg, competition, environment, data protection or financial services) private enforcement can play an important compensatory function. Private collective damages actions for victim compensation should follow on from infringement decisions adopted by public authorities and rely on them.[139] These are called collective follow-on actions. As mentioned above,[140] these exist in France and the UK. The ratio legis is that the public interest and the need to avoid abuse can be presumed to have been taken into account by the public authority as regards the finding of a violation of Union Law.[141] The follow-on action only deals with the questions of damages and causation. If the proceedings of the public authority are launched after the commencement in court of a collective action, the court should avoid giving a decision which would conflict with a decision contemplated by the public authority. To that end, the court may stay the collective redress action until the proceedings of the public authority have been concluded.[142] However, in the case of follow-on actions, the persons who claim to have been harmed should not be prevented from seeking compensation due to the expiry of limitation or prescription periods before the definitive conclusion of the proceedings by the public authority.[143]

5.2. Transnational context

Another context that is of importance is the transnational or global one. Although this probably has less to do with why European class actions are not so successful, I think it nevertheless should be noted here. It is a given fact that many mass harm situations are of a cross-border nature (eg, PIP breast implants case, the Volkswagen case, the Fortis case, the Apple case[144] etc).

The Recommendation stipulates that the Member States should ensure that where a dispute concerns natural or legal persons from several Member States, a single collective action in a single forum is not prevented by national rules on admissibility or standing

138 Art 31 Recommendation. See in general on punitive damages in Europe E Büyüksagis, I Ebert, D Fairgrieve, RC Meurkens and F Quarta, 'Punitive Damages in Europe and Plea for the Recognition of Legal Pluralism' (2016) 27 *European Business Law Review* 137; H Koziol, 'Punitive Damages. A European Perspective' (2008) 68 *Louisiana Law Review* 741; LRC Meurkens and E Nordin (eds), *The Power of Punitive Damages? Is Europe Missing Out?*, Intersentia, Cambridge 2012, p 533 and C Vanleenhove, *Punitive Damages in Private International Law. Lessons for the European Union*, Intersentia, Cambridge 2016, p 260.

139 Art 33 Recommendation.

140 See above subchapter 3.1.2.

141 Recital (22) Recommendation.

142 Art 33 Recommendation.

143 Art 34 Recommendation.

144 That turned out to be a more successful example of pan-European enforcement of consumer law (M Durovic, 'The Apple case today: Factual and legal assessment', EUI Working Paper LAW 2016/03, <http://cadmus.eui.eu/handle/1814/39054> accessed 27.01.2017).

of the foreign groups of claimants or the representative entities originating from other national legal systems.[145] Any representative entity that has been officially designated in advance by a Member State to have standing to bring representative actions should be permitted to seize the court in the Member State having jurisdiction to consider the mass harm situation. The Commission believes that in transnational or cross-border cases the current rules on judicial cooperation in civil matters are satisfactory to initiate a single collective action in a single forum. National rules on admissibility or standing may not prevent this. According to the Commission, the European rules on jurisdiction, recognition and enforcement of judgments in civil and commercial matters[146] and the rules on the applicable law (i.e., the Rome I and II Regulations[147]) are suitable and applicable in cross-border mass cases, and there is no need for specific rules.

The latter statement is simply not true. The coordination of cross-border collective relief has not been sufficiently addressed by the Recommendation and the Brussels Recast Regulation is not satisfactorily flexible for the effective enforcement of mass claims: 'cross-border uniformity is a remote prospect; indeed the Recommendation's limited provisions on cross-border standing raise the prospect of discrimination between representative entities from different Member States, forum shopping, and complex legal arguments over jurisdiction and applicable law, all of which will constitute additional barriers to justice for consumers'.[148] As some have rightly pointed out, 'consumers, potential litigants, lawyers and courts could at least have expected a clear framework of private international rules. Although, or even because, the issues of international jurisdiction and enforcement involve controversial arguments and require a balancing of different national interests, it is up to the European Union to take the lead and to use its core competence for regulating cross-border issues'.[149]

145 Art 17 Recommendation.

146 Regulation 1215/2012/EU of the European Parliament and of the Council of 12 December 2012 on jurisdiction and the recognition and enforcement of judgments in civil and commercial matters (recast) [2012] OJ L 351/1.

147 Regulation 593/2008/EC of the European Parliament and of the Council of 17 June 2008 on the law applicable to contractual obligations (Rome I) [2008] OJ L 177/6 and Regulation 864/2007/EC of the European Parliament and of the Council of 11 July 2007 on the law applicable to non-contractual obligations (Rome II) [2007] OJ L 199/40.

148 R Money-Kyrle, 'Legal Standing in Collective Redress Actions for Breach of EU Rights: Facilitating or Frustrating Common Standards and Access to Justice?' in B Hess, M Bergström and E Storskrubb (eds), *EU Civil Justice. Current Issues and Future Outlook*, Hart Publishing, Oxford 2016, p 251. See also B Hess, 'Cross-border Collective Litigation and the Regulation Brussels I' (2010) 2 *Praxis des Internationalen Privat- und Verfahrensrechts* 116; SI Strong, 'Cross-Border Collective Redress in the European Union: Constitutional Rights in the Face of the Brussels I Regulation' (2013) 45 *Arizona State Law Journal* 223 and BA Terradas, 'Consumer Collective Redress under the Brussels I Regulation Recast in the Light of the Commission's Common Principles' (2015) 11 *Journal of Private International Law* 143. See also MWF Bosters, *Collective redress and private international law in the European Union. Issues regarding jurisdiction and the recognition and enforcement of judgements in cross-border mass disputes relating to financial services*, Wolf Legal Publishers, 2015, p 330 and D Fairgrieve and E Lein, *Extraterritoriality and Collective Redress*, Oxford University Press, Oxford 2012, p 496.

149 A Stadler, 'The Commission's Recommendation on common principles of collective redress and private international law issues' (2013), 4 *Nederlands Internationaal Privaatrecht* 483, 488.

Besides the procedural efficiency rationale, such a coordination could fend off forum shopping, especially in the light of the Dutch case law claiming international jurisdiction.[150]

6. Alternative and new approaches of enforcement

6.1. *Consumer dispute resolution*

A second policy reason is the existence, in some sectors and in some Member States, of alternative and new approaches of enforcement,[151] that seem to be more efficient in offering redress compared to judicial processes. The first one is the out-of-court resolution of (mass) (consumer) disputes.

On the one hand, the Recommendation pays attention to this. It states that the Member States should ensure that the parties to a dispute in a mass harm situation are encouraged to settle the dispute about compensating the victims consensually or out-of-court, both at the pre-trial stage and during civil trial.[152] Appropriate means of collective ADR should be made available to the parties before and throughout the litigation. Use of such means should depend on the consent of the parties involved in the case.[153] Any limitation period applicable to the claims should be suspended during the period from the moment the parties agree to attempt to resolve the dispute by means of ADR until at least the moment at which one or both parties expressly withdraw from it.[154] Where a settlement is reached, its legality should be verified by the courts taking into consideration the appropriate protection of interests and rights of all parties involved.[155] Most recent class action regimes provide for such out-of-court avenues. The Dutch Collective Settlement Act is entirely based on this model.[156] In Belgium, for example, a collective settlement is possible in each phase: before the proceedings (in which case the parties can ask the court to approve the settlement), during the mandatory negotiation phase after the class action has been certified or during the procedure on the merits of the case.[157] Similar provisions exist in France.[158]

150 See above subchapter 3.1.3.

151 C Hodges, 'Mass Collective Redress: ADR and Regulatory Techniques' (2015) 5 *European Review of Private Law* 829. This subchapter is based on C Hodges and S Voet, 'Consumer Dispute Resolution Mechanisms: Effective Enforcement and Common Principles' in B Hess and XE Kramer (eds), *From common rules to best practices in European Civil Procedure*, Studies of the Max Planck Institute Luxembourg for International, European and Regulatory Procedural Law, no. 8, Nomos/Hart Publishing, Baden-Baden 2017, forthcoming.

152 Art 25 Recommendation.

153 Art 26 Recommendation.

154 Art 27 Recommendation.

155 Art 28 Recommendation.

156 See above subchapter 3.1.3.

157 S Voet, above n 28, p 134–36.

158 A Biard, above n 31.

On the other hand, a new world is emerging in the field of consumer redress: CDR (consumer dispute resolution).[159] CDR uses the traditional ADR techniques but within the context of a dispute resolution structure that is entirely separate from the courts. The CDR architecture encompasses a number of possible structures: arbitration, sometimes with mediation as a first stage; official quasi-arbitration but non-binding adjudication; regulated arbitration; complaint functions within public regulatory authorities; private sector ombudsmen, sometimes regulated; and statutory ombudsmen. CDR also encompasses ODR (online dispute resolution), which uses technology (the internet) to facilitate ADR.[160] The model here is usually binding arbitration, although the process, arbitrators and systems are not always transparent. However, online platforms also usually provide a direct communication channel between consumer and trader, which has a high success rate of negotiated and voluntary redress where the platform includes a self-regulatory feedback feature.

CDR gained momentum in 2013 when the European Parliament and the Council adopted a new Consumer ADR Directive and a Consumer ODR Regulation.[161] The Regulation establishes a free and interactive pan-European ODR platform through which consumers and traders can initiate ADR in relation to disputes concerning online transactions (offline transactions are excluded). National ADR entities receive the complaint electronically and seek to resolve the dispute through ADR. The ODR platform was launched in the spring of 2016.[162] The Consumer ADR Directive promotes ADR by encouraging the use of approved ADR entities that ensure the following minimum quality standards: the entities should be impartial and provide transparent information, offer their services at no or nominal cost, and hear and determine complaints within 90 days of referral. The Directive applies to domestic and cross-border disputes concerning complaints by a consumer resident in the EU against a trader established in the EU.

In the meantime, almost all Member States have implemented the Consumer ADR Directive.[163] In some Member States CDR thrives well, such as the Netherlands, the UK and the Scandinavian countries. They have behind them a long history of well-established and good functioning CDR bodies. CDR has become the mainstream method of resolving small consumer disputes. Other countries (eg, Belgium, France and Germany) have recently

159 N Creutzfeldt, 'The origins and evolution of consumer dispute resolution systems in Europe' in C Hodges and A Stadler, *Resolving Mass Disputes. ADR and Settlement of Mass Claims*, Edward Elgar, Cheltenham 2013, pp 223–25. See also C Hodges, 'Unlocking Justice and Markets: The Promise of Consumer ADR' in J Zekoll, M Bälz and I Amelung (eds), *Formalisation and Flexibilisation in Dispute Resolution*, Brill, Leiden 2014, pp 336–68.

160 J Hörnle, *Cross-Border Internet Dispute Resolution*, Cambridge University Press, Cambridge 2009, p 79.

161 Directive 2013/11/EU of the European Parliament and of the Council of 21 May 2013 on alternative dispute resolution for consumer disputes and amending Regulation (EC) No 2006/2004 and Directive 2009/22/EC (Directive on consumer ADR) [2013] OJ L 165/63 and Regulation (EU) No 524/2013 of the European Parliament and of the Council of 21 May 2013 on online dispute resolution for consumer disputes and amending Regulation (EC) No 2006/2004 and Directive 2009/22/EC (Regulation on consumer ODR) [2013] OJ L 165/1.

162 <https://webgate.ec.europa.eu/odr>.

163 For an overview see P Cortés (ed), *The New Regulatory Framework for Consumer Dispute Resolution*, Oxford University Press, Oxford 2016, p 472.

set up new ADR bodies. The first results are promising.[164] It is clear that these established and new CDR schemes are low-cost, quick and user-friendly. The vast majority are free or of minimal cost to consumers and issues are settled within a short period of time.[165]

CDR has two added values. First, although not particularly designed for this, many CDR regimes have the potential of processing mass problems. They are capable of identifying and processing multiple (similar or identical) claims and have developed aggregation techniques – similar to how courts aggregate bulks of claims – that deliver consistency of outcomes.[166] For example, in the Netherlands the Consumer Complaint Commissions regularly allocates a series of similar cases for hearing on the same day, thereby providing consistency of adjudication. The results of these cases are then communicated to the parties of other (suspended) cases and these parties are invited to settle their case.[167] Similar examples exist in the UK, with the Financial Ombudsman being the leading example.[168] Second, if well designed, CDR can go beyond mere dispute resolution. Hodges identified the five functions of CDR: (1) consumer advice, (2) dispute resolution, (3) aggregation of data, (4) publication of the aggregated data, as feedback to traders/sectors and information to consumers, competitions, regulators and investors and (5) improving market behaviour.[169]

6.2. *Regulatory redress*

Within the broader context of the transformation of (public and private) enforcement,[170] new trends and approaches emerge. One example is regulatory redress, which is redress that is ordered or brought about by the intervention of public enforcers.[171] Its strength is the combined weight of public/regulatory enforcement tools and civil/compensatory

[164] In Belgium for example the new Consumer Mediation Service (Belgium's residual ADR body), which was launched on 1 June 2015, received 2,921 complaints in 2015. The average handling duration was 38 days. In 48.5% of the cases a global settlement was reached. In 38.5% a recommendation was issued because a settlement could not be reached. In 19.5% of the cases the trader followed the recommendation. See <www.consumerombudsman.be/en>.

[165] C Hodges and N Creutzfeldt, 'Transformations in Public and Private Enforcement' in HW Micklitz and A Wechsler (eds), *The Transformation of Enforcement. European Economic Law in a Global Perspective*, Hart Publishing, Oxford 2016, p 128.

[166] C Hodges, above n 151, p 834–35.

[167] F Weber and C Hodges, 'The Netherlands' in C Hodges, I Benöhr and N Creutzfeldt-Banda, *Consumer ADR in Europe*, Hart Publishing, Oxford 2012, p 148–49.

[168] C Graham, 'Consumer ADR and Collective Redress' in P Cortés (ed), *The New Regulatory Framework for Consumer Dispute Resolution*, Oxford University Press, Oxford 2016, pp 427–46 and C Hodges, above n 151, p 836.

[169] C Hodges, 'Consumer Redress. Implementing the Vision' in P Cortés (ed), *The New Regulatory Framework for Consumer Dispute Resolution*, Oxford University Press, Oxford 2016, pp 353–54.

[170] See HW Micklitz and A Wechsler (eds), *The Transformation of Enforcement. European Economic Law in a Global Perspective*, Hart Publishing, Oxford 2016, p 424.

[171] For a typology see C Hodges, above n 151, p 841–45 (removing illicit profits; ordering redress to be paid; bringing a collective action; piggybacking civil claimants in public enforcement proceedings; referring assessment of loss to the court; ordering an infringer to create a restoration scheme; ordering an infringer to propose a compensation scheme; approving a compensation scheme proposed by one or more parties; referring a proposed compensation scheme to a court for approval; ordering an infringer to negotiate; etc).

tools.[172] The advantage, and at the same time incentive, for businesses is that all aspects of a (mass) harm situation are resolved in one process, thereby avoiding sequential public (i.e., criminal and/or regulatory) and private procedures and costs. Doing the right thing in providing redress can be incentivized by leniency in enforcement policies or by the advantage of maintaining high commercial reputation. It goes without saying that in order for regulatory redress to work, there need to be sufficient resources and more importantly, safeguards to protect the independence of the public enforcement agencies (such as publication of enforcement policies, fair procedural rules, a predictable and transparent process, ministerial and stakeholder oversight, the possibility for courts to impose more serious sanctions and a mechanism for appeals, etc.).[173]

A leading example is the Danish Consumer Ombudsman, a public enforcer who has exclusive standing to initiate an opt-out class action.[174] She uses the tool as a threat to compel wrongdoers into settlements that include all aspects, such as an agreement to cease infringements, an undertaking not to repeat, the repayment of consumers and the imposition of public sanctions. Companies, that sometimes approach the Ombudsman voluntarily, seem to prefer to resolve the redress issues first, in order to seek lower public sanctions or reputational benefits.

Another example is the UK, which has increasingly paid attention to regulatory redress.[175] The Macrory Principles have been pivotal in that evolution.[176] Macrory developed a set of six Penalty Principles that should underlie a modern regulatory sanctioning system. The two most important are that the purpose of a regulatory sanction is not to punish per se but to get the business back into compliance, and that a sanctioning system should ensure that no financial profit is made from non-compliance. All major UK regulatory authorities have been required to issue enforcement policies that conform to and take account of the Macrory Principles.[177] For example, the Regulatory Enforcement and Sanctions Act 2008 gave regulators the possibility to apply for extended powers to impose civil sanctions, which can include fixed or variable monetary penalties, compliance notices (requiring the offender to come back into compliance), restorations notices

172 See also E Braun, 'Collective alternative dispute resolution (ADR) for the private enforcement of EU competition law' (2016) <http://cadmus.eui.eu/handle/1814/44324> accessed 27.01.2017 ('The successful inducement of collective ADR necessitates a responsive strategy that takes into account the intricacies of behavioural research and the multi-layered incentives that need to be provided for the infringers and their victims. The public enforcer should be assigned the role of inducing voluntary compensation efforts through fine reductions, which necessitates some level of fusion between public and private enforcement.' (ibid, p 97)).

173 Hodges, above n 151, p 870–71.

174 P Kiurunen, N Lindström and M Bylov Rath, above n 26, p 193–94 and C Hodges, above n 151, p 845–46. See <www.consumerombudsman.dk/>.

175 C Hodges, above n 151, p 846–57.

176 R Macrory, *Regulatory Justice: Making Sanctions Effective, Final Report, November 2006* <http://webarchive.nationalarchives.gov.uk/20121212135622/http:/www.bis.gov.uk/files/file44593.pdf> accessed 05.01.2017.

177 Regulatory Enforcement and Sanctions Act 2008 (<www.legislation.gov.uk/ukpga/2008/13/contents> accessed 05.01.2017), Legislative and Regulatory Reform Act 2006 (<www.legislation.gov.uk/ukpga/2006/51/pdfs/ukpga_20060051_en.pdf> accessed 05.01.2017) and Regulators' Code (<https://www.gov.uk/government/publications/regulators-code> accessed 05.01.2017).

(requiring the offender to take steps to put right any damage caused as a result of the non-compliance and address any harm), stop notices and enforcement undertakings (legally binding voluntary agreements offered by those who may have committed an offence and accepted by the regulator). A 2015 recodification of enforcement powers has extended policy and powers on securing redress and changes in behaviour, giving enforcers extensive powers and discretion to fashion the appropriate redress to the particular situation.[178]

A third example can be found in the Italian Consolidated Law on Banking.[179] The law provides that the *Banca d'Italia*, Italy's central bank and a public institution, can issue "orders to redress", which order regulated entities (ie, financial institutions) to redress customers. This is usually done when consumer law provisions are violated. Although these orders do not provide any detail on how redress should be provided, they typically force the regulated entity to provide details on the number of consumers to be redressed and the sums involved. The orders can be published on the website of the *Banca d'Italia*. A fine can be imposed if the order is not complied with.

7. Conclusion: connecting the dots

7.1. End of the traditional public vs private model

In closing, four conclusions can be made. One, the binary and traditional classification of private vs public enforcement is outdated and unfit to properly address the issue of mass harm situations. Traditional private law has become public private law and public law has been privatized. Both have been replaced by a 'multilayered framework of regulation, lawmaking and law application'.[180] In the collective redress area, this is evidenced by empirical findings and shifts in policy. On the one hand, empirical research shows 'that a public/private dichotomy is of little use in analyzing legal responses to mass harms. Their relationship is more like a complex origami figure than two adjacent boxes. Actors, processes and outcomes overlap and intersect on a number of levels'.[181] Hensler and Thornburg discern three levels: (1) public processes often rely on private fact-gathering and the viability of private processes often depends on the outcome of public regulatory investigations and criminal prosecutions; (2) the actors in these mass action dramas play multi-faceted roles (eg, public entities appearing in private litigation) and (3) the outcomes of actions that are

178 Consumer Rights Act 2015 (<www.legislation.gov.uk/ukpga/2015/15/contents/enacted> accessed 05.01.2017).

179 Legislative Decree No. 385/1993 (<https://www.bancaditalia.it/compiti/vigilanza/intermediari/Testo-Unico-Bancario.pdf> accessed 05.01.2017).

180 This is a translation from Dutch to English of the title of the pivotal work in Belgium of Van Gerven and Lierman: W Van Gerven and S Lierman, *Algemeen Deel. Veertig jaar later. Privaat- en publiekrecht in een meergelaagd kader van regelgeving, rechtsvorming en regeltoepassing*, Kluwer, Mechelen 2010, p 515–23.

181 DR Hensler and E Thornburg, 'The public dimension of private collective litigation: A comparative analysis' in DR Hensler, C Hodges and I Tzankova (eds), *Class Actions in Context. How Culture, Economics and Politics Shape Collective Litigation*, Edward Elgar, Cheltenham 2016, p 276.

conventionally labeled as public and private overlap and interact (redress can act as regulation and public regulatory or criminal findings can provide a legal basis for redress).[182]

On the other hand, there are clear policy shifts. New approaches of enforcement and redress are emerging: 'a range of new techniques are being developed to deliver the objectives of behavioural compliance and of redress. Those objectives constitute restatements of what used to be called regulation and compensation, respectively delivered through criminal, administrative and/or regulatory structures and private law'.[183] According to Hodges and Creutzfeldt three aspects of the traditional public-private division have changed: (1) substantive law: the principles of the private law of damages still underpin payment of compensation or redress when a compensation order or consumer redress scheme is invoked in criminal or regulatory processes, but the details of damages law are in practice often of little importance, (2) forum: there is a shift from courts to CDR entities, ombudsmen and regulators, and (3) actors: besides lawyers in private litigation, regulators and CDR bodies have entered the stage.[184]

In other words, contrary to what the European policy makers continue to trumpet, the public vs private angle alone is unsatisfactory to efficiently address the problem of mass harm situations. One should look at other and novel angles.

7.2. Re-orienting collective redress mechanisms

It is clear that collective redress mechanisms, as components of private enforcement, are gaining momentum in Europe. A growing number of Member States has created class action or class action-alike tools to master mass harm situations, or is in the phase of doing so. Remarkably, most jurisdictions do not adhere to the principles as laid down by the European Commission in its 2013 Recommendation. Legislators follow their own course and craft legislation that best fits their legal-cultural system.[185] Nationalism is a sticky thing. Consequently, there is a panoply of models and a large variation in procedural schemes.

However, the number of actual cases being brought in most Member States is low, as the table in subchapter 4.1. shows. Much has to do with the – sometimes deficient – procedural design regarding scope, standing and other procedural modalities and features. The (occasionally exuberant, and not always substantiated by hard empirical evidence) fear of abusive or frivolous litigation has forced legislators to build in safeguards, thereby possibly inducing a catch-22 situation. Moreover, most jurisdictions do not provide appropriate and suitable funding and financing mechanisms. They assume that class action procedures can and will be financed in the same way as individual procedures, which is not the case.

There are two possible solutions to deal with this. On the one hand, one can plead for procedural reform and a more coherent (and binding?) European policy. This might be a naïve solution. Most European class action reforms are the result of a political compromise

182 Ibid.

183 C Hodges and N Creutzfeldt, above n 165, p 130–31.

184 Ibid, p 131.

185 See J Walker, 'Session 5. Cultural Dimensions of Group Litigation. General Report' in D Maleshin (ed), *Civil Procedure in Cross-Cultural Dialogue: Eurasia Context*, Statut, Moscow 2012, pp 413–58.

trying to reconcile the diverging interests of opponents and proponents. In other words, achieving the most optimal and efficient device is usually not the primary goal. The same applies for the European policy. The Recommendation 'is a political compromise based on the realistic estimation that, for political reasons, nothing else would be possible'.[186] It 'only offers a potpourri of diverging topics without giving any guidance or indicating any priority'.[187] Currently, there are no indications that after 2017, when the Commission will assess the implementation of the Recommendation in the Member States, this will be different. Class actions will remain a controversial issue and devising them will always be balancing on a thin line. Moreover, the specific legal culture of a jurisdiction will at all times affect the strength and features of any class action tool. The Dutch system will always prioritize a consensual and out-of-court model. Any German model will maximize party autonomy. The Belgian and French models will adhere to organizational or associational plaintiffs as class representatives. In the Scandinavian models, public bodies will continue to play a key role in defending collective interests. Developing general principles that transcend the national contexts seems a utopian, at least herculean, effort.

On the other hand, one should not throw the baby out with the bathwater. One should take a step back and look at the broader conceptual (dispute resolution) framework. In light of the alternative and new approaches that have come to the fore (see subchapter 7.3.), the way forward seems to be to re-orient the private collective redress model. Class actions should be molded and adjusted so they can fit into an integrated national framework (see subchapter 7.4.).

7.3. Alternative and new approaches

It has been shown above that new enforcement and redress mechanisms are appearing. In some Member States, CDR (consumer dispute resolution) has become, or is becoming, the mainstream method of resolving small consumer disputes. If well designed, CDR can capture and resolve mass problems. Because many CDR schemes can aggregate data, that can be exchanged with regulators, the mechanism can go beyond mere dispute resolution. Regulatory redress, which is redress that is ordered or brought about by the intervention of public enforcers, is still terra incognita. Nevertheless, the examples mentioned above show that it works and that in some contexts it can offer real, sustainable and impressive solutions – again, if it is well designed. There need to be sufficient resources and safeguards to protect the independence of the public enforcement agencies.

Although one may criticize these changes,[188] and despite the existence of caveats – there is no such thing as an ideal world –, these techniques are here to stay. In many jurisdictions CDR and regulatory redress were not the consequence of a well-targeted

186 A Stadler, above n 149, p 484.

187 B Hess, above n 87, p 12.

188 For example German scholars have fiercely criticized the CDR technique (eg, H. Eidenmuller and M Engel, 'Against false settlement: designing efficient consumer rights enforcement systems in Europe' (2014) *Ohio State Journal on Dispute Resolution* 261).

policy, but were developed and implemented by the sectors and actors themselves, making them market driven and thus unstoppable.

Moreover, and from a broader perspective, much also has to do with the dysfunctionality of some European justice systems and (again) national culture. Uzelac recently touched on the topic of the institutional and organizational incapacity of some European civil justice systems (including his own Croatia) impeding the development of different forms of collective litigation into serious procedural vehicles.[189] In many European countries, the (expensive (eg, UK), slow (eg, Belgium and France) or lamentable (eg, Italy)) state of the judicial system – 'the (European) wheels of justice grind slow'[190] – created a push towards alternative (ie, out-of-court) and new approaches. These will not go away. Hodges underlined the cultural aspect of CDR: 'one of the European Commission's motivations in developing CDR was that the EU is not, at heart, an adversarial culture, but seeks to build society based upon compromise and consensus. (…) The core moral idea is that one who has morally wronged another person must do somet*hing about it and make amends'.[191] From a collective redress perspective, these two broader perspectives should be taken into consideration.

7.4. Connecting the dots: a multilayered framework of regulation, lawmaking and law application

The bottom line is to connect the different dots. To put it simply, the approach should be 'and …and' and not 'or … or'. It is not choosing between white or brown bread, it is looking at how it is baked. The ultimate goal should be an integrated and holistic framework, or, as was mentioned above, a 'multilayered framework of regulation, lawmaking and law application'. Arguments to 'replace' public enforcement mechanisms by private or other mechanisms, or vice versa, are based on the wrong premise. The focus should be on exploring and optimizing *all* options for mass harm situations. Even more important is to connect these options so they can form an integrated (dispute resolution)

189 A Uzelac, 'Why no class actions in Europe? A view from the side of dysfunctional justice systems' in V Harsági and CH van Rhee (eds), *Multi-Party Redress Mechanisms in Europe: Squeaking Mice?*, Intersentia, Cambridge 2014, pp 53–74. Uzelac refers to three problems: '1. if a judicial system is not capable of securing litigation within a reasonable time in conventional, 'one-on-one' litigation, it will not be able to do any better in collective litigation; 2. if the effectiveness of judicial protection is limited due to the excessive availability of means of recourse that impede finality and prevent final enforcement, collective litigation cannot fulfil its main purpose; 3. if a civil justice system does not dispose of organizational and procedural mechanisms and case-management techniques for handling complex multi-party and multi-claim matters, any collective litigation device will be inappropriate and will be perceived as 'legal irritant'' (ibid, p 61).

190 'Europe's civil courts. The wheels of justice grind slow', *The Economist* 20.02.2016. See also The 2016 EU Justice Scoreboard, Communication from the Commission to the European Parliament, the Council, the European Central Bank, the European Economic and Social Committee and the Committee of the Regions COM(2016) 199 final 11.04.2016. See Chapter 3.1. Efficiency of justice systems: 'The length of litigious civil and commercial cases has in general improved (…). However, for the broad 'all cases' category (…) and for administrative cases (…), the length of proceedings has worsened in more countries than it has improved', ibid, p 16.

191 C Hodges, above n 159, p 365.

framework.[192] Only a broad and integrated instrumentarium, as a 'dispute resolution continuum',[193] which can avoid empty enforcement gaps, can tackle mass harm situations effectively and efficiently.[194]

Many models, again depending on the national context, are possible. In the CDR orbit, statutory forms of cooperation exist. Article 16 of the Consumer ADR Directive provides for cooperation and exchanges of experience between CDR entities. Member States have to ensure that CDR entities cooperate in the resolution of cross-border disputes and conduct regular exchanges of best practices as regards the settlement of both cross-border and domestic disputes. A network of national CDR entities has been set up. Article 17 focuses on the cooperation between CDR entities and public regulatory authorities, including the exchange of information on practices in specific business sectors about which consumers have repeatedly lodged complaints. It also supports feedback on market behaviour to traders, competitors and customers. The latter function can be vital in the resolution of mass consumer disputes. If a CDR entity or an ODR provider detects a collective problem – which they can easily do because they receive and store complaints electronically – and provides fast feedback to a regulator, the latter can intervene quickly to avoid an escalation of the dispute, or the CDR entity can itself apply a consistent generic approach to all of the similar individual complaints it receives. Such a scheme allows an integrated approach. If the regulator concludes that collective restitution should be provided, then it could cooperate with the relevant CDR entity.[195]

One of the conclusions of a recent study, analyzing the implementation of the Consumer ADR Directive in the various Member States, is the need for interconnection between courts, enforcement bodies and CDR.[196] In this study, Hodges noted that '[a] pathway should be built between [CDR] entities and the courts as well as regulators when statutory interpretation is at stake. A system of preliminary reference between [CDR] entities and regulators, which could in turn trickle up from regulators to national courts, should be put in place to ensure an adequate application of consumer law'.[197] Graham noted 'that an added value of [CDR] is that it can go beyond individual complaints, and provide redress to others entitled to it, but who have not complained'.[198]

192 See also E Bauw and S Voet, above n 40.

193 J Stuyck et al, *An analysis and evaluation of alternative means of consumer redress other than redress through ordinary judicial proceedings. Final Report.* 17.01.2007, <www.eurofinas.org/uploads/documents/policies/OTHER%20POLICY%20ISSUES/comparative_report_en.pdf> accessed 07.01.2017, p 5.

194 E Braun, above n 172 ('Ultimately, the enforcement toolbox should be diversified not only to ensure the successful fulfilment of the regulatory goals, but also to facilitate the transformations that are occurring in the enforcement landscape more broadly.' (ibid, p 1)).

195 C Hodges and S Voet, above n 151.

196 P Cortés, 'Conclusion. Ensuring the Provision of Consumer Dispute Resolution' in P Cortés (ed), *The New Regulatory Framework for Consumer Dispute Resolution*, Oxford University Press, Oxford 2016, pp 465–66.

197 Ibid, p 465 and C Hodges, above n 169, pp 351–69.

198 P Cortés, 'Conclusion. Ensuring the Provision of Consumer Dispute Resolution' in P Cortés (ed), *The New Regulatory Framework for Consumer Dispute Resolution*, Oxford University Press, Oxford 2016, pp 465 and C Graham, above n 168, pp 427–46.

In other words, 'when integrated into regulatory systems, [CDR] and dispute resolution models can enable private redress, enhanced public norms enforcement, and regulatory objectives of economic and market re-balancing (reallocating the cost burden of illicit behaviour from consumers to perpetrators), monitoring and behaviour control'.[199]

In conclusion, one can say that in Europe 'wild things' do exist. Nevertheless, and as in Sendak's book, they turn out to be not that wild at all. Moreover, they can and should be tamed so that one day they can live in harmony with other species.

[199] R Money-Kyrle, above n 148, pp 247–48.

Jaap Hage*, **

SHOULD AUTONOMOUS AGENTS BE LIABLE FOR WHAT THEY DO?

1. Introduction

After decades of developments in information technology and artificial intelligence, 'autonomous' systems have come to play important roles in our society. In the Netherlands decisions about study grants are in first instance taken by a computer programme. Computer programmes keep track of the stocks of shops and order new supplies if necessary. These orders are accepted by other computer programmes, which prepare the physical delivery of the ordered goods. Websites offer goods for sale, and sometimes make the price dependent on information they gather about potential customers.[1] These events and acts all take place in a virtual world, but also physical things have become autonomous agents. For quite some time already aircraft autopilots play an important role in air planes.[2] Weapons have been developed that take decisions about life and death without direct human interference, and the development of self-driving cars has drawn much attention.[3] The 'internet of things' is still on the brink of emerging, but it seems a safe prediction, that some of these 'things' will turn out to be autonomous systems.[4]

These new developments raise many questions. How will human beings respond to autonomous systems if they have to interact with them?[5] Is it morally right to have

* Universities of Maastricht and Hasselt, jaap.hage@maastrichtuniversity.nl.

** The author thanks Antonia Waltermann for valuable comments on an earlier version, and the participants in the workshop on Liability Law of the Ius Commune Conference on 24 November 2016 in Maastricht for illuminating questions after presentation of this article.

1 See, for instance, https://www.cnet.com/news/now-showing-random-dvd-prices-on-amazon/ (last visited on 22-11-2016).

2 See https://en.wikipedia.org/wiki/Autopilot (last visited on 22 November 2016).

3 E.g. https://ikhlaqsidhu.files.wordpress.com/2013/06/self_driving_cars.pdf (last visited on 22 November 2016).

4 See the contribution of Marco Loos to the present volume.

5 See, for instance, the overview of developments concerning sex robots on www.mirror.co.uk/all-about/sex-robots (last visited on 22-11-2016) and the development of 'social robots' (https://www.researchgate.net/publication/308928172_A_Human-Robot_Competition_Towards_Evaluating_Robots%27_Reasoning_Abilities_for_HRI; last visited on 22 November 2016).

machines take actions in matters of life and death?[6] And – from a legal perspective – is it possible and desirable to hold autonomous agents responsible and liable for what they did?

These last questions represent the core of the present article. Before going into more detail on the arguments to come, we must first mention a preliminary question: does it make sense to write about autonomous agents and their acts if we are not dealing with human beings? Can we say that software applications and automated physical systems really act, or are the real agents always human beings, who may use software and hardware tools to realize their intentions? If the latter is the case, the issues of responsibility and liability do not arise for these other systems. As will turn out later, the answer to the question whether it makes sense to write about autonomous non-human agents is a substantial part of the answer to the question whether it is possible to hold these agents responsible. The answer to this preliminary question can therefore only be given in the context of the main argument of this article.

Although the questions with which this article deals are highly relevant for the way in which law deals with autonomous agents, they are not typical legal questions. They cannot be answered by means of law itself, and traditional legal methods such as invoking legislation, case law and doctrinal literature, are therefore not useful. The argument of this article is mainly philosophical, and the method that is predominantly used is analysis.

In the following sections, the question will be addressed whether autonomous agents can be held responsible for their acts. In this connection autonomous systems are taken to be non-human systems which do things which would be considered acts if performed by humans.

The argument, which leads to the conclusion that autonomous agents can be held responsible for their acts, will be easier to follow if its main lines are presented first. The argument is based on an analogy between human beings and autonomous agents and its main element is that if humans can be held responsible, so can, in principle, autonomous agents. This argument can only be convincing if the relevant similarities between human beings and autonomous agents are more important than the relevant differences. An important part of the argument is therefore aimed at showing precisely this. The main point here is that the argument does not claim that autonomous agents are actually like human beings, but rather that human beings are actually like autonomous agents. This analogy can only lead to the conclusion that autonomous agents can be held responsible if it is assumed that human beings can be held responsible, even if they – as the argument assumes – are like autonomous agents. This will be argued indeed, and leads to the transition from the question whether human beings and autonomous agents can be held responsible and liable to the question whether it is desirable to do so. The answer to this last question is guardedly affirmative: it depends on the circumstances, but yes, sometimes it is desirable to hold human beings and autonomous agents responsible and liable for what they did. Therefore it sometimes makes sense to do so.

6 See www.cc.gatech.edu/ai/robot-lab/online-publications/formalizationv35.pdf (last visited on 22 November 2016).

2. The mental and the physical aspects of acts

The law normally holds human beings responsible for their acts. This claim is somewhat ambiguous, because of the many meanings the word "responsible" can have.[7] In this article we are interested in two senses of responsibility: responsibility in the sense of having performed some act, and responsibility as having to bear the consequences of the act, including legal liability. We will call the former act-responsibility, and the latter liability. In the present section we focus on act-responsibility.

Where act-responsibility is concerned, it is almost a tautology that human beings are typically responsible for their acts.[8] However, if humans are typically responsible while the responsibility of autonomous agents still needs to be argued, there must be one or more differences between humans and autonomous agents which seem at first sight relevant. Two differences which might make the difference are that humans act intentionally and on the basis of a free will, while autonomous agents have no intentions, nor a will, let alone a free will.

Let us assume for the sake of argument that, as a matter of fact, autonomous agents lack intentions and a will. However, they have in common with human beings that their 'behaviour' has a physical aspect and that this physical aspect partakes in the causal[9] processes that govern all of physical reality. Even if human behaviour is intentional, and based on a free will, what actually happens fits in the same causal chain of events in which also the 'acts' of autonomous agents fit. The question is therefore whether intention and free will make a difference; whether they play a role in the causal chains that lead to the physical aspects of acts. If they do not play such a role; they are in that sense redundant, and it seems dubious to base a difference in the attribution of responsibility on such redundant phenomena.

There are many reasons to assume that intention and free will do *not* play a role in the causal chains that lead to the physical aspects of acts. The present physical research paradigm, which assumes that physical events are caused by other physical events, works quite well and this paradigm leaves no room for intervening mental phenomena like intentions or the will.[10] It is completely unclear how physical events might be influenced by mental events and there is no evidence that such influence exists.

7 Hart famously distinguished four main kinds of responsibility (see HLA Hart, *Punishment and Responsibility*, 2nd edition, Oxford University Press 2008, pp. 210–237). More elaborate distinctions are also possible.

8 Almost, because we typically say that somebody is responsible in this sense for bringing about particular results, and not that somebody is responsible for, say, whistling. However, when it comes to acts that consist in bringing about a particular result, having performed the act and being responsible for the act that consists in bringing about the result (e.g. closing the window, committing a murder) are the same thing.

9 For reasons that will become clear in section 3.3, the word "causal" may be misplaced here. "Based on natural laws" would be a more adequate, but also more awkward formulation.

10 This research programme is described as naturalism in the illuminating catalogue of arguments against free will that was drawn up by Nahmias (Eddy Nahmias, 'Is Free Will an Illusion?', in Walter Sinnott-Armstrong (ed.), *Moral Psychology. Volume 4: Free Will and Moral Responsibility*, Cambridge (Mass.): MIT Press 2014, pp. 1–15.

Admittedly it *seems* obvious that mental events such as decisions influence human behaviour, but when we look at, for example, the brain processes which cause muscle contractions, the obviousness disappears. The obviousness of mental events causing physical ones only exists as long as we only look at human acts, and not at their physical manifestations in the shape of muscular contractions. As a matter of fact, even where acts are performed intentionally, there is some evidence that the intention to act only comes into existence after the physical process initiating the act has already started.[11] This makes it unlikely that the intention caused this physical process.[12]

This means that even if humans act on the basis of[13] intentions and free will while autonomous agents do not, this difference does not make a difference for what happens physically. It is therefore not at all obvious that this alleged difference between humans and autonomous agents should make a difference for holding agents, be they humans or autonomous agents, responsible for their acts. Whether such a difference should be made depends on the reasons why we do hold humans responsible, even if the mental aspects of their behaviour do not influence the physical aspects thereof.

3. The attribution of agency and responsibility

3.1. Experience of agency

Typical human agency is intentional, meaning that the acting person experiences himself[14] as acting, and experiences the act as being brought about by him, based on his will to act. This *experience* of one's own acts as being caused by one's intention to act should not be confused with the *perception* of independently existing facts such as seeing that some person acts, or that a will causes acts.[15] The sentence 'Jaap saw that Esther hit Veerle' is only true if Esther, Veerle and Jaap existed, if Esther hit Veerle and if Jaap saw this happening. The sentence 'Jaap had an experience of Esther hitting Veerle', on the

11 See for instance Benjamin Libet, 'Do We Have Free Will' in Walter Sinnott-Armstrong and Lynn Nadel (eds.), *Conscious Will and Responsibility*, Oxford University Press 2011, pp. 1–10. This evidence has been disputed for methodical reasons (e.g. Adina L. Roskies, 'Why Libet's Studies Don't Pose a Threat to Free Will', in Sinnott-Armstrong *o.c.*, pp. 11–22). However, this methodical disputation does not provide evidence for the claim to the contrary that intention and free will do play a role in causal processes, and is therefore not very strong in the argument in favor of a role for intention and free will.

12 It does not make it unlikely that the intention caused the act (even though it did not cause the muscular contraction that is part of the act), but that has to do with the fact that the notions of intention, causation and act all belong to the practice of agency that will be discussed in section 3.3. Within this practice it may make sense to say that the intention to perform some act caused this act (Searle's notion of prior intention, cf. John R, Searle, *Intentionality*, Cambridge: Cambridge University Press 1983, pp. 91–98), but this does not imply that the practice of interpreting acts as being caused by prior intentions makes sense in the light of modern science.

13 This formulation "on the basis of" is left deliberately vague, because, if it is not causation, it is not clear what the relation is between on the one hand intention and free will, and on the other hand acts.

14 Here I follow the convention that if the gender of a person is not relevant for the text, an author should use her or his own gender to refer to humans. In my case this means that I use male pronouns. I can only encourage female authors to use female pronouns.

15 This point was already made, be it in quite different wordings, by Searle in his *Intentionality*, p. 124.

contrary, can also be true if Esther, Veerle and the hitting event were all figments of Jaap's imagination. Therefore it is not without a doubt possible to conclude from the fact that Jaap had such an experience that the event really took place, or even that Esther and Veerle are real existing persons.

However, experiences are the building blocks of empirical knowledge; not infallible building blocks but nevertheless the starting point of theory construction. This also holds for the experience of acting, the experience of freely taking decisions on what to do, and the experience of causing events to happen. Experiences of agency and their abundance explain why humans beings for many centuries, if not millennia, conceptualize many events in terms of acts, agents, intentions and (free) will, and it also explains why legal discourse uses these same concepts on such a large scale and in such central contexts as the attribution of criminal and civil liability. The questions whether this conceptualization is valid in the sense that what is experienced also exists in reality cannot be answered solely on the basis of our experience of our own acts, however. From the fact that we experience ourselves as free agents who decide what we will do and who intentionally do what we decided we cannot derive the certainty that we do have a free will, and that this will determines what we will do. We must also look at the (physical) sciences to get a picture of what exists independent of our experience and to confront our experiences with the results of these sciences.

At their present stage of development, the physical sciences seem to leave no room for intentions and manifestations of will which *as such* cause acts.[16] The question therefore becomes how to fit these findings of the sciences with the way humans experience themselves. A plausible answer is that we should distinguish between two views of agency, the 'realist' one and the 'attributivist' one.

3.2. *The realist and the attributivist view of agency*

According to the realist view, the intention to act and the will that leads to the performance of an act are 'real' things, which exist independently of human experience. Our experience of them is on this view very much like perception, like an awareness of something that exists independent of the experience. Think for instance of the experience we have when we perceive a house. The house exists independent of our perceiving it, and the statement that John sees the house expresses a relationship (seeing) which exists between John and the house as independent entities. If 'intention' and 'free will' are interpreted as referring to 'real' intentions, and 'real' free will, intentions and will should exist independent of our experience of them. If intention and will are seen according to this realist theory, the view that human acts are caused by the intention to act and as the result of a free will, are according to modern science false.

16 The clause "as such" was added to account for the possibility that mental phenomena are in a sense identical to physical phenomena – configurations of the brain are the most likely candidate – and in their quality of physical phenomena cause the muscular movements which count as acts. This view is called the 'identity theory of mind-body'. An overview of several identity theories can be found in David M. Rosenthal, 'Identity Theories', in Samuel Guttenplan (ed.), *A Companion to the Philosophy of Mind*, Oxford: Blackwell 1994, pp. 348–355.

There is no reason to assume that intention and will influence the muscular movements that represent the physical aspect of our acts.

According to the attributivist view, intention and free will are attributed, or ascribed, to human agents. A person who ascribes intention and free will to himself can base this attribution on how he experiences his own acts. Attribution of intention and free will to others is based on an analogy to one's own experience. This attributivist view is supported by the fact that we do not only experience intentions in our own acts but that we also recognize them in the acts of others. Of course we cannot see these intentions, because – as the saying goes – we cannot look into somebody else's head.[17] However, going by the context in which a physical act was performed, we can recognize the intention in the act, very much like we recognize the will in juridical acts. This recognition does not concern some independently existing entity, but is essentially the attribution of an intention to acts, based on facts that we can 'really' see, or perceive in some other way. If somebody does something which is understandable and which does not seem to be caused by an external force, we take it that the agent acted intentionally. And if there are no reasons to assume that the act was caused by a factor that should not have caused it, we also assume that the act was the result of a free will.[18] Since it is up to us which factor we consider as illegal causes, it is up to us to determine which acts we count as based on a free will, as voluntary. Free will is on the attributivist view a matter of attribution, very much like intention.

3.3. *Expansion of the attributivist view*

From a purely physical (realist) point of view, there is little ground to distinguish between acts and other events; there are only events and in some of them human bodies are involved. This is different from the attributivist point of view. From this perspective, not all events in which human bodies are involved count as acts, while some events (or even absence of events) can count as acts even though no human body was involved. This is the case when omissions count as acts.[19] So, on the attributivist view, acts are the result of attribution too, and – since agency presupposes acts – the same holds for agency.

Moreover, it also holds for causation. As any lawyer who has studied the legal notion of causation knows, it is not a discovery of an independently existing fact when some act or other event is found to be the cause of particular damage, but it is a matter of attributing

17 Of course we can look into somebody else's head. What we cannot do is to look into somebody else's mind. However, we cannot look into our own mind either, since minds are not things that are amenable to being looked into. Our minds consist of *experiences*, and only our own experiences constitute our minds. We cannot experience somebody else's experiences, although we can have similar experiences.

18 Notice that this "should" makes freedom of the will a normative phenomenon. More on this normative notion of a free will in Jaap C. Hage, 'Rechtstheoretische analyse van de partijautonomie in het overeenkomstenrecht', in Ilse Samoy (ed.), *Evolutie van de basisbeginselen van het contractenrecht*, Antwerpen: Intersentia 2010, pp. 241–262, in particular sections 26 and 27.

19 See for the status of omissions as acts the illuminating account in Johannes Keiler, 'Commission versus Omission', in Johannes Keiler and David Roef (eds.), *Comparative Concepts of Criminal Law*, Cambridge: Intersentia 2015, pp. 47–77.

the status of cause to the act or event.[20] In social and physical sciences it is not very different. The reasons for attributing the status of a cause to something may differ from one field to another, but causation is always a matter of attribution rather than discovery.[21]

This, finally, leads us to act-responsibility for an act that consists in causing some result. If agency and causation are a matter of attribution, then responsibility must be a matter of attribution too. On the realist view, responsibility does not exist. There is no responsibility to be discovered in the 'outside world' analogously to the way we can discover a pond in the forest or a birthmark on somebody's skin. We cannot discover that somebody was responsible for some act, although we can discover facts that are grounds for attributing responsibility to somebody. For instance we can discover that Jane pushed a button and use this discovery as a ground to hold Jane responsible for the fact that the light went on and the fact that a prowler was chased away.[22] Responsibility is best accounted for on the attributivist view, and is then the result of attribution, rather than a 'real' phenomenon.

3.4. *The reality and relativity of what is attributed*

We should be careful not to assume that attribution is really nothing. What is the result of attribution is not 'real' in the sense of existing independent of human experience, but that holds for practically everything in law. Legal rights, legal duties, competences, judges, and criminal suspects, they are all the result of the application of a legal rule and as such the result of attribution.[23] We should not make the mistake to assume that what is the result of attribution does not really exist. What is the result of attribution is by definition not 'real' in the sense of mind-independent, but it does exist as the result of attribution. There are facts which are the result of attribution, and the sentences describing them are true in the same way as sentences describing 'real' facts. The sentence that Willem-Alexander was in 2015 the King of the Netherlands is as true as the sentence that in that same year the North Sea bordered on the English east coast.

This parallel to what exists in law is useful to illustrate that attribution is not always what one single person attributes; it can also be what 'we' attribute, or what the law, in the shape of rules, attributes. A person can hold himself responsible for some accident, while others do not agree that he is responsible. The law can have its own view as to whether this person is responsible for the accident. Therefore responsibility is in a sense

20 See, for instance, HLA Hart and T Honoré, *Causation in the Law*, 2nd edition (1st edition 1959), Oxford: Oxford University Press 1985.

21 Notice that this claim about causation in the physical sciences is limited to the notion of causation, according to which one fact or event *necessitates* some other fact or event. The claim that causation in the sense of necessitation is a matter of attribution does not extend to the regular connections that are discovered to hold between physical facts and events. In contrast to causes, these laws *may* exist in a mind-independent reality.

22 Cf Donald Davidson, 'Actions, Reasons and Causes', in Journal of Philosophy 60 (1963). Also in his *Essays on Actions & Events*, Oxford: Clarendon Press 1980, pp. 3–20.

23 Cf. N. MacCormick and O. Weinberger, *An Institutional Theory of Law* Dordrecht: Reidel 1986.

always relative to one or more persons who, or to a set of rules which attribute(s) responsibility.

3.5. Attribution to autonomous agents

What is 'real' does not depend on attribution and is mind-independent. What is the result of attribution, on the contrary, depends on human minds. This mind-dependency may be direct, as when somebody considers what somebody else 'does' as an act. It may also be indirect, as when the members of a tribe attribute the failure of rain to the anger of the gods which makes the anger of the gods the cause of the rain failure even if some members of the tribe do not believe this. It is also indirect when the law attributes the status of owner of a house to the daughter of a deceased person who used to be the owner. (The daughter is taken to have inherited the house.)

Because attribution is mind-dependent, agency and responsibility may theoretically be attributed to anything, and on any ground. It is possible to consider events as the acts of animals or of gods, or as the acts of organizations, and we may hold animals and organizations responsible and liable, even criminally liable, for their 'acts'. If we can attribute agency to organizations and hold them responsible and liable for their acts, we can do the same for autonomous agents. From the perspective of what can be done, there are no difficulties for the attribution of agency, responsibility and liability to autonomous agents. The question is not whether such attributions *can* be made, but whether it is *desirable* to do so.

4. The desirability of attribution

We attribute agency and responsibility to humans, and the reasons why we do so may illuminate our thinking about the attribution of agency and responsibility to autonomous agents.

4.1. Intuitive and reflected attribution

The attribution of agency and act-responsibility to humans beings is in first instance not done with a particular purpose in mind. It is more likely the outflow of how we experience ourselves as involved in agency, an experience which is projected on other humans. Whether we will attribute agency and act-responsibility to autonomous agents depends in first instance on our propensity to see these systems as similar to human agents. In this connection it should not remain unnoticed that we often in first instance seem to attribute agency to non-human actors, as when we say that the dog is asking to be walked, or that the computer formatted our text wrongly. To say that such attributions are merely metaphorical may reflect that we do not think it desirable to make such attributions, but ignores our intuitive analogizing between human and non-human 'behaviour'.

However, we do reflect on whether it is desirable to attribute agency to animals and organizations, and – in extreme cases such as severe mental illness – even to human beings. Moreover, if the outcome of this reflection is negative – it is not a good idea to attribute agency – the result is often that we stop attributing agency. What originally seemed to be an agent – the dog that 'asks' to be walked, or the computer that 'asks' for our password – turns on closer inspection only to be similar to an agent.

4.2. *When attribution of intention is desirable*

When is it desirable to attribute agency to some system, be it human, otherwise animal, or non-animal? To answer a closely related question – the question when it is desirable to attribute intentional states such as beliefs and desires to a system – Dennett introduced the notion of the "intentional stance".[24] Dennett contrasted the intentional stance to the astrological, the physical and the design stance.

On the astrological stance, we explain the past behaviour of a system and predict its future behaviour on the basis of the date and time of the origin of this system and of the 'laws' of astrology. For example, we would predict that somebody will soon find a lover from the date he was born. This stance is never desirable, because the predictions will fail too often and therefore also the explanations become untrustworthy.

The physical stance is desirable if we succeed in predicting the future behaviour of a system and explaining its past on the basis of the systems physical characteristics and our knowledge of the laws of nature. This physical stance works well for much of the non-animal part of the world, and many scientists expect it to work just as well in the long run for the animal part. As a matter of fact, large parts of medicine are presently based on the adoption of the physical stance towards human bodies.[25]

The behaviour of some non-animal systems can even better be predicted and explained from the intentions of their makers than from their purely physical characteristics. Take for instance a television set. If we push a button on the remote control, the set turns on. That it will do so is in our experience so natural that we do not even need the user manual of the set to switch the TV on in this way. We can predict the behaviour of the set, because we expect it to be designed to turn on if the button is pressed. Theoretically it should also be possible to predict the reaction of the set to the button push from the set's physical characteristics, but that is so difficult that most humans are not able to do so. The design stance – assuming that the set was designed to operate in a particular way – is in this case more fruitful than the physical stance. Therefore it is desirable to take the design stance towards television sets.[26]

It should be noted that the physical and the design stance do not exclude each other. We can fruitfully both approach a television set as a purely physical system and as a system designed to fulfil certain functions. It is a matter of what works best whether the physical or the design stance should be adopted, and it is for instance not so that we should take the design stance to things that were designed. If a television set is defect,

24 Daniel Dennett, 'Intentional Systems' in his *Brainstorms*, Brighton: The Harvester Press 1981, pp. 3–22, and 'True Believers' in his *The Intentional Stance*, Cambridge (Mass.): The MIT Press 1987, pp. 13–35.

25 Notice the move from "humans" to "human bodies". Not everybody likes this move in medicine.

26 That the set is a television set, rather than a heap of electronics, is also part of approaching the 'heap' from the design stance.

we'd better approach it from the physical stance. Moreover, it is useful to adopt the design stance to the results of evolutionary processes, even though evolution is not a matter of design. For instance, it makes sense to ask what the purpose is of the long neck of a giraffe in order to explain the neck's length and to predict whether the length will still increase in the centuries to come.[27]

The intentional stance, finally, should be adopted towards a system when the behaviour of the system is best explained and predicted if we attribute beliefs and desires to the system. This works well for human beings: we can predict the presence of students in the lecture hall from their desire to learn (about the exam) and their belief that the lecture will reveal what will be asked on the exam. It also works quite well for higher animals: we can explain the search behaviour of a chimpanzee from its belief that there is food hidden at some place, and its desire to have the food.[28] It even works for non-animal systems: we can predict the move of a chess-playing computer programme from its desire to check-mate and its belief that a certain move will check-mate the opponent.

It may be objected to the last example that the behaviour of the programme can also be explained from the design stance. The observation that the design stance may also lead to explanations of the programme's past behaviour and correct predictions of its future behaviour may be correct, but the adequacy of the design stance does not preclude an even greater adequacy of the intentional stance. In fact, the two may be combined in a fruitful fashion: assume that the system was designed to use a strategy (try to check-mate) and to employ its knowledge of the board position, the possible moves, and the value of the pieces to execute its strategy. The adoption of the design stance may in this fashion lead to the adoption of the intentional stance and to the attribution to the chess-playing programme of desires (the strategy) and beliefs (knowledge of the board position, the rules of chess, and an evaluation function for board positions).

4.3. *When attribution of agency is desirable*

The step from chess-playing programmes to 'intelligent' physical systems such as cruise missiles and self-driving cars is only minor. Although it is possible to approach them from a purely physical stance, and also from a design stance, their behaviour is most fruitfully explained from the assumptions that these systems reach for some goals (destroy the target; arrive at a particular destination), and that they employ their knowledge (about their geographical position, about the location of defense-missiles, or about the availability of roads) to achieve their goals.

Moreover, it is also a minor step from the intentional stance to the agency stance, if these two can be separated at all. The cruise missile adapts its course to avoid defense-missiles, or to correct for heavy winds; the self-driving car breaks to avoid a collision, or

27 However, some see the fact that the living parts of nature are fruitfully approached from the design stance as a reason to assume that these parts of nature must have been designed. This is a central theme of Daniel Dennett, *Darwin's Dangerous Idea*, London: Penguin Books 1995. See also Richard Dawkins, *The Blind Watchmaker*, London: Longman 1986.

28 Cf. Frans B.M. de Waal, *Are We Smart Enough to Know How Smart Animals Are?*, London: Granta Books 2016.

takes a detour because it received info that some road is blocked because of road works. Adapting course and breaking are best explained and predicted on the assumption that these systems *act* on the basis of their strategies and their knowledge. To this extent it is desirable to attribute agency to some autonomous agents.

In addressing the question whether and when it makes sense to adopt the intentional stance towards systems, Dennett focused in particular on the facilitation of predictions about the system's future behaviour. It is desirable to adopt the intentional stance towards a system if this makes it easier (than any other stance) to predict the system's behaviour. Analogously one might argue that it is desirable to adopt the agency stance towards systems if this makes it easier (than any other stance) to predict the systems' behaviour. However, it is not unavoidable to make predictive power the one and only criterion for the desirability of the adoption of the agency stance attributing agency, or – which boils down to the same thing – for the attribution of agency. Other criteria, next to or even instead of, predictive power may also be used. For example, one may have religious reasons to attribute agency only to human beings. Or one may believe that in the end science will reveal that there are substantial differences between humans and other systems, which justify the view that only humans should be seen as agents. However, the somewhat artificial nature of these examples suggests that predictive power may be the best criterion for which stance to adopt, although there is no ground to postulate that it is the only possible criterion.

5. The attribution of liability

The attribution of agency can be contemplated from the perspective of explanatory and predictive power. However, agency can also be contemplated from the perspective of purpose: why should we call something an act and attribute this act to an agent? The answer to this latter question will often be that we attach consequences to agency. If an agent is act-responsible for some event, this is a ground to call this even an "act" and to hold the agent liable for what he did. Moreover, this relation between the two kinds of responsibility works in both directions: we attribute agency because we want somebody to be liable and we hold somebody liable because he performed the act in question and – for some cases of liability – because he thereby caused the damage.

This raises the question why we would want to make an agent liable. The question is very abstract, and to make the attempt to answer it more concrete, we will focus on two questions, assuming that the answers will be related:

1. Why should we want to make one person (a human being) liable for the damage suffered by some other person?
2. Why should we want to make an autonomous agent liable for the damage suffered by some person?[29]

[29] These questions exclude criminal liability, although *prima facie* there is little reason to treat criminal liability differently from civil liability.

The questions do not distinguish between contractual and tort liability, because *prima facie* there seems to be little reason to make the answer to the general liability question dependent on whether there is a contract. Of course that does not exclude that the answer to the question whether there is liability in a concrete case may depend on whether the basis for liability is tort or contract, or still something else.

The answer to the first question can go into two directions. The one direction is that somebody should be liable for somebody else's damage because he deserves to be liable, most likely because he caused the damage. We will consider this direction in more detail in section 6. The other direction is that liability serves some purpose, such as prevention of future damage, the achievement of distributive justice, or popular satisfaction. Popular satisfaction as ground for liability is strongly connected to the idea that the liable person deserves to be liable, because the idea that the person who caused damage must compensate it is quite popular and the effectuation of this idea may therefore lead to greater popular satisfaction. We consider the purposive direction in section 7.

6. Deserved liability

One representative of the view that an agent is liable for particular damage because he deserves to be liable is Ripstein.[30] According to Ripstein, tort law is based on two principles. The one principle is that people accept reciprocal limits on their freedom. For our present purposes, this principle is not very relevant. The second principle is that people bear the costs their unlawful conduct imposes on others. This principle is reformulated as the principle that if one person wrongs another, the latter's loss becomes the former's to deal with. It is this last formulation which suggests the relevance of desert for liability. Apparently the fact that the behaviour that caused damage was a wrong is a reason to make the wrongdoer pay for the damage. This only makes sense if a wrongdoer somehow deserves to become liable, because if that is not the case, it is still an open question why somebody who violates a norm of conduct should become liable for the resulting damage. That question might be answered by pointing out desirable consequences of moving liability from the victim to the wrongdoer, but then the justification is not based on the wrongness of the act anymore, but on the purpose of moving liability. Seeing in wrongness a reason to attribute liability makes only sense on the assumption that a wrongdoer somehow deserves to become liable.

6.1. Justification within a practice and justification of a practice

When it comes to the explanation of how tort law operates, or – perhaps better – how tort law has operated in the past,[31] Ripstein is likely to be right. Somehow people assume that it is not always allowed to damage somebody else's interests, and that if one does so

[30] Arthur Ripstein, 'Philosophy of Tort Law', in Jules Coleman and Scott Shapiro (eds.), *The Oxford Handbook of Jurisprudence and Philosophy of Law*, Oxford University Press 2002, pp. 656–686.

[31] As is well-known, there is a development in tort law from fault liability (based on desert) to strict liability. This development is in line with the argument of this article, although the view that liability is

nevertheless, this is a reason why the tort-feasor has to compensate the damage that resulted from his illegal behaviour. This is part of the practice of tort law, a practice which also assumes that it is possible to identify acts, agents, and damage, and to identify some act as the cause of particular damage. Working from this practice it is possible to attribute particular damage to a particular act and a particular agent, and to attribute responsibility for the damage to the agent. That this practice presupposes that the agent deserves to be liable can be seen from the demand, now less commonly made than it used to be, that the agent could be blamed for his act. Given this practice, the judgement that some person is liable for the damage of some other person can be justified if the conditions for liability specified by the practice are satisfied. This is how tort law operates, and how tort law justifies liability.

However, justification of liability on the basis of tort law only makes sense if the practice of tort law itself makes sense. To see this dependence of justification from within a practice on the justification of the practice itself, it is useful to consider a practice which many people do not consider to be justified, the practice of rain dancing. This practice uses dancing as a way to make it rain. Suppose that a rain dance, if it is to work, must satisfy certain demands, such as a sacrifice of a goat preceding the dance. Is this sacrifice justified? Yes it is from the perspective of the practice, because if the sacrifice is not made the rain god may be insulted and does not reward the ensuing dance with rain. However, if we step outside the practice, as the readers of this text will most likely do automatically, the sacrifice does not make sense, because there are no rain gods that can be insulted by not sacrificing a goat, and a rain dance will not work anyway. Therefore the sacrifice of the goat, if it makes sense at all, only serves to placate the ignorant observers who demand this sacrifice to be made.

Perhaps many readers will not like the parallel, but a similar argument may be made about the practice of tort law which attributes liability to agents because they deserve to be liable because of their unlawful act. Only if this practice as a whole makes sense, including its presuppositions about acts, agents, damage, and causation, it makes sense to justify the attribution (and enforcement!) of liability from within this practice.

6.2. *The hermeneutic fallacy*

It is tempting to justify the practice of tort law by trying to understand it 'from within'.[32] The justification then consists of identifying the elements of the practice and justifying

the result of purposive attribution was not necessarily the main cause of the development as it has actually taken place.

32 Lucy writes in this connection about the "methodological injunction": the demand that "... any adequate theoretical account (or explanation or understanding) of any social action, practice or institution must, in first instance, capture the way in which that action, practice or institution is understood by those whose patterns of behavior and thought constitute that action, practice or institution" (William Lucy, *Philosophy of Private Law*, Oxford: Oxford University Press 2007, p. 272. As long as this methodological injunction is seen as a technical norm, prescribing what is necessary if one wants to understand a social practice, it may be well defendable. However, it becomes problematic as soon as this understanding of a social practice starts to function as a justification.

them on the basis of the principles underlying the practice. This is what Ripstein did when he tried to justify tort law by identifying two principles which could in his opinion explain the more detailed rules of tort law. We find a similar approach in the work of Weinrib, when he tried to understand – but understanding is meant as justification here – private law from its internal purposes, rather than from external purposes which are served by it.[33] Moreover, the same approach to the attribution of liability can be found in the work of Dworkin, who also claims that the practice of law must be understood from within.[34]

Understanding is a psychological category, which has no other standards than the feeling that one understands and there is nothing wrong with attempts to understand a practice from within if such attempts lead to the feeling of understanding. However, given the psychological nature of understanding it cannot justify a practice that is understood. It is a fallacy to assume otherwise, and we may well call this common fallacy the hermeneutic fallacy: a social practice is justified if we understand why it does what it does. This hermeneutic fallacy is a special case of the fallacy to derive how something ought to be done from the way it is actually done. From the fact that some social practice, e.g. tort law as it used to function, exists, it cannot be concluded that it should continue to function that way, or that the practice should continue to exist. This does not mean, of course, that the practice is wrong, but only that the reasons for its existence cannot be found within the practice itself.

Rain dancing cannot be justified by understanding it, and neither can liability law. So, even if Ripstein is correct in his finding that tort law is amongst others based on the principle that people bear the costs their conduct imposes on others, this does not show that it is right to attribute liability for damage to some person for the reason that this person caused the damage and therefore deserves to be liable.

6.3. *Capacity and desert*

The argument of the previous two subsections only rebuts one type of argument why liability is based on desert, the argument from understanding the practice as it actually is; it does not attack that conclusion itself. It is now time to address the conclusion: should people be held liable for damage for the reason that they deserve to be liable?

The answer to this question depends on whether people sometimes deserve to be liable. If nobody would ever deserve to be liable, it is rather useless to sustain the practice of holding people liable because of desert: nobody would ever be liable. As a matter of fact, we do assume that people sometimes deserve to be liable and we do sometimes attribute liability to persons because they deserve it. However, the question is not whether this practice exists, but whether it is justified, whether it makes sense. That depends on the reasons why we assume that people sometimes deserve to be held liable. Which reasons are actually recognized is a matter of empirical investigation, but here we will investigate

33 See Ernest J. Weinrib, *The Idea of Private Law*, Oxford University Press 1995, chapter 1.

34 Ronald Dworkin, *Justice for Hedgehogs*, Cambridge: Harvard University Press 2011, pp. 227–231. On page 229 Dworkin almost explicitly presents interpretation as a means of justification.

one such a reason which may be the most important one. Somebody deserves to be liable because through what he did he caused damage to somebody else and he should not have done what he did because of the damage it would cause.[35] This reason makes sense on the presumption that people can avoid wrongful acts for the reason that they recognize that wrongfulness. In the vocabulary that is nowadays fashionable one might say that desert depends on reason-responsiveness.[36] Are people reason-responsive in the sense required for the assumption of desert? It depends on how we understand reason-responsiveness, but it will be argued that in the most relevant sense people are not reason-responsive.

However, first we need to consider a brief note on the attribution of capacity. The question what a person could, or could not, do depends in an important sense on the capacities we attribute to this person. Capacity and therefore also reason-responsiveness are a matter of attribution, just like act, agency, causation, responsibility and liability. The argument for this claim will be presented in section 6.6, but if we assume that the claim is correct, the observation – or rather attribution – that somebody is reason-responsive does not help us much further in our search for the foundation of liability. The broad practice of agency attribution, which does not only include the attribution of agency, but also the recognition of acts and causation, cannot be justified by the nth element of this very practice. In order to avoid this complication we will replace the question whether a person could have avoided his damage-causing behaviour by the question whether it would have been possible that he avoided this behaviour. The questions may seem the same, but the crucial difference is that the former question is typically answered through the broad practice of agency attribution which includes the attribution of capacities, while the latter question has no direct ties to agency and does therefore not depend on this practice.

6.4. *What is a capacity?*

Let us assume for the sake of argument that an agent has the capacity to do something if it is possible that he does it. But what does that mean? Possibilities are the most interesting in case they were not realized, because if something is the case it is obvious that it must have been possible. It is notoriously difficult, however, to establish the existence of possibilities in case they were not realized. To deal with this problem, a thinking device was constructed: possible worlds theory.[37] The basic idea underlying possible worlds

35 Not coincidentally, this reason is very close to the second principle underlying tort law which was identified by Ripstein.

36 See for instance Stephen J. Morse, "Criminal responsibility and the disappearing person", *Cardozo Law Review* 28 (2007), pp. 2545–2575, and Michael McKenna and D. Justin Coates, "Compatibilism", in *The Stanford Encyclopedia of Philosophy* (Summer 2015 Edition), Edward N. Zlatan (ed.), URL = <http://plato.stanford.edu/archives/sum2015/entries/compatibilism/>.

37 The idea of possible worlds theory can be traced back at least to the German philosopher Leibniz (1646–1716), who in his *Theodicies* defined necessity as that what is the case in all possible worlds. A technical account of possible worlds, under the for logicians usual name of model-theoretic semantics or model theory, can be found in several chapters of Brian F. Chellas, *Modal logic; an introduction*, Cambridge: Cambridge University Press 1980.

theory is that something is necessary when it is the case whatever else may be the case. For instance, whatever the other facts may be, in any case every colored object has a surface and whatever the other facts may be, the number 5 is bigger than the number 3. Therefore, necessarily every colored object has a surface and necessarily 5 is bigger than 3. A different way of expressing that something is the case whatever else may be the case is to say that it is the case *in all possible worlds*. In all possible worlds every colored object has a surface and in all possible worlds the number 5 is bigger than the number 3.

Something is possible if it is the case *in at least one possible world*. The actual world consists of all the facts as they happen to be, while a different possible world contains a set of all facts as they might have been under different circumstances. In the real world John has brown hair, but under different circumstances, in some other possible world, John is red-headed. Because there is some alternative possible world in which John is red-headed, it is possible that John is red-headed. In fact, he is not, but he might have been. Something is possible if it is the case in some possible world. That may be the actual world, but that is not necessary.

This idea can also be applied to acts and agents. In the actual world, Jane did not visit her mother, but in some other possible world she did. Therefore, actually Jane did not visit her mother, but it would have been possible that she did so. In this sense, Jane had the capacity to visit her mother. This captures the notion of a capacity quite well. That would mean that an agent has the capacity to do something (including omission) if there is some possible world in which he does it. Notice that this notion of capacity avoids the use of attribution, at least that seems at first sight to be the case.

6.5. *Possible worlds and constraints*

We now have a definition of what it means that a person has a certain capacity, but it may seem that this definition has replaced one problem, the nature of capacity, with another problem, the nature of a possible world. What makes a set of facts a possible world? Here the notion of a constraint plays a role.[38] Not all facts can go together. To give an obvious example: the fact that it is raining (here and now) cannot go together with the fact that it is not raining. Incompatible facts cannot be part of one and the same possible world. That is a constraint on possible worlds. A logical constraint in this case, because it is a matter of logic that these facts cannot go together. Next to logical constraints, there can also be physical constraints. The laws of physics can be interpreted as constraints on worlds that are physically possible. It is, for instance, physically possible that a metal bar is red, but it is physically impossible that a metal bar is heated but does not expand. There is no physically possible world, no world that satisfies all the physical constraints, in which a metal bar is heated but does not expand. And neither is there a physically possible world in which something travels faster than light in vacuum.

[38] More about constraints and their relation to possible worlds in Jaap Hage, 'The (onto)logical structure of law', in Michal Araszkiewicz and Krzystof Pleszka (eds.), *Logic in the Theory and Practice of Law Making*', Cham: Springer 2015, pp. 3–48.

We are now in a position to define possible worlds more precisely. A possible world is a world that satisfies a set of constraints. A logically possible world satisfies the laws of logic; a physically possible world satisfies the laws of physics. A particular world counts as possible if it satisfies a set of constraints. Only relative to such a set does it make sense to ask whether something is possible or necessary. Necessity or possibility *tout court*, without being made relative, does not make sense.

Both logically and physically it is possible that John is red-headed, but is it still possible if we take into consideration that John just finished dying his hair brown? That is apparently not the case, and it is worthwhile to consider more closely why that is not the case. Both with logical and with physical necessity (and possibility) the necessity is the result of constraints that consist of laws, the laws of logic and of physics respectively. A law expresses a necessary general connection between *types* of facts, for instance the type of fact that something is a metal bar that is being heated and the type of fact that this something expands. When we speak of possible worlds, such laws are the most obvious constraints to take into account. However, it is not necessary to take only laws into account as constraints. There is no fundamental reason why particular facts should not be considered as constraints too. One such a fact might be that John just finished dying his hair brown. Given that fact, it is necessarily the case that John's hair is brown, and impossible that his hair is red. And given the fact that the train Marco was on departed five minutes ago, it is impossible that he was seen at the railway station one minute ago. In particular in connection with capacities it is important not to take only laws into account as constraints on possible worlds, but also facts. If it is claimed that Jane could not visit her mother, this claim will probably not only be based on the laws of nature (purely physical necessity), but also on facts concerning Jane's personal history.

6.6. *The relativity of capacity*

An agent has the capacity to do something if there is a possible world in which the agent does it. Now we know that this specification of capacity is still too vague: we also need to specify relative to which set of constraints the capacity exists. The crucial question is: which set of constraints should be taken into account in determining whether a particular agent had the capacity to perform some act, or to refrain from performing it? Here we will not attempt to answer this question in abstract, but focus merely on the characteristics of individual agents.

It is clear that in determining the capacities of a particular agent, we should take some personal characteristics of this agent into account. Going only by the laws of logic and of physics, which are the same for everybody, every agent would have the same capacities. That would be an unattractive finding, and to avoid it, we must take personal characteristics into account in determining which capacities some agent has.[39] But which personal characteristics should be taken into account? If the agent cannot drive a car, we should most likely take that into account. So if Jane could not drive a car, she did

[39] A related account of what an agent can or cannot do, is Tony Honoré, 'Appendix: Can and can't' in his *Responsibility and Fault*, Oxford: Hart Publishing 1999, pp. 143–160.

not have the capacity to visit her mother (let us assume) and most likely she should not be held responsible for not visiting her.[40]

Stepping back from this casuistry, the general issue is the following: if all facts regarding an agent are taken into account, as well as all physical and other possibly relevant laws, there are two possibilities. On a deterministic world view, only one possible course of the world is possible if all previous facts and all laws are taken into account. On a non-deterministic view, it is arbitrary what the course of the world will be, even if all previous facts and all laws are taken into account. However, on both views it does not seem reasonable to attribute responsibility to an agent for what he did. In the deterministic case not because the agent could not do anything else than what he actually did. In the non-deterministic case because it is arbitrary what the agent does, and therefore not dependent on the agent himself.[41] There is no middle way according to which the agent determines what he will do, because everything about the agent that might be relevant for the determination what he will do is *ex hypothesi* included in the set of all constraints. Given these constraints the agent is either determined to do what he will do, or his act will be arbitrary, and therefore not dependent on the agent himself. In neither case there is a ground for attributing responsibility.

The distinction between what an agent did and what he had the capacity to do makes only sense if not all facts are taken into account as constraints on what is possible. For instance, in determining whether Charles had the capacity to avoid the car accident we do take into account that in general Charles is capable to drive a car, but we do not take into account that on this very occasion he was distracted by his quarrelling children on the back seat. Therefore we conclude that Charles could have avoided the accident, and since he did not avoid it, we hold him responsible and liable for causing the accident.

When we take this approach, the question arises which facts should be taken into account, and which facts should not. Capacity becomes a normative issue, the issue which facts *should* be left out of consideration to determine what else the agent could have done next to what he actually did. Perhaps this seems an acceptable approach; after all it is what lawyers are actually doing when they ask whether a defendant could have acted differently than he actually did. We should realize, however, that if we make capacity a normative notion, it becomes a matter of attribution (as already mentioned in section 6.3) and we can no longer adduce the capacity of an agent as a reason for holding the agent responsible. What we actually do is to give one single normative judgment concerning both the capacities and the responsibility of the agent. Either we judge the agent to have the relevant capacities and to be responsible, or we judge him to lack the capacities and not to be responsible. This judgment cannot be founded in the capacities of the agent, because these capacities are themselves part of the judgment. To do otherwise would be a circular argument.

40 That might be different if it was Jane's fault that she cannot drive, but for now we will ignore the possibility of responsibility without capacity and constructions like *culpa in causa*.

41 Cf the first four essays in Timothy O'Connor (ed.), *Essays on Determinism and Free Will*, Oxford: Oxford University Press 1995.

6.7. *Conclusion on deserved liability*

To summarize the above argument: we are left with two options. The one is to take all constraints into account in determining what an agent had the capacity to do. If we take this approach, the behaviour of the agent is either determined or arbitrary, depending on whether one accepts determinism. In neither case the agent deserves to be held responsible and liable for damages. The other option is to count some constraints in and to discount some other constraints in determining the capacities of an agent. This is what lawyers actually do. However, then the social practice of counting or discounting constraints determines capacity: capacity has become a matter of attribution too. This practice cannot be adduced as justification of the practice of agency attribution. If we assume that responsibility should be attributed on the basis of desert, capacities would be the main justification for the practice of agency attribution, and if this justification does not cut ice, the practice would not be justified at all.

7. Purposive attribution of liability

However, desert is not the only possible foundation for a practice of agency attribution, including the attribution of responsibility. The alternative is that agency and responsibility are attributed for some purpose. Attribution based on desert is backward looking and requires that the past could have been different than it actually was. If determinism is correct, the past could not have been any different and it does not make sense to attribute agency and responsibility because the agent deserved it. If determinism is incorrect, the past was a random affair, and also then it does not make sense to attribute agency and responsibility because the agent deserved it.

This dilemma is avoided if attribution takes place in order to serve some purpose, because such a practice would be forward looking. It would make sense if what we do now, attribute agency and responsibility or not, influences the future. In section 7.2 it will be argued that purposive attribution of agency makes sense for humans and in section 7.3 the argument will be extended to autonomous agents. However, first we will in section 7.1 rebut an objection against purposive attribution, an objection based on the misguided idea that according to determinism it does not matter what we do or decide. Finally, we will in section 7.4 devote a few words to the way in which responsibility for autonomous agents can be implemented.

7.1. *Determinism and fatalism*

Any act that is performed in order to bring about future effects presupposes that what happens now influences the future. This means that events should not follow each other in an arbitrary fashion. The question whether this also presupposes determinism, the view that the future can only develop in one single way, is not easy to answer, but if determinism is true this does not make purposive action senseless. The view that this is different since if everything is determined it does not make any difference what we do now, rests on a confusion between determinism and fatalism. Because this confusion is quite common, it is useful to devote some attention to it here.

Fatalism is the view that the future will end up in a particular fashion anyway and that what we presently do cannot influence that outcome. This is compatible with the idea that this unavoidable outcome can be reached along different paths. To use a somewhat pessimistic example: whether you exercise a lot or not, in the course of time your strength will decay anyway.

A determinist, on the contrary, can adhere to the view that what we presently do influences the future. The future is determined by everything that is presently the case, but this everything includes what we presently do. Therefore our decisions and acts do influence the future. A different question is whether we are free to act and whether more than one act is possible. If determinism is true, that is not the case: we are only capable to do what we actually do. However, that does not mean that it does not matter what we do or that deliberations on what to do are useless. The deliberations can influence our acts, even though we are not able to deliberate differently than we actually do.

If determinism is true, there is only one possible future, and this seems to confirm fatalism. However, this appearance is deceptive, because fatalism does not only involve that a particular outcome will certainly occur; it also involves that what we presently do has no influence on this outcome. This latter element does not follow from determinism and it is this element that would make purposive action senseless. We see that purposive action is incompatible with fatalism, but compatible with determinism because determinism does not imply this second element of fatalism.

7.2. Three grounds for attributing responsibility to human agents

The practice of attributing responsibility, both act- and liability-responsibility, may be justified if the attribution of responsibility brings desirable consequences. This raises two questions, one evaluative and the other empirical. The evaluative question is which consequences are desirable. In this article the evaluative question will be avoided, by postulating three purposes which are deemed to be desirable:[42]

- influencing future behaviour of the agent to whom responsibility is attributed,
- influencing future behaviour of other agents, and
- satisfaction of the desire of people who believe that agents should bear the consequences, of what they did.

The empirical question is whether the attribution of responsibility to human agents contributes to the achievement of these purposes. The answer to this question can only be found through empirical research, and the following attempt to an answer is therefore speculative.

It seems likely that if agents are held responsible for their acts, and if they believe that this is the case, this may influence their behaviour. It seems also likely that other agents

42 The author adheres to some form of utilitarianism, and believes that the three mentioned purposes are merely instrumental to the maximization of happiness. Cf. Jaap Hage, 'Recht en utilisme. Een pleidooi voor utilisme als richtlijn voor de wetgever', in *Law and Method*, November 2015, DOI: 10.5553/REM/.000011.

will be influenced by the belief that agents in general are responsible for their acts. Finally, it is likely that presently many persons will feel satisfaction if persons are held responsible for their doings because they (falsely) believe that agents deserve to be held responsible for what they do. Perhaps this belief will disappear in the (far) future, but as long as it is still prevalent, it can underlie the practice of holding people responsible.

7.3. *Should autonomous agents be held responsible?*

We spent quite some time considering the argument that humans should be held responsible because they deserve it. Our conclusion was that this argument cannot support its conclusion, and that we need other grounds for attributing responsibility to humans. In the case of autonomous agents it is most likely not necessary to spend time on arguing that they do not deserve to be held responsible, since the reasons why humans do not deserve responsibility hold *a fortiori* for autonomous agents: their 'behaviour' is either determined or arbitrary, and in neither case it can be said that autonomous agents deserve to be held responsible for their doings.

Because it is so obvious that autonomous agents do not deserve to be held responsible, the third purposive reason for holding them responsible may not apply to them either. Since most people do not believe that autonomous agents are 'real' agents, and therefore also not that they deserve to be responsible, there is little gained by attributing them responsibility.[43]

Because human agents presently do not identify themselves with autonomous agents, the argument that autonomous agents should be held responsible because this influences the future behaviour of other agents is weaker in the case of autonomous agents than it is in case of human agents. Weaker, but not completely without force. One reason that the argument still has some force is that humans might believe that if even autonomous agents are held responsible for their 'doings', then certainly humans agents will be held responsible and that this belief influences the future behaviour of human agents. A second reason is that autonomous agents might 'reason' that if other autonomous agents are held responsible, they will also be held responsible, and that this belief influence the future behaviour of these autonomous agents. However, this second reason presupposes that being held responsible can influence the future behaviour of autonomous agents at all. This is a crucial presupposition and we will turn to it now.

Will the future behaviour of autonomous agents be influenced by the fact, if it were to be one, that they are held responsible for their doings? Asking the question suffices for making it clear that it cannot be given a general answer: it depends on the nature of the autonomous agent. Let us first consider autonomous agents which are 'mere' computer programmes such as programmes involved in e-trade or in taking of (simple) administrative decisions. Such programmes can be less or more sophisticated, and their reaction to responsibility depends on their sophistication.

[43] However, Joanna Bryson pointed out to me that (some) people do think that autonomous agents who earned money, e.g. by stock trading, deserve to be taxed. Popular satisfaction would then be increased by making these systems liable to taxation.

If a programme is relatively simple it does not take responsibility into account, and then attributing responsibility to it will have no effects on the programme's behaviour. Then a practice of attributing responsibility makes little sense, at least not for these specific programmes.

A programme can also be more sophisticated in the sense that its programmer has taken into account that the autonomous agent running this programme will be held responsible. For instance, the programme may be made extra careful not to harm other agents, be they human or non-human. If it is allowed to be a little disrespectful to human dignity, this may be compared to eugenics in which the human genome is manipulated to make humans more obedient to rules. Perhaps we would not and should not want this with respect to humans, but in case of non-human agents this might be a desirable development. If attributing responsibility to autonomous agents would contribute to this development, it would be a reason for having this practice.[44]

The variant in which a programmer takes into account that its product will be held responsible makes the effects of responsibility dependent on the reaction of a different system – most likely a human being – to the responsibility of the autonomous agent. The parallel with human responsibility would be bigger if the autonomous agent itself reacted to being held responsible. An intelligent programme may possess knowledge about its potential responsibility and take this knowledge into account in deciding what it will do. This knowledge may be generally available, but may also be the result from being held responsible on a particular occasion. The adaptation of behaviour to potential or actual responsibility presupposes that the agent is not focused on a single task such as taking a particular kind of administrative decisions or conducting e-trade, but that it performs tasks like that in the context of wider tasks such as contributing to the well-being of society, or the maximization of its profits. Presently there are, to the author's knowledge, no practically functioning systems which can do this, but for the theoretical question that is not very relevant. If such systems would exist – and it is quite likely that they can already be created – it would make sense to hold them responsible for their doings, both in abstract as well as in concrete cases.

For systems which are also physically autonomous, such as self-driving cars, cruise missiles, and some robots, the situation is not fundamentally different from that of autonomous agents which are merely computer programmes. A computer programme runs on a machine which typically has peripherals for input and output. The only thing that makes physically autonomous systems different from mere computer programmes is the nature of the peripherals. These different peripherals can make that the nature and impact of what the physically autonomous system does radically differ from what the mere computer programme does, but for the fundamental issue whether it makes sense to hold them responsible this does not seem to make any difference.

44 Elbert de Jong raised the question whether programmers who can make programmes adapt to liability cannot also make them avoid damage causing behaviour. That would directly lead to the desired consequences (less damage) and therefore be preferable to the indirect route of making autonomous systems liable. Liability would still make sense, however, for those cases where a system has a conflict of duties. Then the system can comply with one of the duties and compensate the damage that results from not complying with the other duty.

So there seem to be no fundamental reasons why autonomous systems should not be held liable for what they do. However, this fundamental argument does not show that it is presently desirable to hold autonomous systems liable. Making the programmers or the users of autonomous systems liable for what the systems do may be more efficacious from a purposive perspective. Whether this is the case is an empirical question, and the answer may vary from system to system and may change in the course of time. However, the argument of this paper should have made clear that although the practical desirability may still be an open question, the difference between humans and autonomous systems as such does not justify a different treatment as far as liability is concerned.

7.4. How to implement the responsibility of autonomous agents?

Actually it is not part of the question this article aims to answer, but for practical purposes it is important to know how the responsibility of autonomous agents may be given shape. The answer to this question can benefit from our experiences with autonomous agents which already exist for quite some time and which do function in society on a large scale: organizations. Let us take a company with limited liability as an example, and let us call this company for the sake of exposition C.

C acts in society by means of its peripherals, which are typically called "agents" or "representatives". Some of these agents are humans, but others are also autonomous agents, such as the internet-based programme that sells the products of C to online customers (including some autonomous agents). The events in which the acts of these peripherals are sometimes attributed to C as its acts. Some of the acts performed by C are generally praised, and the rumor goes that C has even been nominated for a Nobel prize. However, some other acts of C have been classified as causes of damage, and C is held liable to pay damages. This means that C has the obligation to compensate the damage and that it defaults on its obligation if it refrains from doing so. In case such a default would take place, the assets of C are collateral for the obligation and are amenable to attachment. In case C would commit crimes the company may be fined, and if the crimes are serious enough, its existence may be terminated.

As this example illustrates, law has already an elaborate set of means to deal with the responsibility of some autonomous agents for their doings. With some adaptations these means can also be made suitable to deal with the responsibility of computer-based and physically autonomous systems. The 'only' thing that is needed is to treat modern autonomous agents as legal persons just as we already do with the more old-fashioned autonomous agents.

8. Conclusion

The main step that needs to be taken to answer the question whether autonomous agent should be responsible for their doings is to stop thinking from an anthropocentric perspective. Intelligence, beliefs, desires, acts and agency, even when attributed to human beings, are no 'real' things which exist in a mind-independent reality, but they are the result of attribution, just as damage and causation. The question is not whether attribution is true or truthful, but whether it is desirable or useful. We have seen that the attribution of agency and responsibility are not useful for the reason that the agents deserve to be held responsible for what they did. Acts are either determined or random, and in neither case does it make sense to attribute responsibility for them to agents. However, it can make sense to attribute responsibility in order to influence the future for the best. This holds for human agents, and also for autonomous agents, for both to the extent that their behaviour can be influenced through the attribution of responsibility. The legal implementation of this responsibility takes place by treating agents, whether they be humans, organizations, or other autonomous agents, as legal persons.

There is only one difficulty: it is very hard for humans to abandon their anthropocentric world view. It is still common to distinguish between humans and animals, and most likely it will stay common for quite some time that humans will treat the differences between them and non-living systems[45] are qualitative rather than quantitative. And yet, stopping to do so is the first step towards an adequate treatment of modern autonomous agents.

[45] The distinction between living and non-living systems may turn out to be as arbitrary as the distinction between agents and non-agents.

Nwamaka
Rosemary Okany*

PRIVATE LAW ANALOGIES AND THE EVOLUTION OF INTERNATIONAL STATE RESPONSIBILITY FOR ACTS OF NON-GOVERNMENTAL ENTITIES EXERCISING DECENTRALIZED/PRIVATIZED GOVERNMENTAL FUNCTIONS

Abstract

Can a State be held legally responsible for wrongs committed by a non-governmental entity (individual or corporation) on the basis that the entity committed them while performing governmental functions on behalf of the State? The affirmative answer of international law to this question relying on concepts that are analogous to concepts of domestic private law constitutes the focus of this article. This article looks at the evolution of a general principle of international law which states that the wrongful act of a non-governmental entity performing governmental functions is to be deemed State action for which the State is responsible. This principle which extends beyond regular government organs, the scope of entities whose wrongful conduct may be attributed to the State for liability purposes, constitutes one of public international law's responses to the increasing decentralization and privatization of public interest functions (such as rail transportation, water supply, social security, health care, prisons and immigration control). Proceeding from the viewpoint that elements of this principle bear a close analogy to legal relations established by the respective concepts of vicarious liability, the non-delegable duty and strict liability in domestic tort law, this article sheds light on the unique manner in which international law has made use of these private law analogies to impose liability on the State for conduct of non-governmental entities. The very reliance of international law, under this principle, on the concept of the governmental functions as a basis for apportioning responsibility has also been criticized as being out of touch with the present day reality of an erosion of boundaries between government/public and private spheres of activity. The article sets out to demonstrate with the aid of international case law that this reliance is not entirely misplaced. Rather, the approach of international law provides valuable lessons for national and regional legal orders regarding the proper division of competences and tortious liability between State and private sectors.

* Ph.D Researcher, Faculty of Law, University of Amsterdam, the Netherlands. The author thanks Chantal Mak and Marco Loos for comments on earlier versions of this article.

1. Introduction

The body of general principles of international law collectively referred to as the 'Law of State Responsibility' represents one of various points of contact between domestic and international law. Despite international law's continued assertion of its autonomy from domestic law, many concepts of international law – and the Law of State Responsibility – are modelled after or constitute analogies of concepts of domestic private law.[1]

This article looks at the role of domestic tort law[2] analogies in the evolution of a principle of the Law of State Responsibility which states that a wrong committed by a non-governmental entity exercising governmental functions is to be deemed State action, for which the State is responsible. This principle, which extends beyond regular government organs, the scope of entities whose wrongs may be attributed to the State, constitutes one of international law's responses to the growing trend of privatization and other decentralizations of public interest functions. As States increasingly farm out, outsource or outrightly abdicate functions such as rail transportation, water supply, social security, health care, education, prisons and immigration control to a variety of non-governmental entities, the principle forms a tool for preserving a measure of State responsibility for how certain decentralized functions are performed by non-governmental bodies. More specifically, it imposes responsibility on the State for acts of non-governmental entities performing certain decentralized or outsourced State functions, where those acts contravene the State's international obligations.

This article takes the position that elements of this principle of the Law of State Responsibility mirror to some extent legal relations established by the concepts of vicarious liability, the non-delegable duty and strict liability in domestic private law. Also, that the identification of the exercise of 'governmental/public' functions as a basis for State responsibility under the principle is heavily influenced by domestic law distinctions between the State as subject of private law (*État personne privée*) and the State as a subject of public law (*État puissance publique*). This article examines the manner in which international law makes use of these private law analogies to impose liability on the State for non-governmental conduct. The operation of the principle under discussion also triggers some questions which are addressed here, viz.: is the resort to analogous domestic law distinctions between 'governmental' and 'non-governmental functions' for apportioning liability at the international level misplaced (as has been argued by some critics)? Also, does the approach of international law to the problem of decentralization and privatization of governmental functions offer any lessons for the domestic legal order?

The body of the article is divided in 5 Sections.

Section 2 provides an overview of the factual context in which the general principle of international law attributing to the State the conduct of non-governmental entities

1 The term private law is used here in the English common law sense – as encompassing not only relationships between private entities, but also relationships between governmental and private actors which are based on the law of contracts or torts as opposed to administrative or other public law.

2 A tort is a civil wrong which causes loss or injury creating liability in damages to a plaintiff. It is distinguishable from a breach of contract or a crime.

exercising governmental functions has emerged: the growing decentralization of public interest functions by governments.

Section 3 introduces State responsibility as a concept possessing a very specific meaning in international law. It identifies the two basic conditions for State responsibility in international law: attribution (the identification of conduct as conduct of the State) and breach of an obligation (the requirement that the relevant conduct must contravene an obligation established in international law). The section also provides a preliminary insight into the relationship between responsibility in international law and responsibility in domestic private law, highlighting in the process the role private law analogies have played more generally in international law on State responsibility.

Section 4 looks at the evolution of the principle providing that wrongs committed by a non-governmental entity while exercising governmental functions are to be considered State acts for which the State is responsible. It discusses key elements of the principle as identified in the writings of jurists, international case law as well as the codification work of the United Nations International Law Commission (UNILC) and other learned bodies. It also looks at how the operation of those key elements in international case law bears close analogies to the legal relations established by the respective concepts of vicarious liability, the non-delegable duty and strict liability in domestic private law. Also examined are several critiques levelled against the resort to domestic law distinctions between 'governmental/public' and 'private' functions for apportioning international responsibility under the principle.

Section 5 revisits the governmental functions concept in the light of international case law. It discusses the relevance of international law's reliance on the concept to ongoing societal debates on the division of responsibilities between various entities (State and private) which cooperate to provide citizens with essential public services or implement social policies expected to comply with certain standards. This approach of international law, it is argued, holds valuable lessons for national and regional legal orders regarding the proper division of competences and liabilities between State and private sectors.

Section 6 summarizes the key points of discussion.

2. Factual background: the decentralization of public interest functions by governments

Every principle of law evolves within a given context and to address a given social phenomenon. The general principle of international law qualifying the conduct of a non-governmental entity exercising governmental functions as an act of the State has emerged against the background of – and in response to – one significant development in the organization of the modern State. The development in question is the increasing vesting, transfer, outsourcing, delegation or outright abdication by governments of public interest functions to persons or entities which do not form part of the official machinery of the State. This development has had a variety of manifestations.

The most prominent manifestation is the advent of the autonomous State-owned corporation. Especially after the Second World War, governments all over the world have established or acquired a variety of corporate entities to perform tasks which serve the public interest. Typical examples include gas, electricity, railway, telecommunications and water supply corporations, as well as hospitals, social welfare organizations, oil or agricultural trading corporations, universities and cultural centres established, owned or nationalized by governments. These entities are often described as 'State' or 'public' because of their establishment or ownership by the State. However, the term 'quasi-public', 'semi-public' or 'parastatal' better takes into account a characteristic many of them share in common: the possession under the laws of their establishing or owning States, of a legal personality separate from that of the government, with powers to sue or be sued in their own names.

The treatment of the 'quasi-public', 'semi-public' or 'parastatal' entity (hereinafter parastatal) as legally distinct from the government may appear artificial to many because of various links parastatals invariably have with the government. Beyond the very fact of State ownership or establishment, those links often include the performance of tasks vested by establishing legislation, management by a board of directors composed of government officials or appointees, State funding or subsidies, general oversight of the parastatal's activities by a government minister or – in the case of trading or commercial corporations – government control of the price of commodities or services. However, this treatment of parastatals as entities separate from the government is well accepted in the laws and practices of many States.

The reasons behind the setting up of parastatals as entities legally distinct from the government vary from State to State. There are, however, a number of reasons many States share in common. Principal among them are the flexibility, efficiency and economies of operation which attend the operation of parastatals as legally distinct entities.

Operation as an entity legally separate from the government frees parastatals from the high level of bureaucratic control regular governmental bodies are normally subject to, thereby enhancing their flexibility and quickness of decision-making with respect to the specific tasks they are established to perform. For parastatals established with a commercial objective, their relative freedom from government control enables them to adapt quickly to market changes and to operate in accordance with private sector commercial principles which emphasize cost-saving and efficiency in the use of resources. It is for this latter reason that the establishment of autonomous commercial corporations has been a tool resorted to by governments post-World War II to generate financial resources needed for post-war economic reconstruction. However, regardless of what may be the reasons behind the establishment of parastatal corporations as autonomous legal entities, an important and fundamental premise behind their legal separateness from the government is their independent responsibility for their own actions or debts.

A second manifestation of the transfer of public interest functions by governments to entities existing outside the official structures of the State is a wide range of governmental initiatives subsumed under the popular label of 'privatization'. One example of the privatization of functions by governments is the total or partial sale of many State-owned corporations (and the resultant transfer of the activities they perform) to the private sector in many countries.[3] However, besides the sale of State-owned corporations,

[3] See FP Feliciano, 'The Doctrine of Sovereign Immunity from Suit in a Developing and Liberalizing Economy: Philippine Experience and Caselaw' (1998) 3 *Austrian Review of International and European*

governments have also engaged in the transfer to the private sector of functions normally performed by the government itself. The forms of transfer range from simple delegations with the government retaining supervisory control, to outright abdications. The functions concerned range from tasks such as post-delivery, health care and water supply to other functions like immigration control, prison management, policing and national defence, which many perceive as constituting part of the very *raison d'être* of the State.

The transfer to the private sector of functions normally performed by the government itself is exemplified by the contracting out of prison and/or immigration camp management to private security companies in countries such as the United States (US), Australia, Canada, the United Kingdom, South Africa and South Korea,[4] the employment of private security guards in parts of Asia to provide security for government officials[5] as well as the hiring of private military companies by governments in Africa, the Americas and Europe to guard embassies or assist in fighting foreign wars against non-State armed groups. It is also exemplified by the scheme under which two major French private companies, Vivendi and Suez Lyonnaise des Eau have managed public water utilities in several Latin American countries as well as in China, The Czech Republic, Germany, Senegal and Poland. Also a relevant and related development is 'liberalization': the lifting of government or parastatal monopoly over particular services to allow private persons or corporations to provide parallel services. An example of liberalization of services is liftings of government monopolies on airport security in Europe and the United States.[6]

A question raised by the afore-described and other instances of the decentralization of public interest functions by governments is how entities which, though not part of the government, perform public interest functions at the instigation or with the acquiescence of the government, are to be perceived where in discharging those functions they engage

Law no 1, 1, 13 where the author refers to the selling to the private sector of government-owned corporations in fields such as transportation, telecommunications, banking, petroleum refining and distribution, shipping, iron and steel as some of the manifestations of privatization in the Philippines.

4 See for example, Commonwealth of Australia, 'Taking Responsibility: Conditions and Circumstances at Australia's Regional Processing Centre in Nauru', Senate Printing Unit, Parliament House, Canberra 2015 concerning refugee processing camps operated in the Pacific Island of Nauru by a private corporation on behalf of the Government of Australia.

5 For example, in 2002, Dyncorp, a private American corporation was hired to provide protection in Afghanistan for Hamid Karzai, then President of Afghanistan.

6 RW Poole Jnr, 'Improving Airport Passenger Screening', Reason Public Policy Institute, Policy Study, no 298, 2002 <research.policyarchive.org/5819.pdf> accessed 13 January 2017, listing European airports that have outsourced passenger and baggage screening; also AH Wen, 'Suing the Sovereign's Servant: The Implications of Privatisation for the Scope of Foreign Sovereign Immunities' (2003) 103 *Columbia Law Review* 1538, n 3.
For other examples of liberalization, see FP Feliciano, above n 3 where he cites the post-Marcos era encouragement of entry by privately owned firms into areas previously reserved to or heavily dominated by the public sector (such as energy generation, water supply and distribution, construction of roads, bridges, airports and even distribution of mail). See more generally, P Starr, 'The New Life of the Liberal State: Privatization and the Restructuring of State-Society Relations' in J Waterbury and E Suleiman (eds), *Public Enterprise and Privatization*, Westview Press, Boulder, Colorado 1990, pp 22–54 for the distinction between, as well as examples of, privatization and liberalization.

in conduct which if emanating from the government itself, would constitute a breach of international law by the State. An example of such wrongful conduct would be ill-treatment or torture in a privatized prison (which would constitute a violation of the international human right to freedom from inhuman or degrading treatment[7]) or a seizure of property by a State-owned investment bank (which could constitute illegal expropriation under international investment law[8]). Since the government is the primary representative of the public interest and these entities perform their public interest functions at the behest or with the acquiescence of the State, are they to be considered State representatives for whose conduct the State is responsible in international law? Or, as is usually the case under national law, separate entities independently responsible for their own actions?

It is in response to this question that the general principle has emerged in public international law that the unlawful acts of a non-governmental person or entity exercising governmental functions is to be considered an act of the State for which the State is responsible. The emergence of this general principle has been hailed as a development introducing a needed element of flexibility to the concept of the act of the State in international law.[9] It also responds to the warning of the legal scholar Friedmann, going as far back as 1938, that international society is in a process of transformation which international law can no longer afford to ignore, and that nothing would endanger international law more than to consider as absolute rules built on a social basis that is undergoing deep alterations.[10] The deep transformation in international society Friedmann was referring to was the advent of the autonomous State corporation as well as the vesting by national legislation of certain public interest functions normally performed by governments on private organizations.[11] The rules he considered had to be adjusted in line with these developments, included the traditional international law rules on State responsibility under which the government was seen as the sole representative of the State in international law, and correspondingly the sole entity through which a

7 See, for example, Art 7 of the International Covenant on Civil and Political Rights of 1966 for an international law prohibition of torture, or inhuman or degrading treatment.

8 See for example, Art 5 of the Agreement on Encouragement and Reciprocal Protection of Investments between the Government of the People's Republic of China and the Government of the Kingdom of the Netherlands of 26 November, 2001 for its provisions prohibiting illegal expropriations.

9 See United Nations General Assembly (UNGA), 'State Responsibility: Comments and Observations Received From Governments', UN Document A/CN.4/488), 25.03.1998, p 36, n 18. Alongside it has also emerged, in response to the afore-mentioned developments, the general principle that the State is responsible for conduct of non-governmental persons or entities acting under the control of the State. The latter general principle however falls outside the scope of this article which is focused on the issue of non-governmental entities exercising governmental functions.

10 W Friedmann, 'The Growth of State Control Over the Individual, and Its Effect Upon the Rules of International State Responsibility' (1938) 19 *British Yearbook of International Law* 118.

11 Ibid, pp 118, 119–123 where he discusses the advent of State-established banks, railways, broadcasting corporations, steel production corporations, etc. operating under State supervision as well as the phenomenon of private undertakings operating with State subsidies or under the management of the State; also p. 144 where he discusses the phenomenon of single party totalitarian States and the vesting in those States by national legislation of supreme powers of political direction normally reserved for the government on the sole political party operating in the totalitarian State.

State can act and incur responsibility.[12] The danger he considered posed to international law by a failure to adjust the rules on State responsibility was the possibility of States evading their international obligations by acting through non-governmental/private entities for whose conduct they bore no responsibility. Now established as a general principle of international law, it is applied by international courts and tribunals for resolving disputes in a variety of fields of international law, in the absence of relevant treaty provisions on State responsibility.[13] It has also been codified by the United Nations International Law Commission, the body that performs on behalf of the United Nations General Assembly (UNGA) the task of codifying and progressively developing international law in Article 5 of its Articles on State Responsibility (ASR) adopted in 2001.[14] Before proceeding to discuss the application of the principle to impose responsibility on the State and the role of private law analogies therein, the next sub-section will introduce State responsibility as a concept of public international law.

3. State responsibility in public international law

3.1. The meaning of state responsibility in public international law

In ordinary language and in law, the term 'responsibility' is often used in either of two senses: first, to refer to an obligation or requirement to act in a certain manner, and second, to refer to the consequences one bears for failing to act in accordance with a specific requirement or obligation.[15] In public international law, the term 'State responsibility' has evolved into a term of art understood in the second sense of responsibility described above. State responsibility, as a term of art in public international law, refers to the legal consequences for a State of its violation of an international obligation. The most basic justification for State responsibility in international law lies in the very existence of an international legal order and the legal nature of the obligations it

12 Other rules Friedmann considered had to be amended included the international law rules governing State immunity and neutrality in times of war.

13 General principles of international law are generally accepted legal principles which are enunciated in international State and tribunal practice and fill gaps in law making left by treaties. In the case of the Law of State Responsibility, they fill the lacuna in law making arising from the fact that international treaties largely focus on enunciating substantive obligations of States, leaving issues of State responsibility to be enunciated upon in the context of dispute settlement procedures. Concerning principles of the Law of State Responsibility as general principles of international law, cf: J Pauwelyn, 'The Role of Public International Law in the WTO: How Far Can We Go?'(2001) 95 *American Journal of International Law* 535, 536–537.

14 See UNGA, Resolution 56/83 of 12 December 2001; also the ASR and commentaries as reproduced in J Crawford, *The International Law Commission's Articles on State Responsibility: Introduction, Text and Commentaries*, Cambridge University Press, Cambridge 2002.

15 Some international treaties nonetheless still use the term 'State responsibility' in the two senses of obligation and consequences of wrongdoing. See, for example, Art 42(5) of the United Nations Convention on the Law of the Sea of 10 December 1982, for a definition of State responsibility as consequences of wrongdoing and Art 139 of the same Convention for a definition of State responsibility as obligation.

imposes on its subjects. In other words, the idea of the State (or any other subject of the law) being responsible – liable, accountable – for wrongdoing is an integral aspect of any rules-based system, be it a system of morality, religion or law.[16]

The basic principles underlying State responsibility in public international law are clearly enunciated in the *Spanish Zone of Morocco Claims*, one of the first known cases to espouse State responsibility as a concept of public international law. In the words of Judge Huber in that case,

> Responsibility is the necessary corollary of a right [or obligation]. All rights of an international character involve international responsibility. If the obligation in question is not met, responsibility entails the duty to make reparation.[17]

The same principles were reiterated by the Permanent Court of International Justice in the *Factory at Chorzow* case:

> ... it is a principle of international law, and even a general conception of law, that any breach of an engagement involves an obligation to make reparation... reparation is the indispensable complement of a failure to apply a convention, and there is no necessity for this to be stated in the convention itself.[18]

The condition of state responsibility is thus in a sense one of obligation – an obligation to make amends for the violation of an obligation or a corresponding right established by international law.

Amends or remedies for a breach of an international obligation recognized in international law include restitution (a duty to re-establish the situation which existed before the wrongful act, to the extent it is not materially impossible), 'satisfaction' (example, an acknowledgement of wrongdoing, an expression of regret or a formal apology) and compensation. Also, the responsible State is under a duty to cease the wrongful act if it is of a continuing nature, and to offer appropriate assurances and guarantees of non-repetition if the circumstances so require.[19]

3.2. *Two basic conditions for state responsibility: attribution and breach*

There is a general consensus in public international law that there are two basic conditions that must be fulfilled for State responsibility to arise:

(a) First, an act (or omission) which is attributable to – in other words, constitutes conduct of an organ or agent of – the State,

16 See I Brownlie, *System of the Law of Nations – State Responsibility, Part I*, Oxford, Clarendon Press, 1983, p 1.

17 *Great Britain v Spain* (1924) 2 RIAA 615, 641.

18 *Factory at Chorzow (Germany v Poland) (Merits)* [1928] PCIJ Rep Series A, no 9, p 21.

19 See Arts. 28 – 37 ASR and commentaries in J Crawford, above n 14, p 192–234.

(b) Second, a breach by that conduct of an obligation binding on the State in international law.[20]

These two conditions flow logically from the legal definition of State responsibility as the consequences for a State of its breach of an obligation. In particular, the requirement of breach – of wrongful conduct – distinguishes 'State responsibility' from 'State liability', another concept of public international law. Unlike State responsibility, State liability is concerned with the consequences for a State of conduct which while injurious, is lawful or at least not prohibited by international law.[21] An example of conduct which may be injurious, but is lawful or not prohibited by international law is industrial activity producing waste which if not properly disposed of, may cause damage to the environment. Although the industrial activity in question is lawful, the State may be *liable* in international law for damage to the environment resulting from that activity.

The reiteration of 'attribution' and 'breach' as two necessary conditions for State responsibility has become a regular feature in international judicial practice. While such reiteration may at first glance appear like an exercise in formalism, it serves to emphasize details of crucial significance subsumed in the two requirements of attribution and breach.

Relevant in this regard is that in speaking of attribution, what is meant is the identification of the conduct as that of the State as a subject of international law. In other words, attribution of conduct in international law is not synonymous with attribution of conduct to the State as a subject of national law. It is a process autonomous and distinct from attribution of conduct to the State as a subject of national law. The autonomy of international law from national law in determining what conduct is attributable to the State entails that international law is entirely free to either disregard the criteria recognized in national law for qualifying conduct as that of the State or to take those very criteria into account.[22] As such, conduct that is attributable to the State in international law may well be unattributable to the State in national law or vice versa. This principle has been consistently affirmed in international law since *The 'Alabama'* case.[23] It was also emphasized by Starke in 1938 in the following statement in which he used the term 'imputation' to refer to what in international law today is referred to as 'attribution':

> The subject of state responsibility is one that touches closely the relation between international law and the municipal law of the state, and … [i]t is always to be remembered that the

20 See ibid, p 81.

21 Cf: A Boyle, 'State Responsibility and International Liability for Injurious Consequences of Acts Not Prohibited by International Law: A Necessary Distinction? (1990) 39 *International and Comparative Law Quarterly* 141.

22 Cf: T Meron, 'International Responsibility of States for Unauthorized Acts of Their Officials' (1957) 33 *British Yearbook of International Law* 85, 87, also n 4.

23 *The Geneva Arbitration (The 'Alabama' case) (United States of America v Great Britain)*, Decision of 14 September 1872 in JB Moore, *History and Digest of the International Arbitrations to which the United States has been a Party*, vol I, p 653 et seq.

imputation of liability results from rules of international law operating in an autonomous manner...[24]

Decades later, the UNILC emphasized the same principle in the following statement:

> The operation of attaching an action or omission to a subject of international law in order to draw conclusions therefrom in the sphere of international legal relations cannot be performed in any other framework than that of international law itself. It is thus an entirely separate operation from attribution of the same conduct to the State as a subject of internal law, and on the basis of internal law, without prejudice to any possible consideration by international law, for its own purposes, of the situation in internal law.[25]

Similar to the position with respect to attribution, the second basic condition for State responsibility – the requirement of breach – also brings into play the relationship between international and national law. It requires that the obligation breached by the State must not only be an obligation binding on the State concerned, but must also be an obligation established by international law and not national law.[26] The source of the obligation could be a treaty or customary international law. It may also be a legal act other than one necessary for the creation of a treaty or customary international law, such as the binding decision of an organ of an international organization like the United Nations Security Council.[27] The obligation may be owed to another State, several States or to the international community as a whole. Also, the obligation owed to another State or several or all States may create rights in favour of individuals, as is the case with, for example, obligations to respect human rights.

Describing the position that the obligation in question must be one established under international law and not national law, Hazel Fox has commented that '[i]n general a tort in municipal law does not itself involve State responsibility...'.[28] In a similar vein, James Crawford, the UNILC's Fifth Special Rapporteur on State Responsibility, has observed that:

> ... a State is not, generally speaking, internationally responsible for the 'private law' acts of its organs (e.g. the breach of a commercial contract entered into by the State)... the breach of a contract is not a breach of international law but of the relevant national law.[29]

24 JG Starke, 'Imputability in International Delinquencies' (1938) *British Yearbook of International Law* 105.

25 International Law Commission, 'Documents of the Twenty-Fifth Session including the Report of the Commission to the General Assembly' (1973) 2 *Yearbook of the International Law Commission* 181.

26 See *Elettronica Sicula S p A (ELSI) (United States of America v. Italy)*, Judgment of 20 July 1989 (1989) ICJ Reports 15, 51 at para. 73.

27 R Ago, 'Third Report on State Responsibility, by Mr. Roberto Ago, Special Rapporteur' (1971) 2 *Yearbook of the International Law Commission* 214.

28 H Fox, *The Law of State Immunity*, Oxford University Press, Oxford 2002, p 315.

29 J Crawford, 'First report on State responsibility, by Mr. James Crawford, Special Rapporteur' (1998) 2 *Yearbook of the International Law Commission*, Part I, p 37, para 174.

Thus, unless conduct can be attributed to the State and that conduct constitutes a breach of an international obligation owed by the State concerned, responsibility does not attach to that State in international law. The persons or entities whose conduct are attributable to the State in international law are set out in the UNILC Articles on State Responsibility (ASR) as follows:

(a) State/government organs (Art 4 ASR)
(b) Persons or entities authorized by the law of the State to exercise governmental functions or authority (Art 5 ASR)
(c) Organs of another State placed at the disposal of the responsible State (Art 6 ASR)
(d) Persons or groups of persons acting on the instructions of, or under the direction or control of, the State (Art 8 ASR)
(e) Persons or groups of persons acting in the absence or default of the official authorities of the State (Art 9 ASR)
(f) An insurrectional movement which becomes the new Government of the State (Art 10 ASR)
(g) Persons or entities whose conduct the State acknowledges and adopts as its own (Art 11 ASR)

The non-attributability to the State of wrongs committed by persons who are not its organs or agents does not, however, exclude the possibility that the State may be held responsible in international law for failing to prevent or punish private wrongs not attributable to it if this is required of it by an obligation established by international law. State obligations to prevent or punish wrongs by private entities are particularly prominent in the field of international human rights law. For example, the duty of States under the European Convention on Human Rights to secure to everyone within their jurisdiction the human rights protected by the Convention requires State parties to prevent or punish wrongful conduct of persons who are not State organs or agents. Where such an obligation to prevent or punish exists, the responsibility the State bears for failing to fulfil it is not for the wrong itself. It is not – as it is often called – 'direct' responsibility. It is rather an 'indirect' responsibility for its own failure, in the person of its organs or agents, to prevent or punish conduct as required of it by international law.

Since the responsibility the State bears for failing to prevent or punish an act unattributable to it is not for the act itself, but rather for its own failure to prevent it, the description of that responsibility as 'indirect' responsibility can be considered a misnomer. The position that the State is responsible only for its own related conduct in cases of 'indirect' responsibility entails that, strictly speaking, State responsibility is always 'direct', regardless of whether it is for harm caused by the State itself or for its failure to prevent harm inflicted by others. Nevertheless, the terms 'direct' and 'indirect' responsibility remain convenient catch-phrases for distinguishing two forms of responsibility whose implications and modalities of operation are different. While 'direct' State responsibility simply requires proof of breach and that the wrongdoer acted as an organ or agent of the State, 'indirect' State responsibility requires proof that the State had an obligation to prevent the relevant conduct in the first place, that it knew or ought to have known the wrongful act was impending, and that it failed to do all that could be *reasonably expected* of it, in the light of available resources, to prevent or punish.[30] In contrast, the 'direct' responsibility the State bears for the conduct of its organs or agents attaches regardless of whether or not the State had an explicit obligation under international law to prevent the wrong by the State organ/agent, knew the wrongful conduct was impending or made best efforts to prevent its organ or agent from committing it.

In the early years of the development of international law, an act of the State contrary to international law was simply described as a 'delict'.[31] No distinction was made, as is the case in domestic law, between various types of legal violations – torts, crimes, breaches of contract, etc. Following a failed attempt to introduce the concept of the 'State crime' as a separate category of offence distinct from the 'delict in international law,[32] this lack of distinction between different types of violations of international law by a State still subsists. However, references to a violation of international law as a 'delict', a term which has its origins in European private law, have receded. Those references have been replaced with the more neutral reference to the 'international wrong' or 'violation of international law'. Regardless, a cursory examination of international practice would reveal that the range of conduct found to constitute a violation of international law includes conduct that would normally fall into categories such as torts, delicts, breaches of contract, e t c, known to domestic private law. Examples of conduct that have been found by international tribunals applying international law to constitute violations of international law include: the seizure of hotel premises by a State's military forces[33] (the equivalent of a property tort), the failure to fulfil a treaty agreement to construct dams on a river[34] (the equivalent of a breach of contract), the placing of explosives in the territorial waters of another State (the equivalent of a crime)[35] and a failure to prevent genocide (an equivalent of the tort of negligence).[36]

3.3. *State responsibility as objective responsibility (responsibility without 'fault')*

Modern international law on State responsibility is founded on the doctrine of 'objective' responsibility. This entails that once there exists conduct on the part of a State organ or

30 See *Osman v United Kingdom*, no. 23452/94, European Court of Human Rights, Judgment of 28 October 1998 concerning the alleged failure of the United Kingdom police force to prevent the killing of a school boy by his teacher. (emphasis added).

31 See, for example, H Kelsen, *Principles of International Law*, Rinehart & Company, New York 1952, pp 5, 19.

32 An attempt made in the context of the UNILC's codification of the Law of State Responsibility. See in this regard, M Mohr, 'The ILC's Distinction Between "International Crimes" and "International Delicts" and Its Implications' in M Spinedi and B Simma (eds), *United Nations Codification of State Responsibility*, Oceana Publications, New York 1987, p 115.

33 *Amco Asia Corporation v. Republic of Indonesia*, International Centre for the Settlement of Investment Disputes, Case no ARB/81/1, Award, 20 November 1984.

34 *Gabčikovo-Nagymaros Project (Hungary v Slovakia) (Merits)* [1997] ICJ Reports 7.

35 *Military and Paramilitary Activities in and Against Nicaragua (Nicaragua v United States of America) (Merits)* [1986] ICJ Reports 14.

36 *Application of the Convention on the Prevention and Punishment of the Crime of Genocide (Bosnia and Herzegovina v Serbia and Montenegro)*, Judgment (2007) ICJ Reports 43.

agent that is not in conformity with an international obligation, a breach of international law is established without more. In other words, there is – as a general rule – no requirement to prove subjective fault on the part of the State organ or agent. Subjective fault could be in the form of wrongful intent (a wilful or malicious intent to violate an obligation – '*dolus*') or culpable negligence (recklessness, or reasonable foreseeability without desire of the consequences – '*culpa*'). The psychological state of the State actor or her motive is, thus, irrelevant.[37]

This modern position represents a rejection of orthodox theories on State responsibility which held sway in the later part of the 19th century.[38] According to those theories, State responsibility depended on the existence of subjective fault on the part of the State actor. The orthodox theory, which grew under the influence of the international law scholar Grotius, was based on a conception of states as moral entities, accountable for their acts and omissions in proportion to the mens rea of their agents.[39] However, by the beginnings of the 20th century, the theory was under attack from scholars such as Triepel and Anzilotti. They argued against the applicability of private law analogies (in this case Roman law from which Grotius' conception of *culpa* was derived) to the horizontal relations between sovereign States. Indeed the reference to fault as an element of responsibility under the orthodox doctrine mirrors the position in domestic private law where tort suits require proof of intent or negligence.

The theory of objective responsibility ultimately prevailed in international practice as the theory best suited to the complexities of international life. Those complexities included the fictional rationalizations inherent in imputing to the State the psychological state of a wide variety of not just individuals, but also legal entities making up the State apparatus.[40] In the words of Anzilotti:

> 'Malice and fault', in the proper senses of the words, express human will as a psychological fact, and one cannot therefore speak of them except in relation to the individual.[41]

Thus, if a State's naval fleet enters another State's territory without permission, the act of entry and the fact that the entry was by organs or agents of the State would be sufficient to ground State responsibility for breach of international law norms prohibiting a violation of another State's territorial sovereignty. An international tribunal would not countenance pleas that the entry was done without any wrongful intent or under a mistake of law.[42]

37 See I Brownlie, above n 16, p. 38; GA Christensson, 'Attributing Acts of Omission to the State' (1991) 12 *Michigan Journal of International Law* 312, 315, n 23.

38 H Lauterpacht, *Private Law Sources and Analogies of International Law (With Special Reference to International Arbitration)*, Longmans, Green and Co, New York 1927, p 136.

39 Ibid, p 137.

40 See, for example, P Dupuy, ' Dionisio Anzilotti and the Law of International Responsibility of States' (1992) 3 *European Journal of International Law* 139, 141 for a discussion of the challenges of identifying the mental State of the State, also I Brownlie, above n 16, pp 38–39.

41 P Dupuy, above n 40, citing Anzilotti, *Corso di diritto intemazionale*, 3rd ed, 1927, reprinted in *Opere di Dionizio Anzilotti*, vol 1, 1964.

42 See I Brownlie, above n 16, p 38; *Jessie Case*, Reports of International Arbitral Awards, vol VI (1921) 57.

However, while objective responsibility is now the general rule, the question of fault remains germane in certain situations. Those are situations where the international obligation breached is one which specifically requires proof of subjective fault as an element of the internationally wrongful act. For example, the International Convention on the Prevention and Punishment of the Crime of Genocide requires proof of a specific intent: an '...intent to destroy, in whole or in part, a national, ethnical, racial or religious group ...'[43] as an element of the wrongful act of genocide.[44] Just as in a case concerning an alleged breach by the United Kingdom (UK) of its human rights obligation to protect the right to life, by failing to prevent the killing of a school boy by his teacher, the European Court of Human Rights adopted a reasonableness test which refers to the mental state of the police officers involved as follows:

> ... The Court does not accept the Government's view that the failure to perceive the risk to life in the circumstances known at the time or to take preventive measures to avoid that risk must be tantamount to gross negligence or wilful disregard of the duty to protect life ... For the Court, and having regard to the nature of the right protected by Article 2, a right fundamental in the scheme of the Convention, it is sufficient for an applicant to show that the authorities did not do all that could be reasonably expected of them to avoid a real and immediate risk to life of which they have or ought to have knowledge. This is a question which can only be answered in the light of all the circumstances of any particular case... As noted earlier (see paragraph 116 above), the police must discharge their duties in a manner which is compatible with the rights and freedoms of individuals. In the circumstances of the present case, they cannot be criticised for attaching weight to the presumption of innocence or failing to use powers of arrest, search and seizure *having regard to their reasonably held view* that they lacked at relevant times the required standard of suspicion to use those powers or that any action taken would in fact have produced concrete results... For the above reasons, the Court concludes that there has been no violation of Article 2 of the Convention in this case.[45]

This interpretation is in line with many interpretations of State obligations to prevent wrongs by persons within its territory as obligations of 'due diligence' – obligations which are not absolute, but rather require the State to act in a diligent manner to prevent or punish harmful conduct.[46]

It is, furthermore, worth noting that the prevalence of the doctrine of objective responsibility has also affected the role under the Law of State Responsibility of two

43 Art 2, Convention on the Prevention and Punishment of the Crime of Genocide of 9 December 1948.

44 Though in terms of responsibility for actual commission of genocide, the Genocide Convention expressly focuses on individual criminal responsibility as opposed to State responsibility, the International Court of Justice in its judgment on the preliminary objections in the 'Genocide Case', acknowledged that States themselves could also commit genocide. The implication of this acknowledgement by the Court is that the Convention constitutes one of the instances where proof of a subjective element on the part of the State would be necessary for establishing State responsibility.

45 *Osman v United Kingdom*, above n 30, paras 116, 121, 122 (emphasis added); see also *Kenan v United Kingdom*, no 27229/953, European Court of Human Rights, Judgment of 3 April 2001, para 90.

46 See *Velásquez Rodríguez v Honduras*, Inter-American Court of Human Rights, Judgment of 29 July 1988, Series C, no 4, para 172; also *Opuz v Turkey*, no. 33401/02, Judgment of 9 June 2009.

other factors found in early international law practice to be relevant for establishing breach of an international obligation: damage (material or moral) and causation.

In orthodox theories on State responsibility, damage and causation were seen as forming part of a multi-stage test of legal liability which required: an unlawful act of the State, damage suffered by the plaintiff, proof that the damage was caused by the State's unlawful act and, furthermore, that the damage was not too remote from the impugned act (i e the act was a proximate cause of the damage). This mirrored the position in domestic law under which a similar multi-stage test is required to establish liability for the tort of negligence. The now prevailing doctrine of objective State responsibility has, however, dispensed with damage and causation as general requirements for State responsibility. Causation and damage however remain relevant for grounding international State responsibility where an international obligation expressly requires or is interpreted as requiring proof thereof.

Thus in a claim brought before the European Court of Human Rights by a leukaemia patient alleging that the UK government by failing to warn her of the effects of her father's exposure to nuclear radiation while employed by the Royal Air Force, violated her right to life (as that failure prevented pre-natal monitoring that would have led to early diagnosis and treatment of her illness), the Court stated:

> Having examined the expert evidence submitted to it, the Court is not satisfied that it has been established that there is a causal link between the exposure of a father to radiation and leukaemia in a child subsequently conceived. As recently as 1993, the High Court judge sitting in the cases of Reay and Hope v. British Nuclear Fuels PLC, having examined a considerable amount of expert evidence, found that "the scales tilt[ed] decisively" in favour of a finding that there was no such causal link (see paragraph 19 above). The Court could not reasonably hold, therefore, that, in the late 1960s, the United Kingdom authorities could or should, on the basis of this unsubstantiated link, have taken action in respect of the applicant.[47]

Regarding material damage as an element of an internationally wrongful act, the Rio Declaration on Environment and Development of 1992, restating customary international law, provides:

> States have, in accordance with the Charter of the United Nations and the principles of international law, the sovereign right to exploit their own resources pursuant to their own environmental and developmental policies, and the responsibility to ensure that activities within their jurisdiction or control *do not cause damage* to the environment of other States or of areas beyond the limits of national jurisdiction.[48]

Lastly, causality and damage may also be relevant for determining the quantum of compensation that can be awarded for breach of an international wrong. Compensation

47 *LCB v The United Kingdom*, no 14/1997/798/1001, European Court of Human Rights, Judgment of 9 June 1998, para 39.

48 Art 2, Rio Declaration on Environment and Development of 1992.

for a breach of international law may only be awarded for material or moral damage and that damage must be caused by the internationally wrongful act. This position is illustrated by the *Genocide case (Bosnia and Herzegovina v. Serbia and Montenegro)* before the International Court of Justice. In that case, the Court while treating causation and damage as irrelevant for finding that Serbia had breached the obligation to prevent genocide, found that compensation was not an appropriate remedy because the facts of the case did not demonstrate that:

> ... there is a sufficiently *direct and certain causal nexus* between the wrongful act, the Respondent's breach of the obligation to prevent genocide, and the injury suffered by the Applicant, consisting of all damage of any type, material or moral, caused by the acts of genocide[;] ... that the genocide at Srebrenica would in fact have been averted if the Respondent had acted in compliance with its legal obligations[;] ... that, in the specific context of those events, those means [available to the Respondent] would have sufficed to achieve the result which the Respondent should have sought.[49]

Also in *CME Czech Republic (The Netherlands) v. The Czech Republic* which involved an alleged breach by the Czech Republic of the Czech-Netherlands bilateral investment treaty, an arbitral tribunal established under the auspices of the United Nations Commission for International Trade Law (UNCITRAL) affirmed the role of causality and damages (harm) in awarding compensation under international law as follows:

> *It is the very general rule that if a tortfeasor's behaviour is held to be a cause of the victim's harm, the tortfeasor is liable to pay for all of the harm so caused,* notwithstanding that there was a concurrent cause of that harm and that another is responsible for that cause ... The Media Council's actions in 1996 interfered with CME's investment by depriving ČNTS's broadcasting operations of their exclusive use of the broadcasting licence, which was contributed by CET 21 to ČNTS as a corporate contribution. *This interference with ČNTS' business and the Media Council's actions and omissions in 1999 must be characterized similar to actions in tort.* The Tribunal therefore is of the view that the above described principles apply in this case.[50]

3.4. The relationship between domestic private and international law on state responsibility

As the previous sections have demonstrated, a discussion of the foundational principles of the Law of State Responsibility inevitably touches on the relationship between international law and domestic/private law. The sections in fact demonstrate that many principles of the Law of State Responsibility have their basis in domestic private law.

49 *Application of the Convention on the Prevention and Punishment of the Crime of Genocide*, above n 36, p 234 (emphasis added).

50 UNCITRAL Partial Award of 13 September 2001, paras 581–582 citing JA Weir, 'Complex Liabilities' in A Tunc (ed), *International Encyclopedia of Comparative Law, vol XI*, Mohr, Tübingen 1983, p 41 (emphasis added).

Ordinarily, these close relations would buttress the views of Hegel that international law is nothing other than an external municipal law.[51] However, the idea of international law as merely an external municipal law has not only drawn considerable criticism from jurists, but is certainly no longer tenable today.

When the Australian international law jurist, J.G. Starke, in his influential 1938 article in the British Yearbook of International Law, stated that:

> The subject of state responsibility is one that touches closely the relation between international law and the municipal law of the state, and...It is always to be remembered that the imputation of liability results from rules of international law operating in an autonomous manner...[52]

he was projecting the then growing repudiation of domestic law as a form as well as source of international law, a repudiation that arose from the triumph of the positivist school of international law. The positivist school's chief postulate was that international law was a self-sufficient system, without a need for recourse to sources other than international custom or treaties as a source of law.[53] In the last century, a century marked by a remarkable explosion in international treaty making, this position of the positivist school has been vindicated. Regardless of its obvious domestic roots dating back to the early stages of its development, international law has through a burgeoning volume of treaty and customary international law asserted its autonomy. It has, importantly, increasingly departed from legal positions adopted in domestic law, and in accordance with its own distinct purposes and interests.

Nevertheless, it would be evident from a comparison of national and international law that many concepts of public international law remain modelled after or analogous to concepts of domestic private law. And in almost no area of international law is the analogy more evident than the Law of State Responsibility. Beyond the continued, albeit limited relevance of domestic law concepts like fault, causation and damages in the Law of State Responsibility, one can point to the defences international law allows to allegations of breach of international law as an area of the Law of State Responsibility influenced by domestic law. For example, self-defence and *force majeure* are domestic law defences which under the Law of State Responsibility can also be raised to claims of breach of international law. Also, the idea of offences committed against the international community as a whole, an idea codified by the UNILC, *inter alia*, in the provisions of the ASR dealing with standing to bring an international claim,[54] bears parallels to the concept of *actio popularis* in national law. Moreover, the idea of a general regime of responsibility applying to different fields of obligation, which modern international Law of State Responsibility embodies, is obviously 'borrowed' from the continental civil law

51 See H Laski, *Studies in Law and Politics*, George Allen and Unwin Limited, London 1932, p. 268 citing and criticizing Hegel's view that international law is merely an external municipal law as not being compatible with the facts of international life.

52 JG Starke, above n 24, p 105.

53 See H Lauterpacht, *Private Law Sources and Analogies of International Law*, above n 38, pp 7–37.

54 Cf: Art 42 ASR, reproduced in J Crawford, above n 14, p 255.

system under the influence of one of the UNILC's special rapporteurs.[55] Such a general regime of liability is largely foreign to common law legal systems.

The analogy existing between principles of the Law of State Responsibility and liability principles existing in various national legal systems is understandable bearing in mind that States, the makers of international law are first and foremost subjects of their respective national legal systems. As such they bring to the international fora where international law is created, ideas shaped or influenced by their respective national laws. At the same time, the nature of international law as law uniting different legal cultures and forms of social organization entails ultimately that the private law analogies existing in international law are not necessarily homogenous in meaning or content with their domestic law counterparts.

The following sections will now look at the evolution in public international law of the principle attributing to the State the conduct of non-governmental persons or bodies exercising governmental functions and the role of private law analogies therein.

4. State responsibility for wrongs by non-governmental entities exercising governmental functions

4.1. Early writings of international law jurists

As recognised by Art 38 of the Statute of the International Court of Justice (ICJ Statute), the provision which sets out the generally accepted sources of international law, treaties ('conventions') and customary international law constitute the dominant or primary sources of international law.[56] However, the Law of State Responsibility including the principles governing State responsibility for conduct of non-governmental entities exercising governmental functions is an area of international law in which the writings of jurists, international law codification and the decisions of international tribunals have

55 Roberto Ago. an Italian jurist and 2nd Rapporteur of the UNILC on State Responsibility had initiated the idea of codifying at the Commission general and trans-substantive rules on State responsibility (in place of an earlier preference expressed at the Commission for codifying substantive State responsibility rules on the treatment of foreigners abroad).

56 Article 38 of the ICJ Statute implicitly distinguishes between primary and secondary/subsidiary sources of international law as follows (emphasis added):

Article 38

1. The Court, whose function is to decide in accordance with international law such disputes as are submitted to it, shall apply:
   a. international conventions, whether general or particular, establishing rules expressly recognized by the contesting States;
   b. international custom, as evidence of a general practice accepted as law;
   c. the general principles of law recognized by civilized nations;
   d. subject to the provisions of Article 59, judicial decisions and the teachings of the most highly qualified publicists of the various nations, *as subsidiary means for the determination of rules of law.*
2. This provision shall not prejudice the power of the Court to decide a case *ex aequo et bono*, if the parties agree thereto.

played the dominant role in the development of the law. This is because treaties and customary international law usually focus on enunciating substantive obligations of States, leaving issues of responsibility for breach of those obligations to be elaborated upon in the context of dispute settlement procedures. The paucity of treaty and customary law practice on State responsibility has thus entailed that a great deal of the Law of State Responsibility consists of gap-filling general principles formulated by international tribunals as part and parcel of their function of interpreting the requirements of the substantive obligations to which State responsibility attaches. The writings of jurists, beyond providing valuable insights on the law, have also influenced legal thinking as well as codification and tribunal practice on State responsibility.

Initially, the idea of attributing to the State wrongs by non-governmental entities exercising governmental/public functions did not draw the support of international law jurists. The earliest known academic work touching on the subject, Borchard's seminal writings on the right of a State to diplomatic protection for breaches of international law committed against its nationals,[57] had instead advocated the 'indirect' responsibility the State bears where it fails to fulfil an existing international obligation to prevent or punish a wrong (provided that elements required to establish such responsibility could be proven). Referring to the position of persons whom the State had granted 'certain monopolies of public service', he had pointed out that the responsibility of the State in connection to such persons had to be predicated upon some independent action or omission of the government – either failure to afford redress in its courts to the injured individual or to punish the wrong in question. His opinion, which he supported with some authorities, was that the State's grant of a monopoly of public service did not make the monopolists concerned agents of the State and thus capable of engaging its direct responsibility.[58]

A similar conclusion was subsequently drawn by H. Lauterpacht in an article published in 1933 in the British Yearbook of International Law.[59] In the article, he had discussed the phenomenon of political parties such as the Communist Party in the then Union of Soviet Socialist Republics (USSR) and the Fascist Party in Italy which wielded within the State, the supreme powers of political direction normally exercised by the government. Those political parties played such a directing and decisive role in determining the policy adopted by the government that from that perspective, they were barely distinguishable from the official government of the State. Yet, Lauterpacht considered that even though in such cases the government and the political party behind it were frequently indistinguishable, and the party whether as a matter of the constitutional authorization or mere fact had a distinct place in the working of the government, it was extremely doubtful whether the State could be held responsible for the acts of such a party.[60]

57 EM Borchard, *The Diplomatic Protection of Citizens Abroad*, The Banks Law Publishing Co, New York, 1916.

58 Ibid, p 190.

59 H Lauterpacht, 'Boycott in International Relations' (1933) 14 *British Yearbook of International Law*, p 125.

60 Ibid, p 134.

It is significant that unlike Borchard whose views on the phenomenon of private entities exercising public interest powers transferred by the State had come in the form of a sweeping statement on non-attribution to the State, Lauterpacht had actually considered the implications of such non-attribution:

> …[that] [t]his may at times enable a state to do through individuals and private bodies what it is not allowed to do itself.[61]

He however justified his stand on the basis that the rules of international State responsibility were based on the separation of the State from individuals and associations of which it is composed, that the advantages of that separation had at that stage of development of international society been found greater than the concomitant disadvantages of the State evading its international duties, and that in any case, that was the present position of the law.[62]

There were, however, contemporaneous scholarly opinions questioning Lauterpacht's standpoint, including his assertion that such non-attribution represented the position of international law at the time.

Among them were views expressed by L Preuss in an article published in 1934 in the American Journal of International Law.[63] Preuss had, therein, examined a phenomenon which was considered one of the most disturbing features of post-war international society. That was hostile propaganda emanating from the territory of one State, and directed against another State with the aim of inciting the subjects of the latter to revolt against its government. This was seen to constitute an international wrong, to the extent it not only interfered with the internal affairs and right to self-governance of another State, but emanated from persons considered to act on behalf of the State.

Having pointed out that there was a sharp distinction to be drawn in this respect between acts of private persons and those which by virtue of being committed by government officials or agencies can be attributed to the State, that mere toleration by the State of subversive propaganda of persons who are not its officials or agents was not sufficient to engage the State's responsibility[64] and that a survey of international practice had failed to reveal the existence of any legal rule by which a State was obliged to prevent or punish such propaganda by private persons,[65] he had proceeded to consider the significance for international law of the propagandist activity of the powerful political organizations earlier discussed by Lauterpacht. These were organizations which though formally of a non-governmental character, determined State policy and were so closely identified with their governments as to be, in fact indistinguishable from them.[66]

61 Ibid.

62 Ibid.

63 L Preuss, 'International Responsibility for Hostile Propaganda Against Foreign States' (1934) 28 *American Journal of International Law*, p 649.

64 Ibid, pp. 652.

65 L Preuss, above n 63, p 649.

66 L Preuss, above n 63, p 655.

The political organizations he made specific reference to were the Russian Communist Party (as well as the Third or Communist International), the German Nationalist Socialist Party and the Chinese Nationalist Party or *Kuomintang*. Hostile propaganda and subversive activities emanating from these political organizations had been attributed to their respective governments by foreign States. In Preuss' view, the already serious accusation that a government was guilty of conducting hostile propaganda against another State was made even more serious by the imputation of duplicity involved in the accusation that it was pursuing an illegal purpose by evasive means.

Preuss found that while the principle of non-interference in the internal affairs of another State was firmly established in international relations, its operation had, especially since the end of the World War, been reduced to an almost vanishing point by governments evading responsibility by engaging in hostile propaganda through such organizations. The activities of these organizations thus, in his view, presented a new serious problem in international law because they did not *strictly speaking* fall within the contemplation of the then existing rules of State responsibility. Those rules, he pointed out, evolved under a political situation in which the fundamental assumption was that the state acted through governmental organs chosen in conformity with its internal law.

Preuss' conclusion was that the principle of State responsibility had to be applied to the new situation to fasten responsibility upon the State for acts of an organization which by controlling governmental policy and the government itself constituted the effective governmental authority of the State. He believed this proposition to be a statement of international law, because the alternative was the inadmissible conclusion that a State may evade responsibility, and in effect, abrogate an important part of international law, by dissociating itself from organizations which though lacking governmental character by law, exercised the substance of State power. As far as he was concerned, to hold, for example, the U.S.S.R. responsible for the acts of its real and effective government involved no straining of existing legal principles, but was merely to apply them in such a way as to realize their fundamental purpose.[67] Moreover, he noted, foreign governments had consistently acted upon the view that the U.S.S.R was internationally responsible for the acts of the Russian Communist Party. In his view, they were clearly under the guidance of the traditional principles of State responsibility in doing so, even though because of the novelty of the situation, they had not clearly formulated their contention as a principle of international law.[68]

Importantly, in reaching this conclusion, Preuss had voiced his disagreement with Dr. Lauterpacht's view that to make a government responsible for acts of such political parties would play havoc with the established rules of State responsibility.[69] He considered the learned author to have involved himself in an apparent contradiction when he stated that the rules of international law on the matter of State responsibility were based on a separation of the State from the individuals and associations of which it is composed. This separation, he pointed out, was surely broken whenever the government acted

67 L Preuss, above n 63, p 663.
68 L Preuss, above n 63, p 656–657, 663.
69 L Preuss, above n 63, p 668, n 97.

through such persons or associations.[70] A similar critique was later voiced by Friedmann in the 1938 article[71] in which he had considered, *inter alia*, the advent of the autonomous State-established corporation as well as the increasing performance by private sector entities – at the State's initiative – of public interest functions normally performed by governments. Addressing Lauterpacht's statement that to hold the State responsible for the actions of private organizations would play havoc with the established rules of State responsibility, his opinion was that there was nothing sacred in those established rules, especially if their basis, the separation of State and individual, had disappeared. It was, he said, better to play havoc with them, than to maintain an old rule completely out of touch with political reality.[72]

Thus, by the first half of the 20th century, support existed in academic writings for the attribution to the State of conduct of non-governmental entities exercising functions which serve the public interest – usually at the initiative of the State. Greater impetus for the recognition of such attribution as a principle of international law and a better circumscription of the conditions for such attribution would come with the codification work of the UNILC and other learned bodies.

4.2. *Codification outside and under the auspices of the United Nations International Law Commission (UNILC)*

Beginning from the 1920's, several attempts were made by various learned societies, international organizations and private individuals – often at the instance of governments – to codify the rules of international law. Some of these attempts resulted in draft codes of law or general statements setting out existing or desirable law. Several of these codes or statements dealt with issues of State responsibility and also in that context, the attribution to the State of wrongs committed by non-governmental entities exercising governmental or public functions.

Point IV of the request for information sent out to governments by the Preparatory Committee for the 1930 Hague Codification Conference convened by the League of Nations referred to State responsibility for '...acts or omissions of bodies exercising public functions of a legislative or administrative character [communes, provinces, etc.]'.[73] Some governments, including those of Germany and Great Britain, observed in their replies to the questionnaire that the State was responsible for acts or omissions of bodies other than territorial or local governments in so far as those bodies were also required to exercise public functions.[74] The German Government in particular had this to say:

> ...when, by delegation of powers, bodies act in a public capacity, e.g. police an area or exercise sovereign rights as in the case when they levy taxes for their own needs...the principles

70 Ibid.
71 W Friedmann, above n 10.
72 W Friedmann, above n 10, p 144.
73 Roberto Ago, 'Third Report on State Responsibility, by Mr. Roberto Ago, Special Rapporteur' (1971) 2 *Yearbook of the International Law Commission*, Part 1, p 255.
74 Ibid.

> governing the responsibility of the State for its organs apply with equal force. From the point of view of international law, it does not matter whether a State polices a given area with its own police or entrusts this duty, to a greater or less extent, to autonomous bodies ...The remarks in this connection apply in practice principally to legal entities, and particularly administrative bodies possessing the right of self-government; but they are also applicable when the State, as an exceptional measure, invests private organizations with public powers and duties or authorizes them to exercise sovereign rights, as in the case of private railway companies permitted to maintain a police force.[75]

Although the codification work of the committee was subsequently discontinued, the above observations led the Committee to conclude that a State is responsible for wrongs committed not only by territorial local government entities but also other '... autonomous institutions as exercise public functions of a legislative or administrative character, if such acts or omissions contravene the international obligations of the State.'[76]

The above conclusion of the Preparatory Committee had clearly restricted the public functions whose exercise by entities autonomous from the State would be attributed to the State to those of a legislative or administrative character. However the resolution on State responsibility drawn up by The Institute of International Law at its 1927 session in Lausanne did not place any such restrictions. It simply referred to the responsibility of the State '... for the act of corporate bodies exercising public functions on its territory'.[77] Similarly, the 1961 update of the draft convention on 'Responsibility of States for Damage Done in their Territory to the Person or Property of Foreigners' prepared by the Harvard Law School in 1929, in listing persons or entities whose conduct may be attributed to the State, made a broad reference to '... a civilian official or employee of a State and any member of ... a para-military organization'.[78] This reference alluded without any qualification to the type of functions performed to, *inter alia*, persons who were employed by the State to carry out functions. Also, the Draft Convention on responsibility of States for international wrongful acts prepared by Professor Roth in 1932 referred to the responsibility of the State for '... acts contrary to international law of any individuals whom or corporations which it entrusts with the performance of public functions ...'[79]

75 International Law Commission, 'Report of the International Law Commission on the Work of its Twenty-Sixth Session, 6 May – 27 July 1974 (1974) 2 *Yearbook of the International Law Commission*, Part 1, pp 281–282.

76 See International Law Commission, 'Bases for discussion drawn up in 1929 by the Preparatory Committee of the Conference for the Codification of International Law (The Hague, 1930)' (1956) 2 *Yearbook of the International Law Commission*, p 223.

77 Art II of the 1927 Draft on 'International Responsibility of States for Injuries on Their Territory to the Person or Property of Foreigners' prepared by the Institute of International Law, reproduced in 2 *Yearbook of the International Law Commission* (1956), pp. 227, 228.

78 See Art 15, Section D of the update which was titled 'Draft Convention on the International Responsibility of States for Injuries to Aliens', reproduced in 2 *Yearbook of the International Law Commission* (1969) pp 142, 145.

79 See 'Draft Convention on the Responsibility of States for International Wrongful Acts, prepared by Professor Roth in 1932', reproduced in 2 *Yearbook of the International Law Commission* (1969), p 152.

The most comprehensive treatment of the principle and the precise conditions for attribution thereunder remains, however, that contained in Art 5 of the UNILC Articles on State Responsibility of 2001. The provision states as follows:

> Article 5
> Conduct of persons or entities exercising elements of governmental authority
> The conduct of a person or entity which is not an organ of the State under article 4 but which is empowered by the law of that State to exercise elements of the governmental authority shall be considered an act of the State under international law, provided the person or entity is acting in that capacity in the particular instance.

As the commentary to the provision (which uses the terms 'governmental authority', 'governmental functions' and 'public functions' interchangeably) points out, the provision was intended to deal with the increasingly common phenomenon of parastatal entities, which exercise elements of governmental authority in place of governmental organs, as well as situations where former State corporations have been privatized but retain certain public or regulatory functions. More generally, it was intended to deal with the wide variety of bodies: public corporations, semi-public entities, public agencies and even, in special cases, private companies, which though not organs of government, are empowered by the State to exercise '...functions of a public character normally exercised by State organs...'[80] The commentary importantly distinguishes a State authorization or empowerment to exercise governmental authority or functions covered by Art 5, from situations where the State authorizes or permits activity as part of its general regulation of the affairs of the community.[81] A good example of the latter situation would be the case of trade unions or professional associations permitted by law to regulate the affairs of their members.

Art 5, widely considered to constitute a codification of international law, has been credited for providing a much needed expansion of the concept of the act of the State in international law. Notably, both the Article and its commentary pinpoint three conditions for attributing the conduct of non-governmental entities to the State. Those three conditions are that the non-governmental entity must be authorized by the State (thus establishing an agency relationship with the State), that the authorization must be to exercise public or governmental functions, and thirdly, that responsibility attaches to the State without any necessity of proving the wrong was carried out under State control.[82] As demonstrated by international case law, the Commission's explicit reference to empowerment 'by law' is best considered a reiteration of law as the usual instrument through and under which the State authorizes or delegates activity. That is to say, authorizations that are not effected by legislation, for example contractual authorizations, would still be covered by the principle codified in Art 5.[83]

80 Art 5 ASR and commentary, in J Crawford, above n 14, p 100.

81 Ibid, p. 102.

82 J Crawford, above n 14, p 100–102.

83 See in this regard, *Helnan International Hotels v. Egypt* (ICSID Case No ARB/05/19), Decision on Objection to Jurisdiction, 17 October 2006, para 93, which provides support for this reading of Art 5.

International case law demonstrates that the operation of these three conditions for responsibility under Art 5 ASR bears close analogy with the legal relations established by the concepts of vicarious liability, the non-delegable duty and strict liability existing in the legal system of common law countries such as the United Kingdom, the United States, New Zealand, Canada and Australia. In subsequent sections, this article will provide an insight into these three tort law concepts and how international law has made analogous use of them to impose responsibility on the State for the conduct of non-governmental entities.

However, before proceeding to provide this insight, it is worthwhile to examine some criticisms levelled against the UNILC's reliance on the concept of governmental functions as a basis for apportioning responsibility.

4.3. *Critiques of the UNILC's reliance on the concept of the governmental function*

In the commentary to Art 5 ASR, it is stated that:

> If it is to be regarded as an act of the State for purposes of international responsibility, the conduct of an entity must accordingly concern *governmental activity and not other private or commercial activity* in which the entity may engage.[84]

The distinction between governmental/public and private (spheres of) activity made by the UNILC is a core component of liberalism – the dominant political and legal philosophy of the West.[85] It is also reflected in the distinction between public and private law which is common to civil law countries (such as France, The Netherlands, Belgium and Luxembourg) that are heavily influenced by the Roman legal tradition. In these countries, an autonomous body of laws regulating the activities of public authorities and distinct from that regulating relations between private parties forms a prominent feature of the legal system. While most modern legal systems now have laws governing the activities of public authorities, in some countries those laws are not necessarily distinct from the laws governing relations between private parties, but rather subsumed thereunder.[86]

The public/private divide arose from two specific developments in European history. First, the distinction between *État puissance publique* (the State as public power, holder of political and governmental duties) and *État personne privée/fiscus* (the State as subject of private law, owner of commercial or pecuniary rights)[87] was originally a by-product of

84 Art 5 ASR and commentary, J Crawford, above n 14, p 101.

85 See H Charlesworth, 'The Public/Private Distinction and the Right to Development in International Law' (1988–1989) 12 *Australian Year Book of International Law* 190.

86 See E Picard, 'The Public-Private Divide in French Law Through the History and Destiny of French Administrative Law' in M Ruffert (ed.), *The Public-Private Law Divide: Potential for Transformation?*, British Institute of International and Comparative Law, London 2009, p 17.

87 Cf: I Sinclair, 'The Law of Sovereign Immunity: Recent Developments' in *Collected Courses of the Hague Academy of International Law*, vol 167, p 129; H Street, *Governmental Liability: A Comparative Study, Cambridge Studies in International Law, Vol. IV*, Cambridge University Press, Cambridge 1953, pp 13–14; EM Borchard, above n 57, pp 143–144.

the 16th century advent of the modern State as an entity distinct from its subjects for whose benefit the State exercised its powers. It served as a tool for distinguishing the personal/private interests of the monarch (then transformed from overlord to sovereign) from the general/public interests which the monarch was intended to serve and to which prerogatives were accorded. However, by the 18th century, increasing claims of the sovereign to broad prerogatives to regulate individual activity in the public interest gave rise to the liberal idea of distinctively private spheres upon which the State's regulatory power may not encroach. In other words, the public/private divide which was originally a means for distinguishing the interests of the ruled from the private interests of the monarch was reinterpreted as a tool for delimiting a private sphere of liberty free from interference by public authorities.[88]

It is clearly the first interpretation of the public/private divide – as a distinction between public activity and the activity State organs or agents carry out in their capacity as private individuals – that Art 5's public/private distinction alludes to. The UNILC's reliance on the governmental/public functions concept and the distinction it draws between 'governmental' and 'private' activity has however been criticized on several grounds. Some of those critiques are summarized in C. Chinkin's seminal examination of the public/private distinction in international law as follows:

> The dualism between public and private spheres of activity has been identified as a key feature of classical, Western liberal thought. Despite its pervasiveness, its normative consequences in domestic law have been criticized on both practical and theoretical grounds. *For example, it has been argued that there is no reliable or constant basis for the distinction. Concepts of the public and private are complex, shifting, and reflect political preferences with respect to the level and quality of governmental intrusion.* Since there is no constant, objective basis for labelling an activity or actor as 'private', the judiciary regularly resorts to this as a device to avoid ruling on political issues...*Many of these criticisms are equally pertinent to the replication of the dichotomy within international law, which upholds a very traditional view of the role of the state. Its claim to universal applicability assumes a commonly accepted rationale for distinguishing between the conduct of state organs and that of other entities which in fact depends upon philosophical convictions about the proper role of government and government intervention. The location of any line between public and private activity is culturally specific and the appropriateness of using Western analytical tools to understand the global regime is questionable...*[89]

On the face of it, these critiques appear wholly justified and, further, supported by positions adopted by governments and by the UNILC itself during the drafting of Art 5.

First, the distinction between governmental/public functions and private functions as drawn by the UNILC undeniably has its inception in Western thought, whereas

88 See E Picard, above n 86, p 20–21.

89 C Chinkin, 'A Critique of the Public/Private Dimension' (1999) 10 *European Journal of International Law* no 2, 387, 390 (emphasis added).

international standards should reflect an average conception shared by all or at least the majority of States.

Secondly, even if it is conceded that the processes of cultural permeation resulting from globalization have meant that the distinction between public and private functions has also been adopted outside the West, international consensus on where exactly to draw the line between the public/governmental and the private is limited. This much is acknowledged by the UNILC itself where it hesitates to identify precisely what is governmental for the purposes of attribution of conduct of non-governmental entities to the State, pointing out that '[b]eyond a certain limit, what is regarded as "governmental" depends on the particular society, its history and traditions'.[90]

Third, to the extent the distinction is accepted in legal and political discourse, indeed concepts of what is governmental or private are not always static, but change with time and in line with developments or shifting priorities within societies. For example, the perception in several countries in Africa and Asia of the exploration of natural resources as a governmental function reflects the priority that activity still has in those countries as a tool for financing large-scale economic or infrastructural development. That persisting importance is underscored by UN General Assembly Resolution 1803 (XVII) of 14 December 1962 on 'Permanent Sovereignty over Natural Resources' which was strongly supported by then newly independent Latin-American, African and Asian countries. Similarly, the perception of health care and the National Health Service as a uniquely governmental function in the UK reflects the importance attached to public health delivery in the UK at this period in its history. It can be contrasted with the situation in the United States of America where the health care industry is currently dominated by private service providers. Thus, functions are not governmental or non-governmental by nature. They are governmental or non-governmental based on a value judgment – because they are regarded as such.

Lastly, the UNILC's reference to governmental functions as functions normally performed by governments and as excluding commercial activity would seem not to have taken into account one key challenge of transposing a domestic law public/private distinction (especially one in which public acts are defined as non-commercial) to the Law of State Responsibility. This is that the trend of privatization of public functions and the converse engagement of the State itself in trading and other commercial activity has meant that previously sacrosanct boundaries between governmental//public or private spheres of activity have become blurred. Commercial functions formerly considered the province of the private sector are now being performed by governments, just as many public interest functions formerly performed exclusively by governments are now being performed by private entities. This naturally raises questions as to whether the public-private distinction accords with present day reality. In other words, could the UNILC in seeking to expand the concept of the act of the State to fit present day reality itself have relied on a concept that is equally out of touch with present day reality?

The German government appeared to suggest as much when in its 1998 response to the UNILC's invitation of comments from governments, it pointed out that the concept

90 ASR and commentaries, J Crawford above n 14, 101.

of the State lying at the basis of the whole chapter of the ASR on attribution may be rooted more in past than in present conditions.[91] Moreover the idea that the act of the State as a subject of the international order excludes acts of a commercial nature had already drawn critiques in the past, of which the following commentary by Friedmann is illustrative:

> The fallacy of trying to distinguish between State acts of a public and those of a non-public nature lies in the attempt to take as static and permanent a state of affairs and a conception of State functions which are transitory. International society in the nineteenth century was sufficiently agreed upon the function of the State to make a general distinction. International society in 1938 is not. Within the States, such distinctions may be established and altered, from time to time, through legislation or judicial practice, in accordance with social changes... *And to stipulate internationally that the State acts for public purposes only outside the sphere of economics, is an unreal assertion in a world in which every State, socialist, fascist, or democratic, has assumed an increasing amount of control over economic activities. Could it be seriously contended that the British Government, when raising a loan in the United States of America in 1917, was not acting for a public purpose?*[92]

Turning to the response of the UNILC to these critiques, it is instructive that the Commission, though acknowledging the concerns surrounding the governmental functions concept, had not proceeded to expunge Art 5 from the ASR (as had happened with the former Art 19 ASR on the concept of State crimes[93]). It instead attempted to address the questions and concerns raised. This it did by proffering some examples of functions it apparently considered to be governmental for all States. The relevant functions are policing, the administration of expropriated property, the exercise of powers of detention or discipline pursuant to a judicial sentence, as well as the exercise of powers of immigration control. Immigration control, the UNILC noted, could be delegated by the State to private or State-owned airlines.[94] Importantly, the Commission also suggested criteria for determining what other functions may be regarded as governmental. These were '...not just the content of the powers, but the way they are conferred on an entity, the purposes for which they are exercised and the extent to which the entity is accountable to the government for their exercise'.[95]

This attempt by the Commission to provide guidelines for applying Art 5 ASR would be a basis for speculating that just like the liberals of old had reinterpreted the pre-existing

91 The UK government, on its part, had pointed to a lack of shared international understanding of the concept. See International Law Commission, 'State Responsibility: Comments and Observations Received From Governments', UN Doc. A/CN.4/488, 25 March 1998, pp 36–37, discussing the former Art 7(2) of the draft articles, now Art 5 ASR.

92 W Friedmann, above n 10, p 128 (emphasis added).

93 See ASR, J Crawford, above n 14, p 243 et seq. for the reasons underlying the deletion of the former Art 19 on State crimes, one of them being that penal consequences for States are not yet recognised in international law, a penal sanction being the usual consequence of the commission of a crime. The provision was ultimately replaced by Arts 40 and 41 ASR which makes a more neutral reference to 'serious breaches of obligations under peremptory norms of general international law'.

94 ASR and commentaries, J Crawford, above n 14, p 100–101.

95 Ibid, p 101.

16th century public-private divide in accordance with specific 18th century goals of preserving a sphere free from government intrusion, the UNILC had sought to define the governmental function in accordance with the primary goal underlying Art 5. That goal – preventing the State from evading responsibility for wrongs committed by persons carrying out functions on its behalf – was a recurrent theme in discussions at the Commission. As Edvard Hambro (Norway) had asserted during deliberations at the Commission, '[t]he State must never be allowed to evade responsibility for wrongful acts by organizing its activities outside its sphere of attribution'.[96] At the same time, the relative imprecision of some of the criteria provided by the Commission has meant that the task of more clearly defining what is governmental/public for the purposes of the principle codified in Art 5 ASR has fallen on international adjudicatory bodies. And it is in the latter's fulfilment of this task that private tort law analogies can be seen to play a role.

4.4. *Domestic tort law analogies and evolution in international case law*

This section examines how three specific domestic private law concepts – vicarious liability, the non-delegable duty and strict liability – mirror and help explain evolutions in international case law on the attribution to the State of conduct of non-governmental entities exercising governmental functions. Attention is devoted principally to cases decided since the 1980's when Art 5 ASR was first provisionally adopted by the UNILC at its 32nd session in Geneva. As is well known, the codification work of the Commission on State responsibility, regardless of whether or not explicitly cited in the case law, had started to influence legal doctrine on State responsibility even before its final adoption in 2001.[97]

4.4.1. State responsibility for non-governmental entities exercising governmental functions as vicarious responsibility

Vicarious liability traditionally arises where an employer or principal is fixed with liability for the tortious acts or omissions of an employee or agent. As the term 'vicarious' implies, it is conceived in domestic law as a derived or secondary, rather than personal form of responsibility. In other words, the respondent employer need not owe the claimant a duty of care or be in any way to blame for the injury caused by her employee. All that the injured claimant need prove is that a duty was owed by the employee, and that the employee breached that duty in the course of her employment by the defendant.[98]

96 International Law Commission, 'Summary Records of the Twenty-Sixth Session 6 May – 26 July 1974', 1 *Yearbook of the International Law Commission* (1974) p 23, para 23; also p 9, para 21 for Roberto Ago's reference to a shared view that '...the State must not be able to escape its international responsibility by adopting an international system of decentralization'.

97 See for example, *Case Concerning The Gabčíkovo-Nagymaros Project (Hungary/Slovakia)* [1997] ICJ Reports 7 in which both the parties and the International Court of Justice itself relied on Art 33 of the then Draft ASR.

98 See *Woodland v The Swimming Teachers' Association* [2013] 3 WLR 1227. Note that vicarious liability is additional to the primary liability of the employee or agent as both are 'jointly' and 'severally' liable.

The indirect or secondary nature of vicarious liability in domestic private law constitutes a point of differentiation from international law which adopts the fiction that the actions of State organs or agents are the State's own acts, not that of another. However, regardless of this point of differentiation, other aspects of vicarious responsibility as it exists in domestic tort law share similarities with aspects of international law's attribution to the State of wrongs by non-governmental entities performing governmental functions. Those similarities concern the means by which the legal relations forming the basis for vicarious responsibility are established, the scope of wrongs for which vicarious responsibility may be imposed, and the justifications for vicarious responsibility.

The employee or agent relation which forms a basis for vicarious liability in domestic tort law is usually established by an authorization or employment to act on the employer or principal's behalf. The employer or principal is liable only if it can be shown that the tort was committed by the agent or employee in the course of performing authorized functions. Thus, torts which are unconnected with the performance of authorized duties or are committed while engaged in the employee/agent's private business do not fall within the scope of the principal's vicarious responsibility.

Various justifications have been advanced for imposing vicarious liability on a principal/employer. One is the impossibility or difficulty of obtaining redress from an agent/employee who is judgment proof. An agent or employee may be judgment proof either because of possessing limited assets or because of having fled or in any other way being beyond the jurisdiction of the court. Another justification is that an employer that reaps the benefits of the activities of an employee should also bear the risk of injury caused by the employee. Also a consideration behind employer responsibility in domestic tort law is that it fosters deterrence by providing an incentive for employers to take steps (such as better training of employees) to prevent harm being caused by their agents/employees in the course of employment.[99] Indeed, as a matter of law, vicarious liability usually applies when a third party has the right and duty to control the activities of the tortfeasor.

Several of the afore-mentioned aspects of the operation of vicarious liability in domestic tort law are replicated in international case law on State responsibility for non-governmental entities exercising governmental functions:

To start with, international case law demonstrates that a State authorization to perform a governmental function on the State's behalf remains the principal basis for attributing to and thus holding the State responsible for wrongs committed by a non-governmental entity exercising governmental functions.[100] The cases also underscore that for the State to be held responsible, the wrong must have been committed in the course of the entity's exercise of the authorized governmental function and not in the exercise of functions that are not authorized to be performed on behalf of the State.

99 Cf: the decision of the High Court of Australia in *New South Wales v Lepore*; *Samin v. Queenland*; *Rich v. Queenland* [2003] HCA 4 (6 February 2003) para. 196–202.

100 Another basis recognised in international law is the performance of a governmental function in the absence of State authorities as 'an agent of necessity'. This is an exceptional situation dealt with by Art 9 ASR and not covered in this article.

Illustrative in this regard is *Bosh International, Inc, B&P Ltd Foreign Investments Enterprise v. Ukraine*.[101] The case concerned a claim brought by Bosh, a United States (US) registered company and its Ukrainian subsidiary B&P before a tribunal established under the auspices of the International Centre for the Settlement of Investment Disputes (ICSID). Bosh had alleged, *inter alia*, that Ukraine through the conduct of an autonomous but State-owned university had breached certain provisions of the bilateral investment treaty (BIT) between the US and Ukraine. Among the provisions alleged to have been breached was the treaty's 'umbrella clause', an umbrella clause being an exception to the general rule that a breach of contract is not a breach of international law.[102]

In 2003, B & P had entered into a joint venture agreement with the university to redevelop and operate a Science-Hotel Complex. Based on alleged breaches of the contract by B & P, the university subsequently terminated the contract and obtained a court order evicting B&P from the premises of the Science-Hotel Complex. This termination of the contract by the university was considered by B & P to constitute a breach by Ukraine of the umbrella clause in the US/Ukraine BIT.

On the question of attribution of the conduct of the university to Ukraine, Ukraine had argued that certain tasks the university was empowered by law to perform, namely, the provision of education and the management of State property, did not involve an exercise of public/governmental power within the meaning of Art 5 ASR as argued by the claimants. Even if the university was empowered to exercise governmental authority, Ukraine went on, '... the termination of the 2003 Contract was not carried out in the exercise of such authority; it was simply the termination of a commercial agreement, rather than the carrying out of any sovereign act.'[103] The university '... is not empowered to enter into commercial agreements on behalf of the State' and it did not so in relation to the 2003 Contract, Ukraine further asserted.[104]

Responding to this contention, the Tribunal was of the view that the provision of education and the management of State property constituted governmental functions:

'the provision by the University of, *inter alia*, higher education services and the management of State-owned property in accordance with Presidential Decree No 1496/99 of 25 November 1999, the Law on Higher Education (Law No 2984-III), and the Charters of 2000 and 2009 (which were, respectively, adopted by an Order of the President of Ukraine, and an Order of the Minister of Education and Science of Ukraine) constitute forms of governmental authority that the University is empowered by the law of Ukraine to exercise.'[105]

101 *Bosh International, Inc and B&P Ltd Foreign Investments Enterprise v. Ukraine*, ICSID Case No. ARB/08/11, Award of 25 October 2012.

102 The umbrella clause is contained in Article II(3)(c) of the BIT: 'Each Party shall observe any obligation it may have entered into with regard to investments'. Because they are made in a treaty, the reference in so-called umbrella clauses to 'any obligation' are generally considered to elevate what would ordinarily be a domestic law breach of a contractual obligation to a breach of international law.

103 *Bosh International*, above n 101, para 162.

104 *Bosh International*, above n 101, para 161.

105 *Bosh International*, above n 101, para. 173.

However, in determining whether the termination of the agreement by the university had occurred in the course of an exercise of governmental functions or authority, the tribunal concluded that having regard to the nature and purpose of the 2003 Contract, which as indicated by articles of the contract was to secure commercial benefits for both parties, the university was not engaged in the exercise of the governmental authority of Ukraine, but in other private or commercial activity. As such, its conduct in terminating the agreement with B & P did not engage the responsibility of Ukraine.

Significantly, the tribunal had arrived at this conclusion after emphasizing that according to the explicit terms of Ukraine's Law on Higher Education, the university had a right as an autonomous institution to engage in joint ventures (such as the one it had entered into with B & P) and was entitled under its Charter to enter into the 2003 Contract in its own right, without the need for any particular authorization by Ukraine.[106] This was in contrast to the university's functions of providing higher education and managing State-owned property which, as the tribunal pointed out, had been vested on it by State law. By this reference to what the university could do as of its own right whether or not authorized by Ukraine, the tribunal had apparently treated the law's reference to the university's right to enter into joint ventures and associated (commercial) contracts as a State authorization/endorsement of activity as part of its general regulation of the affairs of community. The latter had been distinguished in the commentary to Art 5 ASR from an authorization to act on the State's behalf. The *Bosh International* decision thus serves to underscore that in an analogy to vicarious responsibility in domestic tort law, an authorization to carry out a function on the State's behalf (and not on one's own behalf) is the basis for State responsibility for wrongs committed while performing governmental functions.

The position that a State's authorization to act on its behalf is the main basis for attributing governmental acts to the State is equally illustrated by the 1984 decision of the Iran-United States Claims Tribunal in *Schering Corporation v. Iran*.[107] *Schering* was one of several claims filed by American companies against Iran for economic losses sustained in the aftermath of the Iranian Islamic Revolution of 1979. It concerned a claim that Iran was responsible, *inter alia*, for a seizure of the company's assets by the Workers' Council of Schering Iran (a subsidiary of the claimant). Such seizure if committed by an entity whose conduct was attributable to the State would constitute an expropriation in breach of international law. The essential question before the tribunal was whether in the light of Art 104 of the Iranian Constitution, the Workers' Council at Schering Iran could be regarded as an entity authorized *de jure* to exercise governmental functions or authority, for whose acts Iran would be held responsible. The provision stated that Workers' Councils would be organized in accordance with law so as 'to safeguard Islamic justice in the preparation of programs, and in the coordination of progress in the affairs of industrial and agricultural production units.'[108]

In examining this question, the tribunal observed that the constitutional and regulatory framework for the creation of Workers' Councils did not indicate that they

106 *Bosh International*, above n 101, para. 177.

107 *Schering Corporation v Iran*, 5 Iran-U.S. Claims Tribunal Reports (1984-I), p 361.

108 Ibid, p 369.

were to have any duties other than representing the workers' interests *vis-à-vis* the management of the company and institutions and cooperating with the management. The fact that the formation of the Council was initiated by the State, the tribunal noted, did not in itself imply that the Councils '...were to function as part of the State's machinery'.[109] In other words, it did not imply they were authorized to act for the State.

International case law upholding State authorization of governmental activity as a basis for State responsibility for wrongs spans fields of international law ranging from international human rights[110] to international investment and trade law.[111] Significantly, the relevant case law further demonstrates another area of convergence between the Law of State Responsibility and vicarious responsibility in domestic tort law: the type of state authorized functions to which State responsibility attaches.

Domestic law does not place a limit on the type of authorized tasks to which vicarious responsibility attaches. An authorization to act on the employer's behalf and proof that the tort was committed while performing an authorized task would normally ground vicarious responsibility. Many international tribunal decisions, on the other hand, having expressly or implicitly subscribed to a definition of governmental functions as 'normal' or 'traditional' functions of the State, have excluded commercial functions from the scope of functions for which the State is 'vicariously' responsible under Art 5 ASR. However, echoing the more expansive approach of domestic law, it is not all international tribunal decisions that have excluded commercial functions from the scope of what is governmental and thus engages 'vicarious' State responsibility under Art 5. Some tribunal decisions, alongside treating the governmental functions concept as concerning traditional State functions (ie legislative/regulatory functions, executive, adjudication, policing and defence, foreign affairs, education, health care, etc), have also subscribed to an additional, broader conception of governmental activity as encompassing any function, commercial or otherwise, authorized by the State to be performed on its behalf.

That a function commercial or otherwise, is authorized to be performed on the State's behalf (and cannot be deemed as authorized simply as part of the State's general regulation of the affairs of society) is usually read by the relevant tribunals from the circumstances of the exercise of the function concerned. These are circumstances which evince a unique relation between the State and the non-governmental entity – a relation that mirrors the one that the State has with its regular government organs. In those circumstances, the entity's operations are carried out under conditions of State association or involvement that cannot be rationalized as a mere evidence of a public-private partnership. The entity's operations, rather, point to a *de facto* or *de jure* agency relation with the State. In other words, the operations exhibit the markings of State authority or operation as an arm of the State.

109 *Schering Corporation v Iran*, above n 107, p 370.

110 See for example, *Van Der Mussele v. Belgium, no 8919/80,* European Court of Human Rights, Judgment of 23 November 1983; *Carlos Cabal and Marco Pasini Bertran v Australia*, CCPR/C/78/D/1020/2001, UN Human Rights Committee, 19 September 2003.

111 See for example, *Jan de Nul NV v The Arab Republic of Egypt* (ICSID Case no ARB/04/13), Award, 24 October 2008; *Korea – Measures Affecting Imports of Fresh, Chilled and Frozen Beef*, World Trade Organization, Panel Report, WT/DS161/R WT/DS169/R, adopted 31 July 2000, para 763.

One such marking of State authority or operation as an arm of the State recognized in case law is the fact that the entity (or its function) has a public law status under the laws of the State concerned.[112] Another is that regardless of any designations it is given, the function is vested or regulated by administrative law.[113] Other criteria found to render a function governmental in accordance with this broader conception of governmental functions include the exercise of a State-vested monopoly,[114] an enjoyment of rights or privileges (such as immunity) reserved for State authorities,[115] management of State property or of a public utility under the control of the State[116] and performance of a function under the guidance, supervision or approval of the government.[117]

The above-mentioned criteria of governmental functions or authority give flesh and credence to the UNILC's reference to '...the content of the powers ... the way they are conferred on an entity, the purposes for which they are exercised and the extent to which the entity is accountable to the government for their exercise'[118] as tests of governmental activity. Although any one of these factors taken alone may be decisive for attributing wrongs to the State, it may be wrong to say that in each and every case a single factor would be decisive. This is particularly so with regard to the criterion of the public status of an entity under national law, a criterion both case law such as the *Bosh International* case and the UNILC[119] itself suggest to be non-decisive in itself for grounding State responsibility. A reason why a single factor may not necessarily be decisive, is that what tribunals do in many cases is carry out a close examination of the specific facts of the case at hand and balance criteria pointing to action on behalf of the State against criteria pointing to an autonomous or truly separate operation from the State.[120] In any case, it suffices to state that these are criteria of governmental activity for the purposes of State responsibility in international law.

By adopting a second broad definition of governmental functions that encompasses commercial functions, the tribunals can be said to have adopted a 'purely agency' definition of governmental functions which like domestic tort law on vicarious responsibility focuses simply on the fact of empowerment to act on the defendant's behalf. This is opposed to a 'functional' definition that looks further at the regulatory or other traditional governmental character of the function transferred as a condition for Art 5 liability. The definition of governmental functions according to the criterion of 'agency' aligns the principle codified

112 *Yershova v Russia*, no 1387/04, European Court of Human Rights, Judgment of 8 April 2010, paras 58–59.

113 See, for example, *Canada -Measures Affecting the Importation of Milk and the Exportation of Dairy Products*, World Trade Organization, Panel Report (WT/DS113/R), 17 May 1999, para 7.76.

114 *Korea – Measures Affecting Imports of Fresh, Chilled and Frozen Beef*, World Trade Organization Panel Report (WT/DS169/R), 31 July 2000, para 767.

115 *Yershova v. Russia*, above n 112, para 58.

116 *Salini Costruttori SpA & Italstrade SpA v Kingdom of Morocco* (ICSID Case No. ARB/00/4), Decision on Jurisdiction, 23 July 2001, para 33; *EDF (Services) Limited v. Romania* (ICSID Case No. ARB/05/13), Award, October 8, 2009, para 195.

117 *EnCana Corporation v Ecuador* (London Court of International Arbitration Case no. UN3481), Award, 3 February 2006.

118 ASR and commentaries, J Crawford above n 14, p 101.

119 See commentary to Art 5 ASR, J Crawford above n 14, p 100.

120 Cf: Thomas W. Wälde, Investment Arbitration under the Energy Charter Treaty: An Overview of Key Issues, 1 *Transnational Dispute Management* No 2, May 2004.

in Art 5 ASR with the 21st century reality that States also perform commercial functions. By ensuring that States bear responsibility for wrongs of entities authorized to act on their behalf, regardless of the sphere of activity in which they are employed (commercial or otherwise), it ensures the goal of non-evasion of State responsibility is achieved.

Lastly, it is worthwhile to point to analogies that exist between the justification for vicarious liability and the justifications for international State responsibility for non-governmental entities (including those exercising governmental functions). An important justification for State responsibility for acts of non-governmental entities in international law is that non-governmental entities, as a general rule, do not possess direct obligations in international law. As such, they are ordinarily beyond the jurisdiction of international courts as defendants.[121] For that reason, failing to hold the State accountable for their conduct would leave a gap in the protection of rights at the international level. This is comparable to the situation in domestic tort law where the difficulty of obtaining redress from an agent/employee who is beyond the jurisdiction of the courts constitutes an important justification for vicarious liability. Also, as is the case with vicarious liability, holding the State responsible in international law for conduct of non-governmental entities acting on its behalf provides an incentive for the State to exercise better control over them to ensure they act in compliance with the State's international obligations. Indeed some international treaties have sought to emphasize this implication of the State carrying out activities through private or autonomous entities. An example is the Energy Charter Treaty which requires the State to exercise better control over non-governmental entities exercising governmental authority:

> Article 22
> State and privileged enterprises
> ...
> (3) Each Contracting Party shall ensure that if it establishes or maintains an entity and entrusts the entity with regulatory, administrative or other governmental authority, such entity shall exercise that authority in a manner consistent with the Contracting Party's obligations under this Treaty
> ...
> (5) For the purposes of this Article, "entity" includes any enterprise, agency or other organization or individual[122]

121 See, for example M Karavias, 'Shared Responsibility and Multinational Enterprises', *Amsterdam Law School Legal Studies Research Paper* No. 2015-05, p. 7 <https://papers.ssrn.com/sol3/papers.cfm?abstract_id=2572970> accessed 07.01.2017.
An exception to this general rule is the *lex specialis* system of international criminal law enforced at international criminal tribunals such as the International Criminal Court in the Hague. Though corporate criminal responsibility is yet to be accepted in international criminal law, individuals hold obligations in international criminal law and are the defendants in international criminal law proceedings.

122 Art 22 of the Energy Charter Treaty of 17 December 1994. The treaty covers energy investments, trade, freedom of energy transit, energy efficiency and the resolution of state-to-state or investor-to-state disputes.

4.4.2. The non-delegable duty analogy

The concept of a non-delegable duty of care is used to justify imposing liability on a person for the negligence of another to whom the former has entrusted the performance of a task.[123] In contrast with vicarious liability which is a derived form of liability, liability for breach of the non-delegable duty of care is a personal liability. It is for a breach of a duty resting on the employer herself. Obviously, since the 'non-delegable' duty concerns liability arising in the context of the delegation of a task, the description of the duty as 'non-delegable' does not mean that the task cannot be delegated. It rather means that the employer cannot escape liability if the task or an attendant duty of care is delegated and not properly performed.[124] In other words, the employer can delegate the task or duty of care but cannot delegate the accompanying liabilities.

An important role played by the non-delegable duty concept is that it supplements vicarious responsibility in situations where the tortfeasor is an independent contractor and thus an employee/agency relationship which is a condition for vicarious liability is lacking. For example, in Australia, it is well-established that a hospital is liable for the negligence of those who provide health-care services in its name, regardless of whether the provider is an employee or an independent contractor of the hospital.[125] Grounds for recognizing a duty as non-delegable vary. They range from the defendant's control over the location of an activity to a special position of vulnerability on the part of the plaintiff (such as a school pupil or a hospital patient), or the fact that a statute has imposed on the defendant personally a positive duty to perform some function and a related duty of care.[126]

Case law on State responsibility for the conduct of non-governmental entities performing governmental functions contains an analogy to the non-delegable duty concept. This analogy is a definition of governmental functions as including 'core' State functions which the State cannot delegate or abdicate to the private sector without retaining responsibility for the manner of their performance. Though the case law itself does not provide an exhaustive list, the core functions concept evidently refers to certain functions which international society regardless of decentralizations of State functions still considers to constitute the raison d'être of the State, viz: the legislative, executive and judicial functions as well as foreign affairs, security, defence, immigration control and the use of force or coercion in the public interest.[127] Their core governmental nature

123 Government of Australia, *Review of the Law of Negligence Report*, 2 October 2002, p 165.

124 See Lord Hailsham of St Marylebone in *McDermid v Nash Dredging & Reclamation Co Ltd* [1987] AC 906 at 910; *Woodland v Swimming Teachers' Association* [2013] 3 WLR 1227.

125 *Ellis v Wallsend District Hospital* (1989) 17 NSWLR 553.

126 See *Woodland v Essex County Council* [2013] UKSC 66, para 7 https://www.supremecourt.uk/cases/docs/uksc-2012-0093-judgment.pdf, accessed 16 January 2017; also *New South Wales v Lepore*, above n 99, paras 152–155.

127 See the definitions of the 'failed' State in Daniel Thürer, 'The "Failed State" and International Law' (1999) *International Review of the Red Cross*, no. 836; (Dutch) Advisory Council on International Affairs (AIV) and Advisory Committee on Issues of Public International Law (CAVV), Advisory Report no. 35, May 2004, p 8–11; also The African Studies Centre, Leiden; The Transnational Institute, Amsterdam; The Centre of Social Studies, Coimbra University and The Peace Research Center – CIP-

distinguishes them from other functions of government whose governmental character is necessarily dependent on the existence of an agency relation with the State.[128]

Illustrative of the 'core' State functions concept is the case of *Carlos Cabal and Marco Pasini Bertran v. Australia*[129] brought before the United Nations Human Rights Committee. The Committee is the body that monitors the implementation of the International Covenant on Civil and Political Rights of 1966. In that case, the Committee found Australia accountable for the ill treatment of inmates in a prison operated by a private company (Group 4 Correction Services Ltd) under contract with the Australian State of Victoria. In the words of the Committee, '...the contracting out to the private commercial sector of core State activities which involve the use of force and the detention of persons does not absolve a State party of its obligations under the Covenant...'[130]

The 'non-delegable' nature of State functions involving compulsion and detention of persons in the public interest is further underscored by the case of *Yeager v. Iran*. The question before the Iran-United States Claims Tribunal in that case was whether the forced expulsion of a US citizen by an Iranian paramilitary group, the 'Revolutionary Guards' or 'Komitehs', could be attributed to Iran. The expulsion had occurred in the context of the Komitehs' performance of functions of customs/immigration control and security. The Tribunal held Iran to be responsible for the act of expulsion by the Komitehs. Underscoring the 'non-delegable' nature of those functions was the fact that Iran's responsibility in the case was based not on an express authorization to the Komitehs to perform those functions, but rather its acquiescence to their performance. As the Tribunal pointed out, 'Iran cannot, on the one hand, tolerate the exercise of governmental authority by revolutionary "Komitehs" or "Guards", and at the same time deny responsibility for wrongful acts committed by them.'[131]

A second analogy to the non-delegable duty concept in case law on State responsibility for the conduct of non-governmental entities performing governmental functions exists. It is the idea of a function for whose manner of performance the State cannot absolve itself of responsibility because it has expressly or implicitly undertaken at the international level to carry out that function. The exercise of such a function has been regarded in international case law as involving an exercise of governmental authority. It would be remembered that an undertaking by the defendant to perform a duty is one ground in domestic tort law for qualifying the duty as non-delegable.

Thus, in *Van Der Mussele v. Belgium*[132] the claimant had complained that the obligation to grant free legal aid imposed on him by the professional rules of the Belgian

Fuhem, Madrid, 'Failed and Collapsed States in the International System', 2003, p. 3 <www.ces.uc.pt/nucleos/nep/documentos/failed_collapsedStates-Report.pdf> accessed 08.01.2017. The failed State is seen by the international community as one that can no longer perform the core functions of the State as a subject of international law.

128 See the discussion of the 'agency' definition of governmental functions in the preceding sub-section 4.4.2 on State responsibility as vicarious responsibility.

129 *Carlos Cabal and Marco Pasini Bertran v. Australia* (Communication no. 1020/2001), Views of the UN Human Rights Committee under the Optional Protocol to the ICCPR, 19 September 2003.

130 *Ibid*, para 7.2.

131 *Yeager v Islamic Republic of Iran* (1987) 17 Iran-US Claims Tribunal Reports, 92, 105.

132 *Van Der Mussele v. Belgium*, above n 110, para 29.

Order of Advocates constituted forced labour contrary to Art 4(2) of the European Convention on Human Rights. The issue before the European Court of Human Rights (ECtHR) was whether the conduct of the Belgian Order of Advocates in requiring the complainant to grant free legal aid was attributable to Belgium and thus a basis for Belgium's responsibility. In providing an affirmative answer to this question, the Court pointed out, *inter alia*, that the duty of free legal aid for indigent persons was an obligation undertaken by State parties under Art 6(3) of the Convention and in turn imposed by law – the Belgian Judicial Code – on the Belgian Order of Advocates. Imposing the obligation on the Belgium Order, the Court went on, could not relieve the Belgian State of the responsibilities it would have incurred under the Convention if it had chosen to operate the system itself. In other words, the conduct of the Belgian Order in operating a system of free legal aid required of Belgium under the Convention was attributable to the State.

The foregoing discussion has highlighted how the responsibility of the State in international law for wrongs by non-governmental entities exercising governmental functions bears a close analogy to two forms of liability in domestic tort law: vicarious liability and liability under the non-delegable duty concept. The next section looks at the 'strict' nature of these two forms of domestic law liability and how the Law of State Responsibility equally mirrors that strictness.

4.4.3. Strict liability

In the Australian case of *Scott v Davis*, Gummow J. had pointed out that some caution is required in characterizing a breach as a breach of a non-delegable duty '...because the characterization of a duty as non-delegable involves, in effect, the imposition of strict liability upon the defendant who owes that duty.'[133] Indeed an important aspect of liability for breach of the non-delegable duty as well as vicarious liability in domestic law is that the liability is strict. Strict liability entails that liability attaches without any fault (negligence or wrongdoing) on the part of the defendant, and regardless of whether or not the defendant possessed control over the wrong or authorized it.[134] The value of strict liability is that it has a better deterrent effect than liability based on fault. This is because it removes evidentiary problems of proving negligence.

Just like domestic courts exercise caution in declaring a duty non-delegable because of the implications with respect to strict liability, international tribunals also exercise caution about characterizing a wrong as one committed by an entity as a State organ or agent (including one exercising governmental functions). This is because the liability the State bears for its agents or organs, including those exercising governmental functions, is strict. It attaches without proof of any want of care on behalf of the State and regardless of whether it condoned the wrong or had control over its occurrence.

133 *Scott v Davis*, 204 CLR 333 (2000), p 417.

134 Cf: D Neild, 'Vicarious Liability and the Employment Rationale' (2013) 44 *Victoria University of Wellington Law Review* 707, 708 where discusses the rationale underpinning vicarious responsibility.

This position of the law is demonstrated by the case of *B.d.B. et al. v. The Netherlands*.[135] In the case, the claimants had alleged before the European Court of Human Rights that they had been discriminated against by a body known as the Industrial Insurance Board for Health and For Mental and Social Interests (hereafter BVG) in the latter's implementation of social security legislation. They contended that since it was performing the executive function of implementing social security legislation, BVG's acts were attributable to the Netherlands. The Netherlands, on the other hand, argued that though it implemented social security legislation, BVG was not a State representative but an association of employers and employees, managed exclusively by representatives of employers and employees. It also pointed out that like other industrial insurance boards, BVG operated independently without any State influence and that there was no way the State authorities could influence concrete decisions such as those complained of by the claimants.

This argument by the Netherlands was rejected by the Committee. Though the case was ultimately declared inadmissible on substantive grounds, the Committee upheld the applicants' contention that States would easily be able to undermine the basic rights of their citizens if allowed to claim lack of influence over bodies such as the BVG. It observed that the author's complaint related to the application of legal rules of a compulsory nature and for that reason, the Netherlands was responsible for BVG's conduct.[136] Thus, as the commentary to Art 5 ASR rightly observed: '[f]or the purposes of article 5, an entity is covered even if its exercise of authority involves an independent discretion or power to act; there is no need to show that the conduct was in fact carried out under the control of the State.'[137]

The above examination of relevant international case law has highlighted the analogies between domestic tort law and international law on State responsibility for conduct of non-governmental entities exercising governmental functions. It has also revealed two broad perspectives from which the governmental functions concept has been expressly or implicitly defined in relevant case law, viz:

(a) traditional or normal functions of government (a category under which the 'non-delegable' or core State functions are subsumed as those core functions are among functions traditionally performed by governments), and
(b) functions whose qualification as governmental is simply a reference to their being performed in the context of a *de facto* or *de jure* agency relationship with the State.

The next section will revisit the critiques of the transposition of the governmental/private distinction from domestic law to international law in the light of the examination of case law.

135 *B d B v The Netherlands*, no 273/1989, UN Human Rights Committee, Decision on Admissibility, 30 March 1989.
136 Ibid, para 6.5.
137 ASR and commentaries, J Crawford, above n 14, p 102.

5. Revisiting the governmental functions concept: a valuable tool for delimiting liabilities and competences in the 21st century?

Since the adoption of the UNILC's Articles on State Responsibility in 2001, reliance on the domestic law governmental/private functions distinction for apportioning responsibility to the State in international law has gained traction in international practice. This is regardless of the fact that some domestic courts have explicitly eschewed such reliance and that there are still calls for its elimination.

For example, in the seminal 1983 *Bancec* case (the case concerned, *inter alia*, an alleged violation of international law), the US Supreme Court declined the urgings of the US Solicitor General to adopt the governmental functions test for apportioning responsibility between a State and an autonomous but State-owned corporation, pointing out that:

> ...the concept of a "usual" or a "proper" governmental function changes over time and varies from nation to nation.

In support, the Court had also cited previous US case law describing the governmental functions concept as '... too shifting a basis for determining constitutional power and too entangled in expediency to serve as a dependable legal criterion.'[138]

More recently, Van Aartsen has argued:

> The public-private divide is one of the 21st century's flat earth theories ... While scientific use of the public-private divide once had a useful function, its adoption is now unrealistic and harmful. In an era marked by the genesis, continuation and intensification of a wide variety of environmental, political and economic crises we can no longer afford to use this flawed assumption as a fixed frame of reference ... Once a reliable source of social scientific and political stability, this flat earth concept is now at the heart of much social scientific and political impotence in dealing with contemporary social, political and environmental problems. The rules of the game have been rewritten. Social scientific work needs to abandon the positivist confines of the broken political compromise and view the public-private divide as part of the problem.[139]

On the contrary, this author contends that the public-private divide is the solution rather than part of the problem. Put differently, the problem in the midst of the variety of environmental, political and economic challenges faced today is not the public-private distinction *per se* – a distinction Van Aartsen himself acknowledges once served a useful function. It is rather (at least within the context of the responsibility of the State for

138 *First National City Bank v. Banco Para El Commercio Exterior de Cuba (BANCEC)*, 462 US 611, 633 (1983), n 27.

139 C Van Aartsen, 'The End of the Public-Private Divide', *Maastricht University Law Blog*, 14.09.2016 <https://www.maastrichtuniversity.nl/blog/2016/09/end-public-private-divide> accessed 07.01.2017.

conduct of non-governmental entities)[140] a definition of the public-private concept that may be out of touch with present day reality – out of touch with present day reality because it is based solely on the idea of what is 'usual' or 'normal' for the government to do.

What precisely is needed at this point in history is a retooling of the concept in the light of present day realities to serve a useful purpose. In other words, if the distinction once served a useful function, which it did in the 16th and 18th centuries,[141] then it can serve a useful function again – in the 21st century. And it is precisely a redefinition and harnessing of the concept to serve a useful purpose that the Law of State Responsibility has achieved by re-conceptualizing the governmental function for the purposes of State responsibility to include ostensibly 'commercial' or 'private' functions where they are performed by private entities essentially operating as an arm of the public entity, the State. By doing so, the Law of State Responsibility has ensured that States cannot escape responsibility for wrongs by persons truly acting on their behalf by pleading that the functions concerned are 'private' or 'commercial' and thus fall outside the State's remit. Furthermore, by designating certain functions as 'core' functions which the State cannot delegate away responsibility for the manner of their performance by non-governmental entities, international law has ensured that in the midst of blur in boundaries between the public and private, the State retains ultimate responsibility for certain functions on whose effective performance the rule of law, security and stability in the international order depends. For example, if the State, the primary holder of security obligations in international law, can no longer be relied upon to retain final responsibility for the maintenance of law and order within its territory, this could spell chaos for the international legal order.

This pragmatic approach of international law (which balances a sovereign State freedom to delegate functions with a retention of ultimate responsibility in certain cases) offers lessons for domestic as well as regional legal orders. This is particular so at this period in history in which a wide variety of entities – public, private, transnational – are cooperating to provide citizens with public services such as transportation, energy and health care or to implement social policies that are expected to comply with certain standards. Where federal, State or local governments transfer public services to private entities, NGOs or regional organizations, or otherwise work in tandem with them to provide those services, questions regarding accountability to end users as well as divisions of responsibilities/spheres of competences between services providers frequently arise. So also does the phenomenon of buck-passing when things go wrong. Buck-passing is usually only possible where clear rules on the apportionment of (ultimate)

140 In the context of van Aartsen's critique, the problem is apparently one implication that has been given to the public-private divide: that the State cannot intervene in the sphere of private relations to regulate private decision-making that has profound public consequences, consequences that may be even more profound than the consequences of policy making by the government itself. This is a separate problem that is not addressed here since it falls outside the scope of issues forming the central focus of this thesis.

141 See discussion in Section 4.3 above on critiques of the UNILC's reliance on the concept of the governmental/public function.

responsibility are lacking.[142] International law's approach of declaring a core set of governmental functions for which the State retains ultimate responsibility, could – where adopted at domestic and regional levels – help to resolve uncertainties regarding liability and spheres of competence brought about by the blur in previously sacrosanct distinctions between governmental and private tasks.

It is therefore noteworthy that concerning the tangentially related issue of mergers and acquisitions of formerly State-owned companies, the idea of delimiting a core of strategic industries over which a State retains a special responsibility (in the form of a special power of oversight of acquisitions) recently came to the fore in parliamentary discussions in the Netherlands. The pertinent discussions concerned a bid by the partly Belgian State-owned postal company, Belgian Post (Bpost) for a takeover of the fully privatized Dutch postal company (PostNL). The idea was raised in the midst of uncertainty and growing controversy as to who should have the final say on the proposed (though ultimately failed) acquisition bid: the shareholders of PostNL or the Dutch State. This issue was problematic considering that the task of providing universal postal services was a task vested pre-privatization on PostNL by Dutch public law and, in the eyes of some, the task concerned 'vital communication infrastructure'.[143] A clear delimitation of industries which because of their strategic national importance may need to be protected from foreign acquisitions was considered in some quarters to be a solution to uncertainties surrounding the propriety or otherwise of foreign acquisitions of companies like PostNL. Though this example deals with an issue that is only tangentially related, it is an example that points to the utility of clearly delimiting what tasks fall under the core responsibility of the State.

6. Conclusion

The transfer or outsourcing to the non-governmental/corporate sector of functions normally performed by government remains one of the most significant evolutions in the organization of the modern State. This phenomenon, variously referred to as the 'retreat of the State', has led to debates in various disciplines – from economics and politics to the applied sciences – about the proper role of government and how society should deal with the phenomenon of the 'shrinking State'. Public international law has brought a voice to the debate through the manner in which it has addressed the reality of non-governmental entities performing tasks formerly performed solely by governments. It has, notably, done this by relying on concepts which have analogies in domestic law, namely vicarious responsibility, the non-delegable duty concept and strict liability.

By designating an exercise of governmental functions as one basis for attributing to the State wrongs committed by non-governmental entities, the international legal order

142 Cf: generally, R Mulgan, 'Government Accountability for Outsourced Services' (2006) 65 *Australian Journal of Public Administration* no 2, pp 48–58.

143 Cf: A Weissink, 'Kabinet moet PostNL in bescherming nemen', *Het Financieele Dagblad*, 15 November 2016 <https://fd.nl/economie-politiek/1175737/kabinet-moet-postnl-in-bescherming-nemen> accessed 17 January 2017.

has catered to its systemic need to ensure States retain ultimate responsibility for certain functions on whose effective performance the rule of law and stability in the international order depends. By so doing, international law has demonstrated that the centuries old domestic law public/private divide, which served to preserve a private sphere free from government intrusion, can be transposed to the international level to serve new needs of the 21st century. International law's reliance on the centuries old distinction is therefore not misplaced. This is to the extent it has re-conceptualized the distinction to fit modern day conditions.

The use of domestic law analogies in international law on State responsibility draws attention to the opportunities for a beneficial cross-fertilization of ideas between the domestic and international legal orders. Just as international law has occasionally drawn inspiration from domestic law, international law's approach to the decentralization/privatization of State functions arguably offers lessons for national and regional legal orders. Should the domestic legal order adopt international law's approach of designating certain functions as 'core' governmental functions for which the government retains ultimate responsibility, such designation could be one way of ameliorating any concerns that a transfer of public services to the private/commercial sector can lead to reduced accountability to the end users of those services. Such concerns would usually stem from the reality that governmental actors are usually subject to higher standards of public accountability than private entities and corporations. Also – whether rightly or wrongly – private contractors, because they usually operate with a profit motive, are often expected to pay less attention to the public service element compared to governmental entities.

Naturally, it is primarily for the legal order or society concerned to decide for itself the functions for which the government should bear the ultimate responsibility, irrespective of whether those functions are performed by non-governmental entities. At the same time, the increasing interface between international and national legal orders warrants the conclusion that this is an area of discourse in which dialogue between domestic and international law as well as national and international decision makers can only increase. More so, as both legal orders compete with each other in regulating the activities of their (primary) subject, the State.

IUS COMMUNE EUROPAEUM

A peer-reviewed book series in which the common foundations of the legal systems of the Member States of the European Union are the central focus.

The *Ius Commune Europaeum* series includes horizontal comparative legal studies as well as studies on the effect of treaties within the national legal systems. All the classic fields of law are covered. The books are published in various European languages under the auspices of METRO, the Institute for Transnational Legal Research at Maastricht University.

Editorial Board: Prof. Dr. J. Smits (chair), Prof. Dr. M. Faure, Prof. Dr. Chr. Joerges, Prof. Dr. J. du Plessis and Prof. Dr. E. Vos.

Recently published:
Volume 146: *The Citizen in European Private Law: Norm-setting, Enforcement and Choice*, C. Cauffman and J. Smits (eds.)
Volume 147: *Legal Certainty in Real Estate Transactions: A Comparison of England and France*, B. Du Marais and D. Marrani (eds.)
Volume 148: *Scarcity and the State I. The Allocation of Limited Rights by the Administration*, P. Adriaanse, F. van Ommeren, W. den Ouden and J. Wolswinkel (eds.)
Volume 149: *Optional Instruments of the European Union. A Definitional, Normative and Explanatory Study*, W.A. Bull
Volume 150: *The European Union and National Civil Procedure. A Smooth Process or a Rocky Road for Member States?*, A. Nylund and B.H. Krans (eds.)
Volume 151: *Different Paths Towards Sustainable Biofuels? A Comparative Study of the International, EU, and Chinese Regulation of the Sustainability of Biofuels*, T. Yue
Volume 152: *Regulation of Cross-Border Establishment in China and the EU. A Comparative Law and Economics Approach*, G. Shen
Volume 153: *The French Contract Law Reform: a Source of Inspiration?*, S. Stijns and S. Jansen (eds.)
Volume 154: *Convergence in European Consumer Sales Law. A Comparative and Numerical Approach*, C. Goanţă
Volume 155: *Quality and Speed in Administrative Decision-Making: Tension or Balance?*, C. Backes, M. Eliantonio and S. Jansen (eds.)
Volume 156: *Letter of Intent in International Contracting*, E. Pannebakker
Volume 157: *Revisiting Procedural Human Rights*, A. Uzelac and C.H. van Rhee (eds.)

www.ingramcontent.com/pod-product-compliance
Ingram Content Group UK Ltd.
Pitfield, Milton Keynes, MK11 3LW, UK
UKHW051927100926
8556IPUK00022B/1416

9 781780 686028